D1562858

Traveling My Way:
Cannibals to Communists to Dining with the Queen

James F. Bruce

This book is dedicated to my wonderful, understanding, patient wife, and our fantastic family, including our daughters, their husbands and our grandchildren.

Also, thank you to the great, welcoming, generous and friendly people in different countries that made these memories possible.

Finally, thank you to my parents who gave me such a deep appreciation for other cultures.

God bless you all.

Table of Contents

Introduction: Window of Opportunity

We live in an incredible, unique window of opportunity - a moment of potential appreciation, a moment of potential learning.

An incredibly, unique opportunity because 50 years ago was about the first time in the history of our planet that we could visit any part of it with any degree of safety or economy. We could see the beauties of it and its inhabitants, and realize the extent of our potential losses. What will our world and we, its inhabitants, be like 50 or 100 years from now? And what will we have done to affect this outcome, for better or worse?

Change has always been with us, but not at today's rate. The wonderful advances of today can help us make a better world – or destroy it. These advances can also help us appreciate the fabulous cultures of different lands, including the different ways people picture their relationship to God.

This book was written with an appreciation of a few of the world's people and cultures. It encompasses trips for cultural anthropology, theology-themed trips, family explorations, and medical missions. We all have different ways of doing things. I tried to discover what worked for others, and why – from marriages to ways of running countries, maybe even how we think this life will affect the next life.

It's important to truly appreciate differences, and not overly judge the person or the ways others live their lives.

Jim Bruce

Caribbean - 1954

My parents, Harold and Millie Bruce, never paid any attention to my official vacation times at St. Robert's Grade School (in Shorewood, Wisconsin, where I grew up), so I was told to ask the teachers for homework for the two weeks we were going to be gone. Both of the teachers I remember from St. Robert's were nice nuns. I asked the first one, though, and she was quite put out. She said I'd never catch up.

The second teacher was excited for me. She asked where I was going.

"Venezuela" I said, remembering only one of the countries the ship was going to visit.

"Oh wonderful!" she said. I asked about homework. "Oh don't worry about it; you'll catch up in no time. You'll learn more there than you'll ever learn here."

I have never forgotten that wise advice. Thank you, Sister. Even as a kid of 14, I admired her broader perspective.

The ship was the Santa Paula. At about 15,000 tons, it wasn't big compared with ships 10 times that size years later. The Queen Mary was the largest passenger ship at the time at 86,000 tons. In those days, travel - especially aboard a ship - was much more formal than after the early 1960s. You dressed for dinner, and at least one night a week men wore tuxes and ladies beautiful formal dresses.

There were two waiters for our table, one an assistant proudly learning to be a professional waiter. Never talking to each other, they would stand over to the side, not staring, but if you needed something, all that was necessary was a turn of the head and they were there. Your glass of water would automatically be refilled when it got to be half empty. The chair was always pulled out for Mom when Mom was seated. I didn't say "she" because that wasn't considered polite a term for a lady, and Mom was a lady.

Panama and the Panama Canal were interesting. The ship only went in through maybe one lock. To see the big gates close and the water rush in was exciting. The water would raise or lower the ship to the next level in just minutes. We also visited Panama City in the evening, and I remember bar after bar on the main street with loud American fifties music blaring from within.

Near the mainland of Panama were the San Blas Islands. We were told we were only the second cruise ship to visit there. The Cuna (or Kuna) Indians lived on the islands, which were small and all within sight of each other, all sand and only a few feet above sea level. Young boys swam out to greet our ship. People aboard would throw coins in, and the boys would dive in and get them. I didn't have any money, so I threw a bottle cap. The reaction was not good after one boy dove under and came up with it. I felt guilty. It was a dumb thing to do.

Dad, Mom and I got into a small boat with a group and went ashore. Few others followed. The Cuna people were very nice and had a few things to sell. I had no money, and found myself separated from my parents. Betty White, the television and movie personality, gave me a quarter and a pack of cigarettes to barter with. That was nice. I can't remember what I bought.

Then I saw something really strange - several of the Cuna were very blond, with very light skin and pink eyes, unlike most of the Cuna, who had darker skin and dark hair. I was told the blond Cuna were albinos (which is caused genetic mutation). The longer we were there, the more I saw. There must have been at half dozen of them. Wow – different.

The next adventure came in Venezuela. We disembarked and took the "million dollar a mile" highway to Caracas, the capitol. One of the passengers told us that foreigners get stopped by the police around

Christmas time. He said he was stopped on that highway and given a ticket for going through a stop sign (there were no stoplights or stop signs on the entire highway). It was assumed that foreigners were rich, didn't pay enough taxes, and the ticket was their tax. He paid the ticket and kept the receipt so he wouldn't have to pay twice.

Another kid and I decided to race up a little mountain. We got maybe halfway when we both had to lie down because of the altitude. It was the first time I ever felt the effects.

The next day we were back at the port again and aboard our ship. Across from our ship was the president of Venezuela on another ship, where a big reception for him was going on. There were five armed guards at the base of the gangway and six at the top. I was watching all this with a Catholic priest who had been very nice to me. The priest had told me he was not dressed in the usual black with a white collar because people would think he was Protestant. He went to his cabin and came back dressed exactly that way! Why?

He said, "Come on." We went down our gangway to the dock. He told me not to say anything: "Follow me and let me do the talking." I didn't know what we were doing.

We walked across the dock to the ship where the president was, right past the five guards at the bottom of the gangplank and the six at the top. No one stopped us! We walked around a little on the ship and then went back to ours. What a different adventure! When we got back, we laughed at what we had gotten away with.

Mequon - 1956

I don't know how it happened, but my parents were asked to host a man and woman for dinner as part of a cultural exchange program. The guests were from the Soviet Union. I was 16, and knew all about the Soviet Union as any 16-year-old at the time would: It represents all lies, nuclear bombs, atheists and anything else bad. America, on the other hand, was strong, wonderful, truthful, God-fearing and everything that's good.

Dad and I picked the Soviet pair up at a hotel in downtown Milwaukee and drove to our home in Mequon. The man and woman seemed nice! It turned out the woman was an economist from Poland. She said very little. The man was more interesting. He was a card-carrying Soviet Communist and the news announcer for Radio Moscow. Wow!

Mom's dinner was excellent, as usual. Our guests really seemed to enjoy it. The man and I had some great conversations. I found him very engaging, but deep down I wondered about the truth of whatever he said. After dessert I asked him the question that would tell me if he was all baloney or not: "If you could read just one newspaper for the rest of your life, would it be the New York Times or Pravda?" In my mind, the Times was the newspaper that told the unbiased truth for America (that was then). Pravda was the official mouthpiece for the Communist Party of the Soviet Union. One represented truth, the other propaganda. Simple.

His answer amazed me. I will never forget his words, a brilliant answer to my question. He changed the discussion from black and white, truth and propaganda, to shades of gray: "Oh Jim, if I could read only one newspaper the rest of my life, it would be the New York Times, of course. We manage our news, you manage your news. We just manage ours a little more."

A lesson indeed for a 16-year-old.

Cuba - 1958 and 2003

In the late 1950s, Cuba had Las Vegas excitement and Florida beaches all on one wonderful island. It was a common getaway vacation for people from the United States. Casinos and night clubs were popular. Mom and Dad had taken me along on this trip. I'd been to Cuba years before when a cruise ship we were on made a stop there.

Fulgencio Batista was the dictator in 1958. Dictators were common in many of the Caribbean and South American countries at the time. We also knew about the rebel, Fidel Castro. He was hiding in the mountains with his revolutionary force. Many people thought Castro was a hero and a champion of the people, which has turned out not to be the case.

Dad hailed a cab. The driver seems to be a happy-go-lucky, fun man. Dad ended up hiring him for the whole day to give us a tour of the surrounding area. I rode shotgun in the front. Dad and Mom were in the back. We were all making jokes and getting along well.

Then I asked the driver, "What direction are the hills that Castro's in?"

The man abruptly pulled the car over and stopped. He didn't look at me at all but turned in his seat and pleaded with my father with his hand waving: "Please, senor, please. I know nothing! I know nothing!"

He was scared, really scared. I don't ever remember seeing a man really scared before. My dad said, "It's OK, it's OK, he's just a kid, he doesn't know."

I was 18 but I never felt more like a kid in my life. It took a few blocks, and even then we never quite got back to normal.

My parents explained later, you don't talk politics anywhere south of our border - ever. Most locals try not to take sides. It doesn't pay. If the other side wins the latest revolution, you lose - maybe your life, maybe some of your family, maybe just your business or job. You just don't talk politics.

Shortly thereafter, on January 1, 1959, Castro and his revolutionaries took over. In a few years it was obvious that the common man was not going to be the winner.

Forty-five years later in 2003, I was in Havana again with a very generous man and a very generous surgeon. Both had done much good in the world by shipping hospital equipment to third world countries, building hospitals, and providing surgeries for poor people during medical missions. Both had also been to Cuba before.

The surgeon knew a man who ran a small hospital in Havana, so we made a stop there. The man greeted us with big hugs. The hospital was definitely third world - peeling paint, mold, dirt. The man explained that they had no medicine and their equipment was as old as the 1950s cars outside. Tourists would be given a tour of "the show hospital" in Havana, and be told it was typical.

Soon the Communist head of this little hospital came and pointed his finger at me and demanded: "Who are you?" My best smile didn't help. "You have to leave. Go! Go!" He did not want us to see how life in Cuba really was, especially the "free care" hospitals, but it was too late.

Later, in the early evening, I took a walk in a park near the hotel in which we were staying. Two older men sitting on a bench struck up a conversation. After some pleasant talk, and as we said goodnight to one another, the one man said: "You know we are not free here."

"I know," I said, "I know."

Because of the regulations and turmoil, neither of my friends ended up being able to help the Cuban people. Sad.

East Germany - 1963

West Berlin was like downtown Chicago - busy, lots of traffic and noise. I'd arrived by train using a Eurail pass. In a small cafe, I met a couple guys who had also just arrived, except they had originally started in Egypt and just come in on their motorcycles! I feel like a real amateur, but they're very nice and we get along well. They asked where I was going to stay that night. Not knowing, they invited me to go with them to a church mission. It was six to a room, fairly clean and included coffee and toast the next morning. Cost? About 37 cents in American money. It pays to be open to new friends and experiences!

The two were on their way north the next day. I had plans to go to East Germany through the U.S. Army's famous Checkpoint Charlie at the Berlin Wall. I've read about East Germany and want to see how bad it is, how it compares with America. It's the summer after my graduation from John Carroll University in Cleveland and I am on a trip through much of Western Europe.

The Berlin Wall was put up only two years before in 1961. Many people died trying to escape. The wall was built to keep the Germans essentially prisoners in part of what was their own country, now a Soviet-controlled territory. (Many years later on June 12, 1987, U.S. President Ronald Reagan stood before the wall and famously challenged the Soviet leader: "Mr. Gorbachev, tear down this wall!" The wall did come down in 1989 and was a major link in the demise of the Soviet Union).

However in 1963, the wall was only two years old and lined with guards in elevated guard towers. On the way to Checkpoint Charlie (where I was told Americans could pass through), I saw a child playing alongside the wall. I looked both ways, saw nothing and made my way over to visit him. He was only about 50 feet away. Then, a loudspeaker barked out orders in German. I looked up, way up. An East German tower guard looked down at me with an automatic weapon in his hands. The guard couldn't see the kid but he could sure see me. A quicker about face has never been done.

At the checkpoint I showed my passport first to the American soldier, then 30 feet further to the East German guard. I used the toilet near the guardhouse, where the paper was basically a Time magazine on a nail. Walking along the streets in East Berlin was a real revelation. Where West Berlin was crowded and busy, the streets in East Berlin were nearly deserted. Where West Berlin had a lot of car and truck traffic, the only thing in East Berlin was a horse-drawn buckboard like we'd see in an old Western movie. Six men were shoveling gravel out of the buckboard to fill potholes in the street. Never have I seen more convincing, concrete evidence of the success of capitalism and the failure of communism.

After a few mostly vacant blocks, I found a little cafe with a few people inside. It all seemed quite normal. There was a chunk of sausage in my pocket left over from the day before. That and a liter of chocolate milk on the counter would be my lunch. The milk was the type where you had to shake it to mix the chocolate at the bottom. I did.

To pay, I placed a West German mark on the counter. The man nervously shook his head at me and looked around. Something was very wrong. One has to remember this is a police state. I had given him a West German mark, not an East German mark. So what? The official exchange rate was one to one. The black market rate was at least four times that. I had nothing else. I apologized, sheepishly put the milk back, and took the coin back. Just then an older woman touched my arm and put an East German mark on the counter. She turned around and left the cafe before I could even say "Thank you." Wow, how nice! I took the milk.

After sitting and eating, I left too. Outside was the woman waiting for me. Ha! The skeptic in me realized what was up. She, of course, wanted a West German mark in exchange. That was fine with me. Instead, though, she took my hand and said in broken English that she "just wanted to do something for an American." I felt ashamed of what I had thought, and grateful - and then she was gone.

Ireland - 1968 (about)

I met my wife, Katherine Davidson (but everyone calls her 'Squeakie') riding horses at the Milwaukee Hunt Club.

We were married in 1965, and a few years later we went on a fox hunting trip in Ireland with the Nace Harriers hunt club! We were told we were the first outsiders to go with them in more than 10 years. We splurged and stayed at the oldest inhabited castle in Ireland. A Mercedes limo was parked in front. We got the cheapest room at only $25. I think it was probably the dog kennel originally, but that was alright. It was Castle Kilkea, just south of Dublin. What a treat!

We met another American as we walked around the castle. He seemed to know a lot about the history of the place, and I mentioned that to him. His response: "Well, as the saying goes, I own the joint!"

He then asked if we were going to stay long because "we don't get many young people here." I confessed we were just staying one night because it was pretty expensive for us.

"Could you stay a little longer?"

"Yes."

He called someone, had them pack our bags and take them up to the tower room, which was very luxurious and had a great view. The charge was $10!

The next day was the hunt. Up very early, got the horses, went to the local pub for the traditional "stirrup cup," which is a stiff drink made so that when you fall, it won't hurt quite as much. Everything is somewhat formal, including what you wear. We were fine.

The local people were delightful, as were the participants. We had good horses - pretty fast, too. I remember, about halfway through the hunt, racing across a field with the others. I kept way down in the saddle to help my horse go as fast as possible when, all of a sudden, an Irish noblewomen went past me sitting bolt upright in her saddle. She laughed as she went by, and shouted, "Think you're going fast?" Yeah, I had thought so.

From what we knew, the great majority of hunts do not result in a "kill." This one did. The master of the hunt cut the brush (tail) off the fox and asked his friends to whom he should present the honor? A very nice lady said, "Why don't we give it to our young American friends?" He did.

We didn't know quite what to do with it, so we took it back to the castle and went to the back door of the kitchen. We figured salt would help preserve it. Two chefs came to the door, looking at us. We were filthy from the hunt - mud, wild hair - and we had this bloody tail in our hands. They were nice but looked repulsed. We asked if we could have some salt. One brought me a sterling silver salt shaker, and they both watched. I tried to pour the salt down the hole left by the tailbone, but it wasn't going well. In Ireland the shakers are shaped to a point with only one hole. It made sense to me to stick the pointed end right down into the hole in the tail and shake both together. It worked, filling the hole with the preserving salt. We thanked the chefs profusely.

Bet they threw the shaker out, silver or not.

We still have the mounted tail as a wonderful memento of a wonderful trip.

South Africa and Botswana – 1980

Wow, is it a long plane ride from Milwaukee to the Cape Verde Islands, off the western coast of Africa! The stewardess (now called flight attendant) says they never get off the plane: "It's not worth it." We get off anyway. There are a couple of female soldiers with rifles guarding the terminal. Wet dogs are going in and out. They smell pretty bad. The whole place does. Inside isn't too bad until I go into the bathroom. It's good-sized but the urine and water has backed up about 15 feet from the nearest toilet, so I do what everyone else has done. Back on the plane, we're halfway to Johannesburg, or Joburg as they call it.

Apartheid in South Africa would not be abolished formally until 1991, so the "pass" laws, separate toilets, etc., are still the rule in 1980. Pass laws meant any black person had to have identification papers to be allowed in restricted (white) areas, such as Johannesburg. There were other restrictions, too. Nine out of 10 blacks we encounter are subservient looking, and the tenth seems downright aggressive.

The next day, my wife, Kathy, and I drive a rented car all the way to Kruger National Park, famed for preserving a large area for wildlife. The first animal we see is a giraffe. It is huge and walks across right in front of us. We stop the car and the giraffe looks down at us without any fear whatsoever. Impressive, and so are the other animals we see, including quite a few elephants.

We have previously arranged to ride horses at a private estate near

Kruger that has thousands of acres. The very nice woman who owns the estate with her husband rides with us. After riding and getting to know each other better, she becomes quite open and we have some pleasant conversations. Toward the end of our trip, we are riding past a group of black people camping along a river on the estate. The owner tells us the estate hires them to

The flowers were beautiful, too

help with work when needed. She relates that she really doesn't approve of apartheid. I, trying to be a good guest in a foreign country, say that there are many people in the United States who do not approve of it either.

Besides, she says, motioning to the blacks along the river: "We never have trouble with our blacks."

"Your blacks?" I ask.

She looks at me and explains, "Oh Jim, it's so ingrained, I'm sorry. It's so a part of living here. I just meant those living here on the property."

Next we drive back to Johannesburg to catch a plane to Botswana. When we get to the airport, there are two other people going with us, a nice German couple. The plane is a two-engine six-seater. We have been told to take very little luggage so we just have an overnight-type bag. The Germans obviously have not received the same message. They have a lot of stuff, all of which is put in the back luggage compartment.

Off we go! The pilot and a ranger are sitting in front of us, the Germans behind us. About two hours out of Johannesburg and after miles and miles of flying over the Kalahari Desert, the pilot yells an obscenity and strikes at the instrument board. I look out the window to my right and see one engine is pouring out smoke. The pilot turns it off.

The German woman, who had been a flight attendant, said "Scheisse!"

in German. We didn't need a translation. The pilot quickly figures that with the extra weight, the one engine would not keep us in the air. We're going down.

"Tighten your belts. Just before landing, put your hands over your heads to help protect them, and lean forward." He explains that he will try to set the plane down between two trees to knock the wings off. "That's where the fuel is and that's the danger."

He puts out several Maydays, but no answer. I look at my watch and calculate our descent. We are losing about 100 feet per minute. We had been flying at 3,500 feet. I take a picture of the stilled propeller with a background of semi-desert and elephant trails.

Then the ranger asks: "Isn't Orapa near us?" The pilot thought yes.

Orapa is an Oppenheimer family diamond mine. It is not on any maps. Another Mayday. No response. We turn a little bit to the West. We're down to 1,500 feet and see a dirt strip in the distance. The pilot makes the approach and just before touchdown starts the other engine in the hope that it will give us a little more control. We make it!

We all pile out of the plane and almost immediately see two rooster tails of dust coming toward us. You should know, Botswana formed an army only about two years earlier, so everyone takes care of themselves out here. Two dump trucks full of armed men surround the plane - and us. A man comes over and asks what we are doing here. The pilot explains, and I hear the man saying something on the order of not caring: "Crash next time, don't come here!" Exciting? Oh, yeah.

Another plane picks us up eventually and we do get to our camp. Beautiful! Overlooking a river with hippos down below surrounded by trees and low bush. It's idyllic. There are about six tents, ours is the last one and a large dining tent at the other end. There's one other couple there. We're told not to leave our tent unless accompanied by a guard. Never did see one. A drink in the dining tent and relaxing conversation with the three rangers who are there is fun. As we talk, I see across the river a good-size truck with a half a dozen men in the back with rifles. The ranger next to me sees it, too, but pretends not to.

I ask him, "Poachers?"

Our transportation and rangers

Without looking at them or me he says, "Yup. Nothing we can do about it. We're not allowed to have weapons, and they know it."

After a good dinner, it's time to turn in. I look through the screened tent wall at the river and see a cape buffalo walking up. He's coming near us. They're one of the most dangerous animals for humans in Africa. I tell Kathy, who jumps to the other bed. The buffalo doesn't seem to know we are there, or care. The huge beast changes direction a little and Kathy jumps to the other bed. He passes right by our tent, only feet away! I can hear him breathing and smell him, too. Wow! Exciting!

Sleep comes easily. In the morning, a young man comes around with tea and lets us know breakfast will be served shortly. Twice I suggest that my wife get dressed if she wants breakfast. The second time, she throws back the covers, revealing she never got undressed. She still has her boots on! She mentions something about dying with her boots on. As we leave the tent, we see the huge imprint of an elephant that had walked past our tent. The imprint was no more than 3 feet away. Never heard it.

The several "game drives" in the next few days were fantastic. It seems most of the animals aren't disturbed and allow our truck to get quite close. The animals are so different than the ones we see in a zoo - more alert, more muscular. Our driver is not only a good driver but a little bold. We see a large female elephant going down to the river, so he drives ahead of her and stops right in her way! She keeps coming, and when she is about 60 feet away raises her head and puts her ears forward in a threatening

Two pictures and we quickly moved out of her way

demonstration and keeps walking toward us. Great picture, one of my favorites. We get the heck out of her way and she calmly walks on by.

Later that same afternoon, we are driving along a dirt strip when out of the heavy brush a bull elephant actually charges us. Not a fake charge - this one was for real. The driver guns it and the bull's big tusks miss us by about 10 feet. This is a little too close for comfort. That doesn't stop our driver the next day from driving between the river and a large hippo that is cantering along, glancing at us, for maybe 50 feet. Boy, they're big and it's surprising they can move so fast! Wonderful, successful trip.

The plane that takes us back to Johannesburg a week later works fine. We find out someone had not tightened the plug after changing the oil on the plane that had first brought us here.

Zimbabwe – 1980

From Johannesburg to Victoria Falls in Zimbabwe is a short flight. On the flight are a group of rugby guys coming back from some game. All are very nice, quite loud and having a few drinks and being fun. One has a shirt on that says "Second Place Rhodesian War Games." Naively, I ask him what that means. He explains the whites lost control of Rhodesia and now it's called Zimbabwe. Do I feel stupid! The rugby player goes up to the cockpit but instead of getting kicked out, surprisingly spends the rest of the flight there.

Seeing the world's largest falls is fabulous. The falls are so big, so loud, with a huge amount of water pouring into a valley. The mist created in the wet season is so overwhelming that you cannot see the falls. It rises up thousands of feet, and creates the local name for the falls: "The Smoke That Thunders." Fitting. Amazingly, here in the desert a rain forest has been created by the mist surrounding the falls.

Somehow we arrange for a small plane to get a bird's-eye view of it all. The pilot, who is very nice, can't be more than 19. Up we go, over the falls and down the valley. I am taking pictures like crazy, enjoying it all. Kathy is too, but when I point out something for the tenth time, I find her reading a book. The pilot seems to be having a lot of fun also. We talk with each other – or perhaps yell is a better word. The engine on the little plane is loud. Then he asks if I'd like a real close look. "Sure."

He tightens up on his five-point belt and tells me to do the same.

"Ready?"

"OK!"

With that he takes a dive down into the valley, then abruptly flies up, does a hamerkop turn, and dives again. If we got any closer I would have gotten the camera wet! Yikes!

Only then do I think of my wonderful wife, who we did not warn. I turn around and find her spread eagle, holding on to both sides. She thought she was going to die - twice!

I got sick to my stomach as we landed. Serves me right.

Pablo and family (The Witchdoctor
of the Yaguas) arrives

Peru - 1983

It's only Chicago and already there's trouble. United's plane has developed an oil leak. They send for another plane. I sit near the pilot and we talk. I need to get to Miami to catch the twice-a-week flight to Iquitos, Peru. Joan Gonzalez, my travel agent, is supposed to meet me at the Faucett Peru Airlines ticket counter in Miami when I land to give me the travel vouchers for the rest of the trip. The pilot and I have a great talk. He says he just bought a plane to get to his cabin near Hayward, in northern Wisconsin. I tell him my story. He says he'll really push it. I suggest to the ticket agent to contact Joan in Miami to wait. He does. Hope it works. The estimated flying time of 2:26 hours would land us in Miami after my flight was scheduled to leave. It would be too late.

We arrive earlier. He really did push it. I'm sorry I don't have time to thank him. Before the plane stops, I move up and stand with the forward flight attendant. The door opens, and I'm running. I stop at the Faucett counter. They phone the Faucett gate to ask them to wait. I'm running again. They're calling my name over the loud speaker. I board a bus-like tram, more running, then reach the gate. Joan is standing in the doorway of the plane arguing with the attendants who want to close the door. I grab the vouchers, kiss Joan, and the door closes. People are staring, wondering who the heck they were all waiting for.

I open my vouchers - and a sealed envelope by mistake. In the sealed envelope is a letter of complaint from a travel agent in Encino, California, to someone in Lima: "… filthy, full of cockroaches, wet sheets, the people were so sick they had to stay in Lima before going home." And that was in civilized Lima, the capitol of Peru. I reseal the envelope.

Iquitos is in the middle of the Amazon jungle on the upper stretches of the Amazon River. No roads lead to it. The only way in and out is by plane or boat. Iquitos is crowded, with a population of more than 50,000. It used to be a wealthy city, back when the rubber barons were here. It's not now. When the rains come, the Amazon can rise 43 feet in this area, so a good portion of the town is built so it floats. Edith Olive, my local contact, meets me, and we catch a bus to the hotel.

She asks if I'd like to go with her tomorrow to vote. Sure. Edith and her husband, David, meet me for breakfast. He's helping his friend in the election for mayor. Nice. There are a lot of military personnel and long lines of people waiting to vote. It seems easy enough - you show an ID, vote and get your finger stained purple. It is explained to me that you only vote for the position of mayor, and then the mayor appoints everyone else in government. Everyone seems quite friendly, though David advises to get down if there's gunfire. Seven were killed earlier today in Lima, he says.

Morning brings Gilberto, who will be my guide. He comes with tons of supplies in a taxi: Two mattresses, 20 gallons of water for me, a case of Coke, cooler of food, and much more. We could go around the world with less, and I notice it's not properly packaged for the heat.

Off we go to the dock where our cook meets us. We load everything on a small motor boat and off we go at high speed. In five minutes we're surrounded by dense jungle. It takes only about an hour to get to the drop-off point where we'll wait for the people I am to stay with. A family lives here, and we have some time to get acquainted. The man, Alfredo, invites me to drink a shot of ginger root rum. I take a sip, yell and grab my throat, much to the delight of his kids. He has me take a picture of him as he smoothly dispatches the rest. Sort of a manhood thing.

I'm called gringo loco for coming here. Senora, his wife, is very hospitable and after awhile explains how lucky they are. She's maybe in her late thirties. "I've had fourteen children," she says, "and ten are still living!" That's considered very lucky here. They don't name children until they are about a year old, so as not to "waste the name," they explain.

After a while, the headman, Pablo, who's also the local witch doctor, walks up with a couple others. One glance tells me I'm not in Kansas anymore, but he's nice and quite shy. Pablo and the others are members of the Yagua people, and their skin is reddish, a color quite different than I've ever seen. Most are about 5'2" or less in height. They're all wearing long grass skirts and grass head coverings - nothing else.

The Yaqua were once known for their headhunting and shrunken heads, although they were not cannibals. They placed the shrunken heads on sticks outside the villages and hung some from their homes to serve as warnings to strangers. The heads were taken from strangers who didn't take the hint. The shrinking process was simple: The skin was cut and peeled off the skull. After sewing the eyelids shut and the lips together, the head was partially filled with sand. Then it was shrunk by boiling. It's no longer done in this area - they say.

It takes two trips to carry all the unnecessary equipment. It's hot and very humid, but in 20 minutes or so, we reach their clearing located on a 10-foot wide stream that feeds the Amazon. There are 23 in this family grouping. I'm introduced to each. The women wear a short, wraparound skirt made of cloth. Nothing else is worn, except maybe a necklace or two. Their huts are built of logs held together with vines. Long banana leaves provide the thatching. They have sleeping platforms built inside, plus at the moment two babies are being swung to sleep on hammocks. Some of the children who helped are paid. Gilberto, my translator, doesn't speak much English but he tries and we get along well. He shows me the "shower." It's the stream above the clearing. Then he shows me the "toilet" - the stream just below the clearing. It works.

Dinner's good. I ask what it is and the best he could come up with is that it was just caught and it's "wild chicken." Didn't taste like chicken. A little girl, Jesus, comes up and watches me write. She's about 6 and is a foster child. Bugs are all over everything. No one brushes them away unless they bite.

There's a half a moon out tonight, so it's not a real good night for hunting because the animals see you coming. We go anyway. Mario, the native guide, has a rusty 12-gauge shotgun that's looks more dangerous for the user than the prey. Gilberto had given him two shells.

"What are we hunting?" I whisper.

"Anything that moves" is the answer. They say one type of rat, the fruit rat, is good eating. After nearly an hour, no luck.

When we get back, we laugh and talk around the fire. I don't know what we're laughing at a third of the time but we all have fun. Two babies are crying. Gilbert authoritatively gets out his first aid kit. Is he giving the babies a shot? I hold the flashlight and the mother holds the baby. We're all scrunched together and I notice her bare breast is resting on my arm. All so natural. Gilbert gives the baby an enema. The second baby was sleeping when she got hers. Rude awakening! Hope it works. I ask why they don't take the child to Iquitos. Gilberto says they have many natural cures here, and besides, it's a 5½-hour trip by dugout.

The night ends with me taking a delightful "shower" in the moonlight in the middle of the stream and jungle. Mattress out, mosquito net up. In five minutes I'm sweating again.

My morning tea was made from a plant about 20 feet away. I add coarse sugar. A boy is weaving a hammock. The headman's making several quivers for poisonous darts. Parrots and a huge flock of noisy parakeets fly overhead and are so loud all the talking stops.

There was mild interest by some last night in a bite one of the older men got. The conclusion: From the fang marks, it wasn't poisonous. A mangy dog and two pups walk by a few chickens and us. The conditions of the chickens make the dog look good. Gilbert's giving one baby another "shot." The cook is cleaning my t-shirt to get out the blood stains caused by yesterday's mosquitoes. Talking, bird calls, a fire, gentle laughter all very nice.

The next day we visit Alfredo on the Amazon again and, after another welcome of rum, he shows me a clearing where he has about an acre of pineapples. Before we leave, his daughter Jenny brings me a cut fresh pineapple. A sponge could not hold more juice. It's the best I've ever had. Senora says Jenny, her daughter, is talked about as my lover. There is much giggling. I say I have to go but I would stay if Jenny says yes. Much more giggling. My comprehension is getting better.

Next Alfredo shows me a hole, maybe 4 to 5-foot deep and 4-foot square. For "carbon," he says, meaning charcoal. He proudly shows me how it's done. Hardwood of all kinds, in 4-foot lengths, is put upright in the hole. Then tin covers are put over the hole and the wood is burned for two days and two nights. A bag of the charcoal in Iquitos sells for about 75 cents.

A long walk with not enough water proves too much for me because of the heat. My hands swell up so much I can't close them. When I get back, I lie down and keep drinking water and pouring more of it over my body. It takes most of the day to recoup. The next day, though, we have an easier walk down to the Amazon and then downstream to a little village and its primary - and only - school. All school work stops, of course, and all classes are let out to see the foreigner. They want a picture. Everyone is very friendly and one older boy in the back gives the camera the "OK" sign. Gilberto goes over and bawls the heck out of the kid who sheepishly sits down. I find out that the "OK" sign doesn't mean the same in South America as it does at home. Gilbert won't tell me the meaning, but his limited explanation, "very naughty, very naughty," gives me the idea.

A few more miles beyond the village, there is a house and a friendly owner. It turns out the homeowner makes rum from sugar cane grown haphazardly nearby. He invites us in. It starts to rain, so we stay quite a while and talk. His friend climbs a tree in the back and brings several pieces of fruit, which look like big limes. They peel easily and taste like plums. However, when I later try to wash my hands in the stream, they feel all sticky, and my fingers stick together. When I get back, I notice the residue is like dried glue. It peels off. The homeowner and others laugh. They have no rum left to offer but show me how they make it. Then Gilbert spies on a shelf a bottle that is empty except for pieces of wood in it. "Seven root rum!" he says.

It's supposed to "make an old man feel young." Gilbert gets very excited about it but can't really explain why. Finally, he shows me by walking like an old man, then pretending to drink a little and pointing as he says "Up two weeks, sir, two weeks." Uh huh, got it.

When we return to the village, it's almost time to leave these wonderful people. Most of Pablo's group has followed us down to the river to say goodbye. We're waiting for the motorista. I'm surrounded by men, women and children talking, and am catching a little bit of the conversations. I find out from Edith later that they are very honored to have a gringo actually stay with them. For years they were treated badly, so it is very special to have me there. Certainly is special for me, too. Every time Mario (a Yagua) passes by, he or I mumble "gringo loco" or "Mario loco" and look out of the corner of our eyes to see whether the other caught it. It's our little joke - and connection. No one except Jesus, the little girl, has enough nerve to sit with me right now. Moments earlier I had seen Mario give her a violent push that knocked her down. She didn't cry and isn't hurt. It all happened in a few seconds. I glance at Senora, Alfredo's wife. I don't know if she saw it or doesn't want to do anything about it. We both turn to the talk. It was the first time here I have seen any intolerance.

The motorista arrives, and comes to join in the fun. Gilberto says they are sad to see me go. The motorista gives Gilberto an envelope with money in it. Gilberto makes a big ceremony of giving it out. Pablo gets 10,000 soles, so Mario and the others get 5,000 soles for putting up with me (2,500 soles equal a dollar). I say goodbye to everyone, calling each by name - as many as I can remember. Pablo takes my hand in both of his hands. His gesture seems very genuine and says more than words. He is the witch doctor of all the Yaquas, but as I see him and his wife sitting on the small wooden bench next to mine, they seem very happy and very ordinary. Such good people! We slide down the clay slope to the boat and wave goodbye.

Gilbert and I catch a taxi to Edith's place, where she and Joan are there to greet us with a big welcome. Joan has actually flown down from Miami to see how my trip was. She asks permission to do a pamphlet when she gets back to promote adventures similar to mine. Of course, and I give much praise for the trip and for Gilbert's skill and concern. We get a taxi to the Amazonas Village, where we meet Philip, the manager. It turns out he's a baron, the black sheep of a royal family in Belgium. He's nice guy and we all have dinner together. As Edith is talking, something the size of a mouse runs down the back of the seat and up - twice. Edith bangs the seat while continuing to talk, and we don't see the thing again. It was a cockroach, more than an inch wide and at least two inches long. Later, six more greet me in the metal shower in my bungalow. I bang on the side and they leave me in peace.

Outside, there's a 7-month old capybara (the largest rodent in the world), a wild boar that is quite shy, a toucan, and a few parrots. One parrot, named Pepe, bites women on the ankle. Joan is aware of this, but he sneaks up later and draws blood anyway. They all roam free, except for a caged puma that had recently "got" two village dogs. Phillip was worried about the neighborhood children, so when he caught it stalking one of the kids, a cage became its new home. Do I want it?

Mudmen of the Asaro Valley

Papua New Guinea - 1984

The flight to Port Moresby, the capital of Papua New Guinea, from Sydney, Australia, is uneventful. A nice woman meets me and then gathers four others for our drive by bus to the other end of the runway. It's the headquarters of TALAIR, the Papua New Guinea airline. United doesn't have to worry! A two-engine job, loud and hot, waits for us and what else I don't know. Sweat is rolling off of me. It's a 19-passenger plane, and there is a flight attendant. Think it's hot? She gives out cologne! That's a first. Then juice and cookies are served. The seats are very small seats, and I'm next to an 85-year-old, hearing-impaired, hunched-over Aussie. Whine! It's going to be a long trip.

As we ascend, the vegetation below appears solid. There's not much sign of civilization, just foothills, rolling land and many streams. We land at Goroka, and a mini bus takes us to the Bird of Paradise Hotel. I don't see a white person, except in the mirror. There's every mixture of clothing, from worn American shorts and t-shirts to native dress. One old man near the hotel is right out of National Geographic. Horn in his nose, loin cloth, etc. Wonderful! I didn't want to go to Kansas. My purpose in visiting the Eastern Highlands of Papua New Guinea is to experience the cultures that are different than mine - and perhaps are disappearing.

Breakfast is delicious, and two Aussies and two young women are eating here, too. One of the women – with jet-black skin - comes over and sits with me. She explains the Aussies are engineers and are leaving tomorrow, then asks how long I will be here. She's very nice and one of the more attractive women I've seen. She's from the Solomon Islands. I think she's working here.

Everyone is friendly and a "Good morning" is always returned. Several men actually cross the street just to shake hands with me and say hello. Although some are tall, many men seem to be about 5-foot, 6-inches in height, and women about 4-foot, 6-inches. I have a driver, and as we drive toward Mountain Hagen I am continually amazed at how many people wave. As often as not, if your eye contact is more than fleeting, people smile and wave. There's little traffic and most of it consists of trucks with wire mesh over the windshield. I notice a police car with heavy screens over all the windows. They say it's mainly for protection at night.

On the way we stop at a village in the Asaro Valley. The people here are famous as the Asaro Mudmen. They and their neighbors were enemies. The neighbors came and killed so many that only 20 or 30 survived. The few that survived made use of the superstitions that are common in PNG. The men covered themselves with gray mud and donned gray helmets made of mud. Pigs' teeth stuck out from mouth openings. Then they attacked the panicking neighbors and killed many. The trick worked. To show us, the men dressed up covering themselves with clay and wearing helmets with pigs' teeth. They slowly came toward us from behind their huts with raised hands slowly waving leaves and moaning. The wail of cicadas made the sight even weirder. When they got close, they again became very friendly and had many pictures taken. They were reliving what some of them actually did - or, for a couple younger ones, what their fathers did. They were proud to show us.

The Asaro also showed us their bows and arrows, some 3-foot long and some 5-foot long with a 40-pound pull. I try one. The tree is about 40 feet away, is 2-foot wide and sports a white dot target. I miss the tree. The arrows have no tail feathers, and you tilt the bow at a 45-degree angle, loosely wrapping your left index finger around the arrow. The bow is made of bamboo, as is the string. I ask for one more arrow. It grazes the tree. Interesting - when they shoot, they draw back and release in one fluid motion

After asking for just one more arrow four more times, I hit the tree. Some of the arrows, I notice, instead of having points, have a hexagon nut at the tip. It's made to knock out birds, they tell me. They do have the power. Almost as interesting are the entourage of villagers that join us and watch. They are as curious about me as I am about them.

We stop at another village and are invited into one of the huts. It's made with cut saplings in the ground, with branches tied together overhead and leaves covering it all. There's no chimney or even a smoke hole in the roof, so the smoke is solid 5-foot or higher in the hut. It eventually leaks out the entrance. I am much taller than five feet, so after standing and coughing and getting watery eyes, I learn to duck down. Some smirking is going on. One "bed" is in the corner with nondescript clothes piled on. They're cooking with buried heated stones, covered with banana leaves, then the food, mostly squash, then more banana leaves.

The villagers have been very friendly toward me. They explain that wars are very common in PNG and that they are now in a war with a neighboring tribe. They show me dozens of their fruit trees that were destroyed. About one person has been killed each week. The army came for three months to establish peace, and did. Everyone on both sides told the army they were OK now. The army left, and the war resumed.

"Should I be concerned?"

"No, no, they will not harm you. If it starts up again, the women, the children and we will watch from the nearby hill."

I'm told the men shoot arrows at each other until someone gets hit. Then the women and children run down and drag the man away. They usually don't try to get medical help for anyone wounded because if they do, they're arrested for fighting. As a result some die just from infection, they tell me matter-of-factly.

The topography of PNG consists of many hills, mountains and valleys. The tribe in the next valley is historically the enemy. No contact except to occasionally grab a wife or have a battle. This has gone on so long that languages are distinct from one valley to the next.

The entire trip from Goroka to Mount Hagen is about 130 miles. I've seen only two other tourists (hate that word), and they're in the car with me. I know my tanned skin is awfully pale but I'm glad I at least have shoes on. Not only would my feet be embarrassingly white, but they would seem so dainty next to those of the villagers'. Mine have little toes pointed straight ahead, not spread out, for traction, like theirs are. And the toenails - mine are cut, not split and cracked like those of everyone else here. Their feet seem to be much squarer, too, while mine are long and narrow.

Wealth here is measured in pigs, and they are everywhere. Big ones, hairy ones, little ones. I see men sometimes have necklaces with small 2- inch rounds of bamboo hanging down in rows. Each piece represents a pig that someone owes the man.

On all of my trips, there's one picture I really regret not getting. This time it's of a full-breasted woman walking by with a baby on one breast and a piglet on the other. I'd been told that pigs are highly valued.

Mount Hagen is comparatively modern and contains the impressive St. Paul's Cathedral. After getting a decent night's sleep, I walk a kilometer to the church about eight in the morning. The building is beautiful, and large. Mass is just starting. It's very crowded, so I stand in the entrance with maybe 30 others. I am the only white person here, except for the priest and two nuns. Again, everyone is very friendly. There are lots of stares.

The whole service is done in pidgin English. After awhile I can pick out every fourth word and even understood an idea here and there. Even the hymns, which were projected on a screen, were in pidgin English. I sing right along. One part I remember: "Jisus laikem mi, na me laiken Jisis." Translates fairly well. Good experience. Most locals are Catholics but everybody goes to whatever church has the best "sing-sing." More pidgin English I saw on a sign outside a small business: "Sori, nogat wok".

Lunch is at the nearby Baiyer River Sanctuary, a beautiful place situated in dense jungle. In cages at the sanctuary are birds of paradise, bowerbirds, buzzards, parrots, cockatoos, pigeons, a type of turkey, cassowaries, and more. Farther on are PNG wild dogs, wallabies, several types of tree kangaroos, and spotted gray cuscuses, which look similar to lemurs. They even had guinea pigs!

William, my guide, tells me he doesn't drive at night: "Some bad fellows out there." He warns me about pickpockets, too. Near the roadside markets, we see people selling betel nuts. You can tell the people who chew the nuts. It's obvious when they smile. Their whole mouth is red, even their teeth - if they still have teeth. Red spit is seen all over on the ground. The nut's a mild narcotic and its acidity eventually destroys the teeth. Not great for dating either, I bet.

More impressions: All women have face tattoos, and everyone is outgoing and laid back. A tattooed woman passed me by earlier, saying "Morning!" She had a small child who was doing its best to nurse. Many older men wear a panel of cloth down the front and a bunch of leaves - called "arse grass" – in back. Some men are sitting on the front steps of the little hotel, selling bows and arrows, necklaces, woven bags, axes, and some flutes.

A one-engine Cessna takes us toward our final destination. The dirt landing strip is some distance downstream from a lodge located on the Karawari River. After going down the 200 feet to the river, we take a flat-bottomed metal boat for a 10-minute ride upstream to a little dock. There we get in the back of a little truck, and it slowly takes us and our luggage up the hill to the bluff. There are no roads for hundreds of miles and the only road here is the dirt track we were just on. I can only imagine how they got the truck here - floated down on the river?

Here, in the middle of the jungle, a beautiful lodge built in the "Spirit House" architecture with greatly uplifted eaves, greets us. It would be impressive anywhere, but all the more so here. It's hot and humid. Inside a cool drink is welcome. The lodge has a tremendous number of artifacts, shields and masks, many deeply carved with clay over parts with inlaid shells.

When entering, I noticed the ceiling is supported by a large tree with branches forming a canopy. The bark has been removed, the wood polished, and high above a face is carved. One large root is still attached and you have to step over it as you cross into the dining room. Later I am told what it represents. Lunch is served immediately. I've never had cool orange soup before; it's delicious. The lodge is basically the dining room, and places to sit and visit.

The story of the tree: It's regarding a legend from the nearby village. Seems the origin of the local people began with a man-god from above impregnating the village women. That large, long root that crossed the dining room floor didn't represent a root.

It's a short walk along the bluff to the duplex cottages overlooking the flat, green jungle and the views of mountains 20 miles to the left and to 50 miles to the right. Each cottage has a little porch on which to sit and to take in the views. It's one of the most impressive sights I have ever seen - anywhere.

A few others are staying here. I talk with Peter, an architect who's with an attractive woman from the Solomon Islands. An Italian-American man and his half-Korean wife are here. A Belgium couple asks Peter if he is going to marry the girl. Uh huh. A Jewish travel agent and his wife are nice, too.

Alicison and Bill manage the place, and the three of us talk privately after dinner. They're from Australia, here on a two-year contract that is half over. We talk at some length about the local customs. They show me a cuscus they found last week, saying the natives probably killed its mother. The cuscus has large wide eyes, a long prehensile tail and hands that have two opposing fingers. Gentle, it climbs up on me and rests. Its rear feet have two toes with long claws, two with short claws, and a flat opposing thumb that has no claw at all. They didn't know what to name it and invite me to do so. I named it after one of my daughters.

Alicison and Bill tell me that most of the guests are planning to spend some nights in a boat moored in the river some two hours away. Alicison confides that it's not really worth it. Rather, she says, it would be interesting to spend some time in a village but no one has done that in the year she's been here. More stories. More talk.

Days later, my guide asks if I would like to visit his village, which is downstream. It appears that no one else goes there. Perfect! The people at his village are not quite as outgoing as those in Mount Hagen, but nice enough, maybe just a little more shy. I've been other remote places where children run and hide at the sight of me. It happens here, too. We have a good dinner, or maybe I'm just hungry.

As we're eating, a man walks by. My guide tells me the man is 76 years old (really old here). I smile. He smiles. His smile shows that he's absolutely toothless. My guide says the man likes buttered bread, so I offer some and wave to him to sit down next to me. He smiles and does. Instead of the bamboo pieces representing pigs owed, he has a kina shell hanging from his neck. These are fairly common here, too.

What's different about his necklace are the eight holes drilled in the shell. Because everything has significance, I ask him what the holes represent. The guide asks the man, and translates his reply: "They are for the eight men he has killed and eaten." That's a showstopper! My guide says it's true. The man looks at me. I offer him more buttered bread, and we all burst into a good laugh.

We visit several more villages, seeing along the way cormorants, hawks, eagles, whistling ducks, and a small redheaded bird related to the lily trotter. A lake surrounded by low mountains has a couple of fishermen, and is quietly idyllic.

My other guide, Albert, suggests we go to his village. He, his wife and two kids take me there. PNG is unique in that many different languages are spoken here. Some claim there are 5,000 to 6,000 languages in the world and nearly 400 of those are spoken here in PNG. There are so many valleys and mountains, and villages just miles away often have different languages. That's why now, if they do communicate, they do so in pidgin English (or bows and arrows!). In Ambawari village, Albert's village, the people – there are about 400 people total - speak their own language. No outsiders know their language.

When we get close to the village, it seems like a hundred kids are running along the river bank when they see the whiteface paddling up. I ask Albert what the word for "good-looking person" is. He says it is yapacupon. I practice it several times, then yell it to the kids on the riverbank. They yell it back amid much laughing! This goes on back and forth until we pull up at their little landing. Albert tells them I am here to stay tonight. Big compliment, I guess. They sure think so. Lots of curiosity, lots of stares, helpful, shy. I can't do anything without everyone noticing, commenting, giggling and laughing.

Albert sets to work. It's getting dark and everything is carried to the house. The camp stove is started, kerosene lamps lighted, flashlights brought out, and there is a lot of bustling and more curious eyes. I hand out some candy – a big hit. Then when most leave, some beef jerky. Dinner tonight begins with canned fruit salad, and I take a few spoonfuls and pass the can and spoon on. There's plenty to eat including peas, bread, a delicious lamb stew with mushrooms, tea and soup, potato and pumpkin boiled together. Several boys help to set up for me an air mattress and mosquito netting in the small house where I'm to stay. It's Donald's house, I'm told, and he's gone. His brother sleeps nearby on his own bed.

No one leaves. I go outside and everyone follows. Ten of us take a walk in the darkness, then sit and talk. Some of these boys do speak a little pidgin English. I repeat yapacupon again, and so do they - fast, slow and laughing. I tell them about America and all ask questions. I ask questions about them. Later, when they pass my house, I hear them whisper yapacupon. I whisper it back. They muffle a giggle. I sleep well.

The next day it rains, and rains. My new friends and I sit and talk as we wait for it to end. I copy down about 20 words in their language, spelling them the best I can. They have no written language. Everyone helps me to learn. Some older ones have gone to school by dugout, so they know some English. One of them tells me to ask them to sing. I do. It takes awhile, but soon they don't want to stop! I want to try paddling a dugout, so I leave. Standing is how the men do it. It takes practice and I nearly fall in a few times. Well they are just dugout logs! Most of the dugouts have about an inch of freeboard and are open on the stern. The bow ends in a point with mostly carved crocodile heads. I did see carved pigs, fish, shark, birds, even one turtle, but mostly crocs, the local favorite.

Albert and another guy, Ande, take me on a climb for more than an hour. We go past rubber trees in the jungle that have been tapped, then come to a rubber "factory." It consists of two sets of three wringers, including one with gears that cut the rubber cups into strips. Of course they are all hand-cranked. The cups are formed by the drying in the metal cups that collect the sap from the trees. I walk along the narrow paths, always behind my guides. Andre, who is in the lead, suddenly jumps back, nearly knocking me over. He's pointing to a 7-foot-long brown snake that is hurrying to get out of our way. "Very poisonous," he says.

It's a long walk back to the lodge and to my room to see that fabulous view. Then, a wonderful discovery! A 7-inch flying insect, a walking stick, joins me in my room. Slow flying and in an almost upright position, it lands on the side of a curtain. It has two sets of wings and long legs, and leaves as quietly as it came. Yes, it had two sets of wings - unheard of. What a nice goodbye gift.

Some time ago I got some advice from my wonderful wife: "If the natives ever start looking good, it's time to come home." I've been away a couple of weeks now. Back at the airport on the way home, I spy a girl with tattoos over her face with sweeping lines. It's actually quite attractive.

Time to go home.

Tanzania - 1985

The flight from Chicago to Amsterdam had some delays, and after boarding I find my seat occupied by a crying 2-year-old. The mother is irate. I ask the flight attendant for some help. The woman with the child says she had been told she'd have an empty seat next to her (that she didn't pay for). She loudly demands the flight attendant get her another two seats. I quietly offer to move instead. The flight attendant points across the way to an empty seat in the middle of five. I look at him and suggest nicely that this wasn't quite the direction I had in mind. He says, "Yes sir, follow me please."

We go toward the front of the plane, and he then diplomatically goes through to the other side of the plane, out of sight from the people we just left. He seats me in business class with no one seated next to me and thanks me profusely. The filet was done perfectly.

After a great couple days in Amsterdam, my next flight is to Vienna, Austria, then Khartoum, Sudan, and finally Tanzania. Leaving Vienna, I did steal four seats across the center and got some sleep. However, what was supposed to be a short stop in Khartoum turned out to be a little longer. There are only two planes in the airport - ours and an Egyptian one. The ground crew parked us close behind the Egyptian one, and they have a problem. We are so close the crew doesn't think we cannot get around them. Khartoum doesn't have the tractors that move planes. We cannot get off, so I watch from the open door with one of the flight officers. He tells me that in the daylight hours you can see the armored cars lining one side of the runway, plus two tanks (concealed from the public) that guard the entrance to the airport. A couple of years earlier, 160 people were killed in a coup attempt, he says. They just measured the distance and figure we can just barely swing our plane around the other. We do and it is close.

My guide, Willie, meets me at the airport and introduces Joseph, the cook, and Mustafa, our driver. A short ride takes us to a resort-type of place where I get a chance to freshen up. Next we see a zoo, have lunch and are on the way through Arusha and the desert to the Ngorongoro Crater.

Through all the dust of the desert we make it. Joseph is starting a fire and fixing dinner. It looks like he's cooking enough for the entire Masai tribe. Mustafa, the driver, is helping my guide, Willie, set up our tents and unpack. It's our first night in the Ngorongoro Crater. The giant crater was formed 2 million to 3 million years ago when a huge volcano exploded and collapsed on itself. It's the "world's largest, inactive, intact, unfilled crater," they tell me. The crater is wild and beautiful. No human settlements are allowed, only visitors such as me. The four of us are the only ones here tonight. Ngorngoro is home to elephants, up to 16,000 wildebeest, Hartebeest, Thompson's gazelles, Grant's gazelles, maybe 12 black rhinos, silver-backed and brown jackals, two small groups of hippos, two cheetahs (very rare here), maybe 30 lions, hyenas, warthogs, some fox, Kori bustards, ostrich, vervet monkeys, baboons, zebras, servals, and many others, some only seasonal. On the way here, we see five kills, one where a lone lioness chased away a jackal from her zebra kill. The jackal was definitely trying to draw her away and nearly paid with its life.

After the long ride, I stretch my legs while they're setting up camp. The area has lots of brush, so it's back down the "road" we came in on.

Actually, the road is where a few trucks have pounded down the dry dirt into two ruts, but it works. Within minutes I see a large herd of Thompson's gazelles about a quarter mile away and they see me. Beautiful! Strange, when we were in the Land Rover they didn't seem to even notice us but now when I'm on foot, they sure do. They seem rather alarmed and some are jumping around. Then I notice that they aren't looking at me but slightly to my left. I look to my left and just then crossing the road about 200 feet ahead of me are two lionesses stalking the Tommies. One thought quickly passed through my mind: What the heck am I doing here? I turn and go back to see if Willie or the others need my help.

Outside the crater we mostly see Masai people, and their cattle, goats and donkeys. The local Masai are all friendly, most have little to do and enjoy the diversion of sitting and talking, especially the men. Their homes and unusual food are fascinating. Traditionally, one meal a day is consumed: Blood (taken from a small slit in one of their cows' necks) and milk (from another cow) are mixed in a calabash (gourd). As I understand, a type of porridge is added, especially in the dry season. Two women come up to our camp and Mustafa offers pieces of grapefruit from a can. Both try it at the same time and immediately spit it out, glaring at our driver for an explanation. He just laughed. If you're used to warm blood and milk, I suppose the biting favor of grapefruit warrants a glare.

Many of the Masai people visit us in the next few days, and Mustafa knows some of their language. He definitely has a way with the women. I did catch part of when he asked if they'd like to be his woman, which was met with a lot of giggling.

All the Masai have earrings in the bottom of their ears and some have plugs enlarging the hole. Some also have a 3-inch wire with a few beads, which uses a hole at the top of the ear. Necklaces complete the package. Short hair is the norm for women. The warriors (the men are warriors for about nine years) use red clay in their braided hair.

Their homes are in compounds called bomas. The bomas consist of a 6-foot-high outer ring of acacia branches, complete with thorns, to discourage lions and anything else. Then there are one or two inner rings and finally the hut. At night, the outer ring is for the cattle and the inner ring is for sheep and goats. The hut is made of sticks stuck about 6 inches in the ground, then the tops are pulled together and tied with vines to form an arching network. More branches are woven in between. As a cow walks by and deposits building material, it is mixed with water and clay and added to the structure. When dried, it provides shelter from the sun, wind and some rain. The entrance is arch-shaped and usually has a cowhide flap for a door. In the dry season, there is very little smell. In the rainy season, according to Willie, "It's awful."

Beds are 6- to 8-inch-high stick platforms, with a covering of cowhide and any articles of clothing not used at the time. The beds are the only furniture other than a stone or two to sit on. No birthdays are kept track of and the only indication of age is the "age group" to which a person belongs. Marriage is one of convenience, and the groom is usually much older than his wife or wives. How many cattle and other livestock he owns determine a man's desirability. More cattle mean more wives. A man might have six to eight wives, each with their own boma. At night he visits whomever he wants. Other men of his age group stay with his other wives. Who's your biological father? No one cares. Not important, I guess, or determinable.

Runny noses, diseased eyes and flies are everywhere. The flies are not brushed away. I notice a fly land on a nearby child's cheek. The fly casually walks up to the corner of her eye and drinks, then flies away. The child never seemed to notice.

One of the children was catching several of the milking goats and rubbing manure on the goats' teats. The baby goats won't nurse then, so there will be plenty of goat milk for that Masai family. The boys take the goats out to pasture and are responsible for them all day. These boys appear to be about 6 or 7. Lions don't bother them, the adults tell me, because they are Masai!

We see a grandmother who Willie knows, and after some talk she invites us into her hut. (Oh yes, I forgot to tell you, it's the women who build the bomas). It's totally dark inside and she opens a couple windows - basically 3-inch holes in the dung wall. She opens each window by removing a piece of wood stuck in the hole. Now we can see a little. She then offers me some local brew in a communal mug that looks like it hasn't been washed in a decade or two. There's lots of stuff floating around in it, too. I take a sip and graciously offer it to Willie. It gets passed around. It's offered to a young woman who first sends a boy out to see if her husband is near. (He doesn't like her to drink.) He's not. She takes a sip. You wild thing, you! Thankfully it never gets back to me.

The old woman is still in the other "room." The house is about 9-foot long. There's a fire and because there's no chimney, the smoke goes up the ceiling and out the arched doorway. Presently, the old woman comes out and offers me tea. I mistakenly think it's another brew and try to politely refuse. She lays it at my feet, so I try it. It's delicious. I almost finish the whole thing.

One night after dark, we have the usual fire going between the "staff" tent and mine. It's refreshing to just sit next to the fire and relax with the three of them. Quiet talk. A little laughter. They're good people and earning a good living in a beautiful country. The temperature has mercifully cooled down, and there's a gentle breeze. The stars are all out. Occasionally you hear a lion's roar. Then I see glowing eyes at the edge of our vision about 20 feet away. There are six pair. They're hyenas. Willie says they're curious and won't bother us, especially if we keep the fire going.

Sometimes the dust is up to the hubcaps. With all the blowing, there are times when we can't see the spare tire mounted on the hood, 8 inches from the windshield. Our drive today to Lake Natron is like that. There I meet Marius, a 26- year-old Masai who I take to right away. He's not married, has a hundred cattle, plus goats and donkeys. He speaks very little English. Between Willie and Marius, they try to teach me some Masai. Several other people are there and are amused at my attempts. Two women who are friends of Marius join us. They have some bracelets, which I buy for $10 - too much but oh, well! I also wanted to buy a small calabash but Willie and Marius point out it has a small crack and wouldn't hold the blood and milk. Well, I wouldn't want that.

We take Marius and a friend of his with us to see the thousands of flamingoes on Lake Natron. Yellow-billed storks and pelicans are there, too. Fantastic! A few carnivores are there to pick up the wounded or old.

Dinner consists of onion soup, green beans, pork chops, salad, fruit and cauliflower. I'm roughing it but it'll just have to do!

The next day we drive past beautiful mountains and creeks. We see a group of Masai children leading goats, and stop to visit. I have them look through the camera lens. They all really liked that. Some warriors visit and Joseph feeds them. When Willie sees two women coming, he has them hide and wait because the warriors are eating, and the women supposedly think the warriors are so strong they don't need to eat. Doubt if they really believed that, but they were not allowed to be with the men when they were eating.

A little more than a wonderful week later, it's time to go home. Willie drops me off at the airport almost three hours early, so I have time to kill. (I had asked to be early). The airport is almost deserted. The customs official takes me to a side room, takes my pack and puts it on a shelf, and says it will take much time to go through all my things. One small pack? If I had something for him, it would go much faster. "Go ahead, I have plenty of time," I say. I tell him if I give him money, I won't have enough to buy a beer. He's all smiles. I'm all smiles. He asks if I need my pen. "No, I have another, keep it."

I tell him I'm coming back next year when Julius Nyerere won't be president (he's not a popular president). We talk about his country. He again asks for money but not in a direct way. I look shocked and say, "You don't mean a bribe do you?" He laughs. I laugh. We get along well. I offer to buy him a beer, and we sit and talk. His captain walks by and I invite him to sit with us. We get into more conversation. I buy, then he buys (I have no more local money), then they see the airport manager coming and are quite uncomfortable, and say so. I see the man and invite him to join us. He buys and we split a beer. We talk of how much I like their people and their country. It has such a great future and they need the tourist dollar but Americans don't like corruption. We have to work on that. They all agree. I glance over to my friend who is also agreeing, too - wholeheartedly. I have three new friends. They seem happy to be with the white guy. As I go out to the plane, I'm happy, in more ways than one.

It seems in many places, including the United States, when some people have a little authority, they show it. At the airport, five of the seven officials I've met have asked for money to do their job. The last one is a guard, standing in front of the double doors going out to the plane. He is as tall as I am and has an old M14 rifle across his chest. He stands there blocking my way: "You have something for me?"

I ask if he is married. "Yes" is his baffled answer.

"You have children?"

"Yes."

"How many?"

"Two."

Without looking down from his eyes, I reach into my pocket and pull out a balloon and blow it up - and give it to him. We both laugh. He's showing it to everyone as I pass by.

Masai - A few words:
- Beautiful: zi di na' lee
- Hello: soap' pie
- Fine: ip' pa
- Cattle: in ga tang
- Goat: in ga na
- Sheep: en ger
- Human: al du wani
- Elder: al by an
- Warrior: a mo me ni
- Woman: eng a took
- Goodbye: wal a city

Canada, Nunavut Territory - 1987

I'm stuck in Hall Beach, in Canada's Nunavut Territory, north of the Arctic Circle. The wind's blowing 35 miles per hour and the visibility's under a mile because of the blowing snow. My plane to Igoolik can't leave. Well, they can take off but the problem is the difficulty seeing the runway to land. The friendly manager of the little airstrip takes me to the hotel. There's no sign that says "hotel" or anything. I guess if you're here, you know what it is. All the buildings in this tiny settlement are like this one. They resemble the Wausau prefab three-bedroom, one-story homes.

Pat McDonald, head of the co-op hotel, says the buildings are typical here up north. The Canadian government builds them, and then rents them out. Rent starts at only $25 a month. Still, many people here are behind in their rent. Unemployment is at 85 percent. There are no roads in or out of Hall Beach. Everyone gets their water by truck, and it's delivered daily. It costs an extra dollar a pound to bring anything in because everything is flown in by air, except for the once-a-year supply ship. More about that ship later.

Almost all visitors are from the government, and Pat apologizes that he has to charge me, a private person, $67 for the night. For that $67 I get one small bed in a room of six beds. The bath is down the hall. No one else is here tonight. Dinner costs $17.

I walk a half mile to the end of Hall Beach. It's bitterly cold and my glasses fog up. It's 10:30 p.m. and still quite light out.

The next morning I'm up at 7:30 and soon get a call from Emil's son, Richard. Emil is the Inuit who will be my guide. Igloolik's about 65 miles from here. Everywhere you look, it's all snow and ice. There's not a tree or bush for hundreds of miles. We're already more than a hundred miles north of the Arctic Circle. Richard tells me that if the plane cannot make it, no problem, he will come by snowmobile and get me.

The hotel's cook is not here to prepare breakfast and Pat can't call her because he doesn't speak her language. He says if I want something to eat, "Just help yourself to whatever is in the refrigerator. No charge."

There are large drifts on the runways, strong winds. Then the drifts get plowed. A woman whose husband is the head of the Hudson Bay Company outlet here also wants to go. She calls someone at the airport and finds out we can go, but there's also a drift in the road to the airport. The woman calls the government office, and finds out we maybe we can get a snowmobile ride to the airport. A lot of waiting; the saga continues. A Royal Canadian Mounted Police (RCMP) officer comes and offers us a chance to "see the drift." By the time we get there, a gigantic blower has enough of the 10-foot drift removed for us to get through. After a few other delays, we're off, and minutes later we can see Igoolik and the runway below.

Igoolik's terminal is a beautiful, raised circular building, shaped to withstand the wind and built high enough to escape the drifts. Interesting. There's no one, however, to meet me, as arranged. While I'm waiting, a young woman, Ann Kern (the only other non-native person here), introduces herself. She's with her 14- month-old son. She asks what I'm doing here in Igoolik. I tell her. It turns out she is the first dentist for Igloolik and her husband is the science teacher at the school. The government paid for her education and in exchange she agreed to donate two years' service as a dentist wherever she was needed. She and her husband have been in Igoolik for months but she hasn't seen her first patient. Why? Her dentist chair sits at the bottom of an eight-step stairs to her office. The authorities don't want anyone in Igoolik to carry the chair up because of the possible liability of someone getting hurt and suing the government. Some agency was supposed to fly a couple of movers in just to do that, but it's been months. Yoiks! Some of the guys I see around here look like they could lift a walrus with one hand. Oh, well!

Steve, Ann Kern's husband, offers to take me to town on his snowmobile. We can't find Emil. Several people think he might be at church. We walk toward the church, and on the way we meet a couple of others. They're going to Mass, too. (Actually, it's properly called a service with distribution of communion because the priest is away.) Everyone is very friendly. The service is very nice but in the local dialect. It might as well have been in Latin - I didn't understand much. Emil comes in later; he had been looking for me.

After church, we go to his house, see his sled dogs, meet his wife, have tea and discuss our trip. "We" decide it is too windy today and will go tomorrow. Emil says I can stay with one of his sons, or Steve and Ann, who had invited me to stay with them the first night. I stay with Steve and Ann, who are most hospitable, and we have a good talk accompanied by cups of hot tea. Dinner is baked bread and cheese; we say grace before partaking. Wonderful couple!

Tonight they are working on the "Sealift" package. Everyone in town orders food (or anything else they want) in bulk a year before the supply ship is due. It only comes once a year in about midsummer. There is a little Hudson Bay store and a co-op in town but the ship is much less expensive. The 35- page food list has boxes to check as to what you want and how much - 50 pounds of this, a hundred pounds of that. And to think we go to the store every other day. Ann and Steve tell me they spend about an additional $200 a month for fresh vegetables, milk, etc., by air.

Ann openly nurses her baby several times, then gives Steve a haircut. I feel very welcome. A hockey game is playing on the television. I went to the school with Steve earlier, and was impressed. The school boasts a gym, computers, and very nice library. The government must have spent a fortune here. Steve says he has heard the little school cost more than a million dollars. The population here is about 900, including the 30 "whites," who work for the government in one form or another. Hall Beach was only 350 people.

It's been snowing off and on, and no Emil. I call him and he says, "Maybe leave this afternoon."

At 3:30 I walk over to his house. He's getting ready with the help of his very nice wife. I take his snowmobile back to the Kerns' place and get my pack. Emil looks at my big parka and my newer winter boots and keeps saying, "Take that off." Pretty soon I'm standing there in front of him and his wife in my boxer shorts. He gives me some caribou boots and long sealskin outer boots that go above the knee. They feel wonderful, like moccasins. No socks are needed (only going to walk on snow and ice!). Next I am given caribou britches that come down to the knees. This is all topped off with a caribou parka, over a shirt, over long underwear. They keep the home at 80 degrees and I'm sweating just getting it all on.

We load up our food; they have mostly packaged stuff for me, caribou meat for Emil, and a whole seal for the dogs. The seal was taken from their "freezer," which is the snow on the roof on their home. Off we go! I'm told there are more dogs than people in Igoolik, and they all seem to join Emil's dogs in a noisy welcome. They're barking and howling and are ready to go. Each is staked on their own line so they don't fight and now each is attached to a separate line of different lengths to the kam'utik, the sled. The lead dog is huge, must weigh more than a hundred pounds. Most are about 50 pounds. Later I notice he can walk while the others trot.

The sled is 18-foot long, 3-foot wide, and made of heavy wood with strips of quarter-inch steel nailed to the runners. Twenty-four wood cross braces hold the whole thing together. Fully loaded, it must weigh in the vicinity of 900 pounds! Oddly, it's lying on its side. I'll find out why in a few minutes.

Emil has a 40-foot-long whip of sealskin, and uses it. The dogs cower but jump right up again. They're pulling hard against the turned-over sled. Emil says as soon as the sled is upright, "You get on quick." We lift the heavy sled up and both jump on, "quick." Almost immediately we are going very fast. There's no stopping the dogs for the first mile, he says later. Emil rides in front, then me, then the supply box. We're really moving!

The dogs run at a good pace for more than a mile, then get down to a fast trot, about 5 miles per hour. In a few hours we make a stop - for tea! We chop a little blue ice to melt with his little burner. You use the blue ice because it's not made from the salt water of the Arctic Ocean, which is underneath us, but from the accumulated snow.

By the time we do stop, it's 10:30 at night. Of course being where we are, north of the Arctic Circle in the summer, it's still light. We put up the tent. Some seal is cut up in chunks for the dogs. The howling quickly dies down as they chow down. Emil's son Joe and his friend Leo had gone ahead on a snowmobile and now share some canned stew with me. Emil hacks off some raw caribou and eats outside. The tent's just big enough for all of us, and I sleep well in my heavy sleeping bag pitched on caribou skins. I keep my hat on. It's now about midnight and everyone's still talking. Soon, though, I'm asleep.

I awake in the morning to the sound of Emil starting the little stove. We leave the tent flap open to get a little fresh air. I slept well and kept warm. Breakfast for me is oatmeal with raisins, a cookie and tea. 'Course it's light out; it never got dark.

There's much silence in the Arctic, too. The sounds I hear: the low talking of Emil and Leo, the constant gas flame of the stove and the gentle folding of the tent flaps from a breeze. Even when we were traveling yesterday, there were few sounds - just the squeak and crunch of the runners on the snow and ice, the occasional encouragement of Emil to his dogs (very little direction), sometimes a yelp from a dog's encounter with another. My immediate favorite is the huge dog I call the "friendly bear."

It's snowing again. They swear it hasn't snowed like this for a long time. The lack of precipitation makes the Arctic technically a desert. However, when it does snow, the snow stays. Emil goes back to his sleeping bag. Joe never got up.

The snow has stopped and soon we're on our way again. We travel for hours, with Joe driving the snowmobile and the rest of us on the sled. Joe suddenly stops. Caribou. Joe, Leo and I take off running and Emil stays with the sled and snowmobile. At 24 and 29, they have an advantage. I'm getting warm, so I take off my gloves and hat and occasionally pick up snow and put it on my forehead to keep cool.   We come to a spot overlooking the two caribou, which are out on the ice. I am 75 feet behind. Joe and Leo decide to circle around. I decide that where I am is a good vantage point.

Joe and Leo get close. The caribou spot them and off they go. Emil tries to go down a mile or two to head them off. Joe takes several shots. Seems too far. The two caribou must be a thousand feet way. One goes down! The other just stands there. By this time, Joe and Leo are almost to the ice and Emil swings past and picks them up. Now I am about a half mile away. They follow the caribou and more shots are fired. I walk to catch up. Two miles? In the snow and ice combination, it seems like 10. Joe comes back for me when I'm only about a half mile away, but still out of sight. Now we're traveling on sea ice between large islands. They killed one caribou and wounded the other.

"This one's not so good", Emil says. "For dogs." It's butchered and loaded, and after a little hot tea, we're off. All was done very leisurely, except the running. We go for several more hours and see lots of tracks but no more caribou.

We're near where Joe wounded the second one, so they climb up to see if it died. They find it and bring it down, and it's butchered. The caribou are in "velvet" (the fine hair covering the growing antlers). The first thing they do is to cut off the tips of what was growing into an antler. Joe and Emil cut off the hair and eat the bloody stumps. I think it's the only thing on any trip I have ever declined. The blood is running down Joe's arm as he's smiling and enjoying. They crack open a leg. I do try the marrow - tasteless. We load up and head back to camp.

When we reach camp, big chunks of the caribou are cut up and given to the dogs. Emil is busy filing smooth the steel runners on the sled. Joe and Leo are resting in the tent with me. The sun is very bright. The sky is an awesome blue. It's not too cold. The air is clean and fresh.

I tell them that back home we have saying about "seeing a man about a horse." They change it to "checking the dogs" here. Seems more appropriate. I understand it's a new expression in the far north now when you excuse yourself to go to the toilet.

Lessons learned:
- The dogs eat anything - hair, bones, whatever. Their poop is black soup.
- A mixture of blood and water frozen on the runners make the sled go better; water alone doesn't stick as well.
- The liver of a female caribou that's pregnant is Emil's favorite food. Each of them has their own favorite food.
- You don't "check the dogs" until you really have to; 10 feet outside the tent is fine.
- Garbage stays where it is when it hits the snow.

Tonight Emil is preparing stew with fresh caribou meat. (It's good raw, too, I shared some with him while he was cutting it up.) It's also good together with a can of Lipton's beef-vegetable soup and snow. This afternoon Emil thinks we ought to go the "flowage" (the open water of the Arctic Ocean) to hunt seal. In the summer you shoot a seal in the water; dead they float. Walrus you shoot on ice; dead they sink. Good to know.

Caribou hair is everywhere. Emil, smiling, says I will take some home. The little left-over caribou-Lipton soup hits the spot.

We take off for the open water of the Arctic Ocean. We make camp about 25 miles later when we're close to the open water. We're just about there when Emil sees a seal on the ice near a breathing hole. The snowmobile quickly gets turned off. Emil takes his rifle and his one shot misses. The seal is gone. We spot maybe 10 more seals in the next few hours. The guys got off shots at almost all of them. None are killed.

We give up about 11 p.m. The sun is beautiful on the ice. On the way back to camp, we hit a bad bump and Emil falls off, hurting his elbow. It's getting cold. We spent most of the day standing or sitting, waiting for seals. Now I'm getting warm again - in my bag.

Morning: It must be somewhere between 10 below zero to 10 above, and quite windy, maybe 35 miles per hour. Emil calls walrus fat his lipstick. He's great! He's outside now sitting in the wind, sharpening his knives and filing those sled runners. One day the ocean was absolutely calm. Gray and black seals would pop up, and Emil and Joe would try to get a shot. A seal came up close to me, but I have no rifle. Emil was 200 yards to my right, Joe was way to the left. They came running but too late. The seal dove under the ice and us and headed for its breathing hole far out of sight, in back of us.

It's too windy for seal hunting today, so Emil picks up a saw. He cuts blocks of ice about 1½-by-2½-foot (the blocks are bigger for bigger igloos). He cuts about 12 before he starts to lay them. He shaves a side of the bottom a little so they lean in, then shaves the ends so they match the next one. He's almost around, so he cuts the first one diagonally so he can spiral the rest to the top. My job is to fill the cracks with new snow (powder). For the last block, he calls Joe over to lift it from the outside to him on the inside. He uses large kitchen knives to shave the ice. It's not like the ice we know. The consistency is more like Styrofoam and it's also quite light.

I tell him I'd like to sleep there tonight. It's big enough for just one person. Caribou and dog skins are brought in. The igloo is built over the hole we made by cutting the ice. It leaves a place to stand inside. I put my bag on the flat ice next to the hole. The standing area height inside is about 6-foot. The outside height is only about 4-foot. The arched entrance is just big enough to crawl in and out. I can't believe I slept in "my" igloo in the Arctic in a raging wind and snow. Last night I knew it must be bad when they built a 4-foot windbreak for the tent because Emil thought it might collapse. The igloo was much better.

The next morning I wake up to discover a few inches of snow covering my sleeping bag. The strong wind had blown all night. The person who filled the cracks on my igloo did not do a perfect job.

I'm remembering different happenings on the 7-hour trip back to Igloolik. Two dogs went through a snow-covered crevice; lots of scrambling but they made it out safely. Our 18-foot sled is so long, it had no problem. One dog out of the 13 simply gave up about a half mile from Igloolik. Emil kept going and the dog was dragged behind the sled the rest of the way. After we get back, I go over to check the dog. Emil asks me if he's dead. "No." They're working animals, not pets. They seem to be proud of their dogs, but I didn't see any affection.

Emil had showed me where his first wife is "buried." They bury their dead here by putting them under large flat stones on a ridge - frozen forever and safe from the bears and fox. One night he had told me that some years ago, his father, mother and aunt went on dogsled trip. At night their dogs somehow got away, and they were left stranded. Several days went by and his father told his wife that he would die in three days and they should eat him to survive. They said they would never do that. Three days later he died. Two days after that they did what he said. A week later someone found them and they were saved.

We don't see any polar bear but see plenty of fantastic sights. One night, while cruising on the back of a snowmobile, I notice two polar bear skins stretched out on frameworks. The frameworks are leaning against a home. Both skins appear enormous. The roof of the one-story home is about 10 feet off the ground. The framework stretches above that. The "armpits" of the largest bear are over the roofline! Wow!

Later, I pay $120 for a carved soapstone bear at the co-op to have as a wonderful reminder of all my memories on this trip. When they don't have any Arctic char at the co-op for me to buy, Leo gets me one from their "freezer" on the roof. It's beautiful and must weigh 20 pounds. I thank him, and especially Emil and his wife, for a great time. Emil is wonderful. A hard worker and a good person. I take the char to the Kerns as a gift for being so hospitable to a stranger. They love it. Steve cuts the char into 1½- inch portions for the future, and prepares some for tonight's dinner.

Steve says promiscuity is rampant here, as is disease. "If AIDS comes, it will wipe out the population." He also tells me that garbage is strewn all over the town, covered by the snow. There's a terrific stench in the spring as the meat rots, he says. Everyone goes to "summer camp" near the open water. When they leave, the animals come in and clean up the town, eating anything that's left.

The Arctic char dinner that night is excellent.

Inuit – a few words:
- One: Atansiq (an tau' sic)
- Two: Marruq   (mar rook') (coughed out)
- Three: Pingasut (ping' ga sut)
- Four: Disamat (di' sam mit)
- Five: Dallimat (da lim' mat)
- Good: Piujuq (per'ry uk)
- White man: Qallunaq (qua lun' nak)
- One person: Inuk
- Two persons: Innuk
- Three persons: Inuit
- Dog: Qimmiq (cum mik')
- Caribou: Tuktu (tuk'tu)
- Polar bear: Nanuk (nan' nuk)
- Wife: Nuliaq (Na' lee ak)
- Daughter: Panik (panic)
- Son: Irniq (r' nik)
- Sled: Kamutik (kam' u tik)

Russia, Moscow – 1991

My ticket says Soviet Union, but just weeks ago it became Russia and 15 separate, independent states. It's a most interesting time to be here, right after the breakup and attempted coup. Moscow's the first stop for a taste of the former Soviet Union.

The number of planes lined up is impressive as we fly into Moscow. Both sides of the runway and beyond are lined with airplanes of all types. Impressive, that is, until a closer look reveals missing engines, flaps, even wheels on every parked plane. They've been cannibalizing these for years to keep others flying.

Alexsey and Irina are right there to greet me, and we drive to their friend's apartment, about a 15-minute drive away. Their friend prepares some meat, shredded beets, coleslaw, bread with caviar and cream cheese, and more - as a snack! They are delightful people and great hosts. We talk until about one in the morning - then to sleep.

The apartment's 10-by15-foot living room is my bedroom; their bedroom is 8-by-9-foot. There's a kitchen, 6-by-8, and a bath. The apartment is very clean; decorating style is early attic. Irina is a part-time Spanish teacher. Alexsey works, for what was, just days before, a broadcasting company owned by the USSR. He was on top at the Russian White House, (home of the Soviet parliament), setting up a satellite relay for CNN when Russian President Boris Yeltsin made his world-famous speech from the top of a tank. Wow!

The next morning, Alexsey leaves for work and Irina drives me on a tour of Red Square, the Kremlin, the famous St. Basil's Cathedral, and then we drive past the White House, right where Yeltsin had made that speech that faced down the tanks and the coup itself. Odd, to be right here at the very spot he had been. I even recognize the background and surroundings from the television coverage in the United States.

My overall impression as we drive around Moscow is "drab." Everything's in need of repair. The old buildings, pre-Stalin, are beautiful. The others, built in the Communist era, are plain or worse. The hall to their friend's apartment smelled of garbage and whatever. Irina says it's the smell of Moscow. Everywhere outside is completely unkempt, as is their car. The sour expressions on the faces of the people complete the picture. Irina, ironically, mentions that what impressed her the most when she visited the U.S. was how many people smiled. She also says they'd always been told that Americans watch their diet and exercise, so she was surprised to see so many overweight people.

According to Irina, Alexsey's father is old school. He cannot believe his son would talk to an American, much less have one at his house. He thinks we are all spies and that they shouldn't even talk about it on the phone. Maybe his son is now a spy, too, because the American might have put something in his tea. He's an old-line Communist and can't change, Alexsey says. My visit here with them is too short. I would have liked to meet his father.

Moscow is served by three main airports and one smaller one. Each one is worse than the next. My plane to Tbilisi, in Georgia, is going to be late because of the shortage of fuel. In many of the major cities, there is a separate area, sometimes a separate building, at the airport for the non-Soviet, or Intourist, passengers like me. The ones for Soviets are crowded. The Intourist areas and buildings are mostly empty. We buy ice cream cones and talk.

All of a sudden there's a rush. Time to go! The soldier who is supposedly checking boarding passes is so interested in doing nothing that I could have walked past with a horse. It's a short bus ride to the plane for Intourist passengers. Everyone else walks. The planes used for international flights are fairly nice. This is not. The old torn carpeting, the smells and the seatbacks that don't stay up aren't a surprise. Intourist passengers get on first and we have our choice of seats. There are only a couple of us on this flight. A woman in a heavy sweater, who I later find out is a flight attendant, politely motions me to a seat near the door. Finally the locals are allowed on. An old man with two bags gets on. He's having trouble. He shows his ticket to the woman and asks where he should sit. I couldn't translate, but "Go find your own damn seat" would be close. He has no reaction except to pick up his bags and trundle down the aisle. I feel sorry for him and wonder about the rudeness. As I travel through the former USSR, I find rudeness from employees is everywhere. Tellingly, the old man's lack of reaction is common, too. The doors close. Now the two attendants are having a snack. I notice one passenger who got on late has to basically squat for the entire flight because his seat had rotted away. Later the attendants sell strips of fried bread for 2 cents each. They're not bad, actually, or maybe I'm hungry. As we take off, a cabinet door flies open. A passenger kicks it shut, four times. It stays open. He gives up.

My stay in Moscow was good but too short. However, glad I went. I got a good taste of it, or at least a taste.

Tbilisi, Georgia - 1991

The flight from Moscow to Tbilisi, the capital of Georgia, is uneventful. The plane should have been on the rubbish heap, along with what passed for the two female flight attendants. Ouch! Sorry! They all were rough. Gia meets me right away and off we go to his home. I'm staying with families on this trip. It's much more interesting and productive. Gia, about 46, is a physicist and lives in a nice duplex with his wife, daughter, son and grandmother. The daughter, Natia, 16, is my translator. She's delightful and speaks English well. They are atheists but she says she is Christian. It's late afternoon by now and Gia tells Natia to take me to the park, which contains a beautiful memorial to the World War II dead. The huge statue, beautiful falls and pools, colored lights (most of which are broken) are all rather unkempt but interesting. We end up with an ice cream cone each.

Gia has planned for us the next day a trip by helicopter into the mountains. Gia, Natia and I drive to a tiny airport some ways out of town. On the way, I notice he doesn't pay any attention to lanes. Just a few days ago, he tells me, the left lane was only for high Communist officials. There's very little traffic. We're in the left lane - a lot.

My airplane tickets said Soviet Union, but by the time we landed in Moscow, it was Russia. Now I'm in Georgia, a former Soviet republic that is now a free country finding its way under the distinct shadow of the Communists next door.

Soviet transportation

We're a little late, so Gia is driving his Lada extra fast. He takes pride in his country being freed but because of all the unrest in the country, there are roadblocks to check for weapons. A well-armed officer signals for us to pull over. Gia points to me and keeps going! Very soon the officer's squad car forces us to the side of the road. The cop is not happy.

Gia says: "Get out with me."

"Pardon me?"

We get out. Gia points to me and says that I am an American - and a guest. The cop bawls Gia out, saying he should have stopped and explained. He lets us go. Now we're a little later. We're going a little faster. The next policeman thinks so, too, and pulls us over. We get out. I know my job. Before the cop can even come over, Gia tells him I'm an American guest. This cop doesn't say anything, just turns around and gets back in his car. We get back in ours. I say to Gia: "I'm a real convenience, aren't I?" He agrees, laughing, and serving around the squad car. Secretly, I don't like thumbing our noses at authority. It doesn't seem right - even here.

The helicopter's an old, beat-up Soviet model, but big. There are no real seats, just benches on either side. Up we go, not high. Instead, we

Wonderfully friendly sheepherder greets us

snake our way up through the valleys. There's no working door to close the huge opening on the side, so it's a bit windy. I see some shepherds below. Their horses panic as we whirl our way down to drop their supplies. Several jump a fence. Supplies unloaded, we continue on. It's beautiful up here. All the hills/mountains are covered with inch-high grass, evenly cropped by thousands of sheep. There used to be 2 million sheep, but now it's down to 200,000, Gia says.

A shepherd's been flying with us. He's going to rejoin his family and flocks. Gia introduces himself. They have the same last name! We are all instantly good friends. At his stop, we're introduced to the shepherd's family and are warmly welcomed. The pilot agrees to pick us up on his way back, so we can stay awhile. The shepherd invites me to return with my family as his guest for a week. When I show him pictures of my daughters, he promises to find them good husbands! He kisses me on both cheeks as we say goodbye. He gives Gia a note – a very special note, I find out later.

The helicopter returns and soon we are on the way back. When we arrive, instead of going home we go down a bunch of side streets to the shepherd's cousin's house. Inside are many cheeses.

"No, these are special for the family," the old woman says. Gia produces that note. The old woman is now our friend and shows us the cheeses. Some are poured into a whole sheep skin and weigh about 25 pounds. Gia and I try a sample. I take a pretty big piece. After a taste, I'm sorry I didn't take less. The two cheeses Gia bought at the market yesterday were more to my taste. He buys more here, including a whole wheel. He tells me later that he can trade for other things he wants. It's what you do.

The next day, Gia gives me a tour of Tbilisi, including a beautiful Catholic church. There are many lighted candles but not the inferno that we find in the Georgian Orthodox church. The paintings and architecture are interesting. Next Gia drops me at the zoo. Although the animals seem to be in good condition, the zoo, including the deserted areas, is the worse I've ever seen. Bright spot? I told the ticket taker "Ya Amerikanis" or

Gia and my translator - Natia

something like that and she waved me through so I didn't have to spend the 3 rubles that Gia gave me. Oh, by the way, instead of the official rate of 6 rubles to the dollar days ago when the black market rate was 31:1, now the official rate is about 35:1, so the ice cream was about 3 cents.

When Gia picks me up, his son, Peter, is driving and we head to the university where he is in his first year. Officials have delayed the opening of school because they are afraid of getting students together and starting

Behind the tank barricade with 6,000 others

riots. We start to drive past the parliament building near the school. There's a large crowd in front and tank barricades have been put up to protect them. The Russian president has locked the parliament members in! He also outlawed all Communist members, so the parliament went from 250 to 175 members. Several members have escaped through a back door and given the news to the crowd. Today they have voted to dismiss the president and 73 have joined in. Now news comes out that the parliament has been released!

Gia greets two friends. One's the Georgian minister of education, who is delightful and explains to me at some length what is going on. He jokes that if there are two Georgians, there'll be three political parties. A bigger crowd gathers. Exciting - history in the making! There's to be a big meeting tomorrow by many of the political parties to decide what happens next. The president had been elected by an 80 percent majority but now has done things that look more like a dictatorship.

At dinner we toast to the independence of Georgia. My hope and my toast is that they experience the same freedom that America has had. Americans are admired here and it's taken as a compliment. We watch television tonight to see if it all is covered. The Tbilisi TV station had been closed for a time on orders of the president. On the way home, Gia points out an empty traffic circle. Three years ago they had torn down a statue of Lenin. It's a start.

We just turned on the TV to listen to the 9 p.m. local news. It is announced that all political news is cancelled. After several minutes of nothing, CNN is also cancelled, too. An old Georgian movie comes on. Shortly thereafter, they run the president's speech in parliament from earlier in the day today, showing crowds of people supporting him. Gia points out the supporters are from outside Tbilisi - brought in for just this purpose.

The next day Gia gives me a tour of the original Georgian capitol building a short distance away. Included is an old monastery on a hill, still used, and a church built in the 8th century. It hasn't lost any of its charm. After lunch Peter takes me to a cable car that takes us to the top of a hill where there's a museum and a lake. The museum is closed today, but the lake boasts an unusual attraction: It has posts where ropes pull skiers, without a boat, around the lake. Ingenious!

It's now early Tuesday and my plane is supposed to leave at 5:35 a.m. It's dark outside but at least the lights are back on. Then they mysteriously go out a few minutes before the early morning Russian and local news. We're concerned but then we see some lights a block away, so we realize that the problem is localized, not political.

Gia takes me to the airport, where we head to the separate terminal for Intourist passengers. Only four other people are there. Gia takes my passport and tickets. He needs to talk with someone because I have no Tashkent stop noted on my visa. No problem. He and I go through a security checkpoint that's not manned and say our goodbyes. An attendant walks the four of us to a bus but driver is drunk or asleep, so we walk the quarter mile to the plane. Others from the normal terminal are there and are already boarding. It's crowded, there's pushing. It appears some have reserved seats. I do not but find one. The plane is full and not quite as bad as the one from Moscow, or perhaps I'm just getting used to it. The man next to me offers me some cognac out of two small bottles. Nyet. I'd given him some gum before.

Before I had left, Gia had found out to his elation that one of the leader's wives who was in opposition to the president tried to fly to Moscow late yesterday. We had met the day before at the barricades. When it was than halfway to Moscow, the Georgian president ordered the plane back and had both she and her husband arrested. She was to have given a news conference in Moscow. They had not been very important opposition before but will be now, Gia says. "The president did them a favor!"

Gia has told me that the president would not be able to hold them more than a few days, and by doing so he will bring more people against him. He believes the president was so stupid for doing this and that he showing everyone what kind of person he is. It will shorten the time he has left as leader.

When we did some shopping yesterday, Gia had insisted on buying several pairs of earrings, two bowls and a bracelet for my wife and daughters. When I exchanged money (originally), he said with a little more time he maybe could get me 100 rubles to the dollar. The official rate at the time was 3 rubles to the dollar! A short time ago, it was 6 to 1. As Americans, we are so used to money somehow having an inherent value.

Tashkent here I come ...

Tashkent hosts - Michael, his wife, and Ulia, my translator

Tashkent, Uzbekistan - 1991

The plane lands in Tashkent in the former Soviet republic of Uzbekistan, and we wait for two buses – which are really trailers on the back of trucks. One is for the "teeming masses" and one for Intourist passengers, including a student from Sudan, another traveler, and me. The other bus is so overcrowded that half the people must wait. This seems unfair and terribly inefficient.

Michael, my contact, is waiting with his 16-year-old daughter, Ulia, my official guide. Both warmly greet me. He says his car has been damaged, so we take a taxi to their apartment. It's a fourth-floor walk-up, consisting of a living room (about 19- by 12-foot), a bedroom (13 by 13), a walk-through to another bedroom which is about the same size, and a kitchen. It is evident Michael's family is very rich – for the Soviet Union. He tells me that they are planning on moving to New York in a couple months!

The next day Michael, Ulia and I see the zoo, which isn't bad. Many of the parks, buildings and the Metro subway are beautiful. When I start to take a picture, Michael quickly looks around: "It is not legal, but go ahead."

Besides his regular job, he and his wife make hats of beaver and mink. When they have enough in stock, they travel to the border and sell them. They pay 200 rubles a year in rent for the apartment. At the official exchange rate that's about $6 and includes heat! This morning we see more parks, big plazas, pass by the huge KGB building (no pictures allowed), have more ice cream, visit a fabulous museum of fine arts and a horrible museum of natural history (stuffed animals that were old and very unrealistic).

Lunch yesterday was in a cafe, today it is at Michael's home. There's always a lot of food. I seem to be eating dinner twice a day plus lunch, snacks and breakfast.

On the way back to the apartment, we pass through the market behind the building. Michael spies some triangular meat pies; I finish my last one by the time we're supposed to sit down to dinner. After an early dinner, Michael has to work, so Ulia and I go to an Uzbek concert. Fabulous building (built for the Communists), wonderful dresses and tuxes, 45 people in the choir accompanied by a piano. Wonderful voices! The concert happens only once a month, and is very enjoyable. The capacity here is about a thousand but only about 150 are attending tonight. Lucky me to be here at all! Tomorrow night we'll be going to a circus.

Earlier today we also visited Michael's boss. We sat in his office and discussed possible imports to the United States. He and Michael are in charge of two collective farms, a huge coal mining facility, and at least several other enterprises. They bring in a wooden box to show me. How much could we sell this for in U.S.? Beautifully carved, it looks like it could be used for jewelry. They had made a trip to Spain and sold $500,000 worth of contracts. We take pictures under the watchful eyes of Lenin. His boss wants to make an impression and he does, but maybe not the one he wanted.

We then toured the Uzbek area and we saw an Islamic seminary and mosque in a very old section of town. Interesting! Tashkent is about 42 percent Russian and 39 percent Uzbek, plus some others.

Back at the apartment, a shower feels great. The shower is handheld, and you have to turn on the heater in the kitchen to heat the water, and then adjust the cold water in the tub by using a wrench. "Parts are in short supply," Michael tells me. I mention two lights in the chandelier are out. "There are none in the stores," he says. Good one, Jim.

Next I am invited to address Ulia's class of 23 students who are studying English in a school of 2,000. They had heard an American was in town. Ulia takes three buses and a 10-minute walk to get to her school. Michael tells me it's the best school in Tashkent. Hope I do OK. At the school, we find they've combined two classes of about 40 or 50 forty kids. They are all about 16 or 17 years old, bright and in their seventh year of English. As they enter the classroom, I introduce myself to some and exchange a few pleasantries. Four women teachers sit on the side to my right. I'm introduced as an American capitalist. Well, that's OK! I explain what a capitalist really is and give them a few facts about who I am.

After five minutes, I suggest it would be more fun if they asked me questions about what they are interested in. There is a little hesitancy, so one of the teachers asks: "How much do you cost?" I already know that the students generally speak better English than the teachers. Should I? Why not? I answer her by saying what I think she's asking is how much I am worth in money and that in America that is not a polite question, so I will not answer it. Then I tell the students how important it is to know what words mean. I further explain that what their teacher actually asked was that if I were for sale, how much would I cost, and with my hands defiantly on my hips, I turn to the teacher and tell her I am not for sale! The room erupts. The teachers all are laughing, with the exception of one who is trying to crawl under her chair. Now there are many questions - from the students. Instead of the 10 minutes I had been invited for, they kept me for more than an hour, with lots of questions, including about capitalism. From all the discussion, it was obvious they had enough of communism and socialism. Delightful time! I did OK.

Next we visit the Lenin Museum. Excellent! There are three large floors with many - too many - pictures of Lenin. We then meet a friend of Michael's for lunch. For refreshment, I had four glasses of kvass, a drink made from fried bread, yeast and water. Not bad! It's sold from tankers on the street using one glass that's wiped clean after each use.

That night they take me to the circus. It has one small ring, with a dog act, a juggler, a horse, and trampoline with towers from which to jump. Good fun. Dinner at their apartment is an Uzbek specialty - a big bowl of soup with noodles, meat, tomato and onions. It's a nice goodbye dinner with good people.

As I am leaving, Michael and I talk about the Communists and he said they are essentially organized crime. They're so powerful that even now they have special lanes on the main roads that other cars cannot use. We sadly chuckle that the Communist Party is the "servant of the people." No one buys it, even them. Everything seems to be based on privilege.

The dinner on the long flight to Irkutz, Siberia is different: a little package that looks like gum is sugar, a piece of cake, coffee (served but not requested), beautiful foil-wrapped cheese along with a triangle of bread, and then the piece de resistance - on a small rectangular plastic plate, half of a tomato and a lonely bite piece of cold, but excellent tenderloin. A knife is included but no fork, so the knife cuts cheese and meat and the food is eaten by hand. Actually, it's not bad but the presentation makes our Army mess hall service look like the Ritz.

It's dark outside and far below, lights here and there, each one with a story.

My class - delightful kids

Guide - Vatali

Siberia, Russia - 1991

We had left Tashkent hours before. The plane had landed. There are no announcements. Everyone sits like obedient children. OK, here we go - time to look for a sign of "Soviet Home and Host." Instead an attractive woman asks, "Are you Jim Bruce?" Luba is the coordinator and she introduces me to her former student, Eugene, who now teaches English at the foreign language university.

Off we go to his apartment. It's typical: Soviet-style concrete block, rubbish and disrepair everywhere. He lives there with his parents and brother. The parents spend their summers in their dacha (cottage), so they are gone.

I'm up early the next morning - "First day at camp" syndrome. My two guides, Vtali and Sergey, pick me up in the equivalent of a Soviet people's jeep - except it looks like World War II wasn't kind to it. Luba had assured me last night that it runs. We head northeast, weaving in and out of traffic and potholes. I wonder if there were just a few more potholes, wouldn't they all run together and be a smooth road instead? Hmmmm. Fumes, dust; Sergey's in the back with his dog, a Lika. The dog is beautiful, something like our coyote.

It's long drive, and I'm getting tired. "How much longer?"

"About three hours."

Vtali and Sergey speak very little English. Finally, we're "here." "Here" is a friend's small farmstead. Vtali and Sergey suggest we should take a sauna – banyan, as they call it. Now I am not bashful but when a guy you just met and whose name sounds like Sir Gay wants to sit with you in a sauna, naked of course, and hit you with birch branches in stimulate blood flow – well…

First we bake until I am really getting uncomfortable, then we sit outside, back in, hitting each other with branches. Next is a quick walk to the stream. This is Siberia. It is summer but the water is still ice cold. Vtali dives in. No way! Splashing is good enough. Back in the sauna, and then we come out again and wash up with soap and cold water. Boy, am I having fun! We're still not dressed when a young guy and girl come up with the horses. I have the guy take a picture of us resting in front of the sauna. I ask Sergey to at least cross his legs - maybe he forgot. The horses look OK.

After the sauna (I told them to cover up)

The owners of the farmstead are Antoni and his wife. They have two boys. Antoni's wife is busy making lunch for us: potatoes and meat chopped up, heavy brown bread, tea, jam, and round pretzels that have lots of salt. I sure am not going to go hungry. Their kitchen-dining room is plain, with a wood-burning stove and lots of flies. It's not unlike our "Up North" cabins in Wisconsin. There are two bedrooms. They have no refrigerator or electricity. The "bathroom" is out back. Outside there are chickens and a couple of dogs. Antoni's wife makes a wonderful lunch and is very friendly. They lead a simple life - and delightful.

Soon we're ready to go. The horses are saddled, complete with saddlebags. I think back and wonder why the customs woman who went through my bag and camera case in Tashkent didn't bump into the two

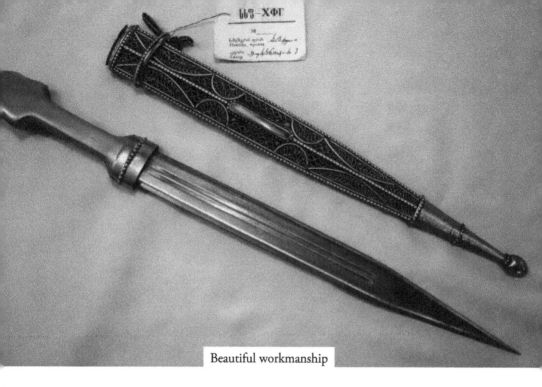

Beautiful workmanship

knives I bought - one which is just over 2-foot long. It's about 5:30 p.m., and a beautiful afternoon. I assume we're going a few miles and will then camp. Wish I could speak Russian and our communication could be more complete. It's basic at best. Vtali is anxious to learn English, and is a lot of fun. Both are, really, but Vtali reminds me of my nephew - tall, good looking, athletic, long hair. Both like playing volleyball!

We've been riding a couple hours. "How far are we going?" I ask. About 20 kilometers is the answer. It's now dark, with moonlight shining through the clouds now and then. Sometimes my horse is following by sound; glad the first horse knows the way. It's slow-going because there are many trees. Sergey warns: "Watch out, go home to America with no eyes!" Comforting thought.

Three, four hours? My hands guard my eyes from the unseen branches. It begins to rain. Can't really complain - we're all in the same boat as I am and it's not going to change the circumstances. Sergey has given me a poncho, so at least I'm dry.

Finally, about 11:30 p.m. we get to a hunter's cabin. It's 50-plus years old, with a stove and a platform bed. The whole hut is 10-by-10-foot. The ceiling height is about 5-foot-6. The platform bed is 6-by-7-foot.

Our cabin and bed for the three of us

Naively, I look around wondering where everyone's going to sleep. The stove's now crackling and soon it's warm and things are drying. The food is cooking. Dinner is rice and canned meat - kind of like corned beef. Excellent! The tea's good.

I'm tired. Now I see - we all sleep on the platform. Less than 2 feet of room for each is a little uncomfortable, but I fall asleep. Then I awake! It's dark. Are those mice or rats I hear? I throw a little piece of dirt. They pause - briefly. I wonder what time it is. What difference does it make? Back to sleep.

Sergey and Vtali are up early but suggest I go back to sleep for awhile. I get up anyway. They're going hunting. I stay and get a fire started to heat up some food and tea. By the time more wood is gathered and I repack a little, they're back. They were gone less than two hours – and had no luck hunting. Breakfast is more canned meat mixed with some type of boiled grain, along with bread and tea. It's filling.

What a wonderful area to explore. It's time to saddle up but two of the horses have taken off. They're soon found. I wonder what we'd have done – hiked, I guess. No huge deal. This is beautiful country. Much of it resembles the woods of northern Wisconsin, but then we get into foothills and it becomes more like Colorado. Pine, birch, aspen and what looks

The Sea of Baikal

like evergreen – Vitali and Sergey call it "larch." They say the needles fall off, and many are yellow and falling. After about 20 kilometers we reach Lake Baikal. Wow! They call it Sea of Baikal, not because it's saltwater but because the god of the lake wanted it to be called a sea, which sounds bigger. Baikal is the largest lake in the world by volume, they tell me, and more than 5,000-foot deep. In the mist we can see mountains on the other side, 40 to 50 kilometers away. Beautiful! There's summer farming here. In some places hay is grown. It's harvested by hand and put it in haystacks to dry and preserve.

We meet the only other inhabitant we've seen, a geophysicist from Moscow. He's been studying the lake for three months every summer for years. He's nice and invites us in. Later I ask Sergey, who has a degree in geology, why he isn't working in that field now, and he replies that it's secret. We've gotten along well, so eventually he tells me. Sadly, he says, he and some others discovered a secret atom bomb testing two years earlier. I can't believe what I'm hearing! The Russians exploded it underground in the desert, Sergey says.

The story is somewhat unclear but he was too open about it at the time, so was fired from his job. He was sent to Siberia and warned that if he tells anyone, he will be in prison and his relatives back home will lose their jobs, too. "Cover up?" I ask.

"Maybe," he says, adding that Russia tells people the U.S. is still testing. I tell him I don't think this is true. (When I return home, I contact Wisconsin Senator Bob Kasten's office and relate what Sergey told me.).

We ride about 5 kilometers more when we come upon another farmstead. The man is fairly rude, but his wife quickly fixes us some dinner. We sleep in a traditional native eight-sided cabin. It's traditional except for the metal hood over the fire, which is usually just a hole in the roof. Tonight I'm going to sleep well.

The man who owns this yurt grouping is a friend of Sergey's, so there's no charge. We eventually ride about 10 kilometers back to where we originally got the horses. When we return, we put the horses in the barn, and pull the saddles and bridles and take them to a nearby house. No one's there. The fairly good-sized house has rather a deserted feeling, almost no furniture and no clothing. It does have a few beds in several rooms, and there was one young man, perhaps in his 20s, who quickly leaves.

As we walk past a fireplace, I glance up. Above the mantle see a "kite" - a large, stuffed bird swinging from the ceiling on a heavy string. Then I see it! On a mantle is a human skull, minus a jaw, mostly cleaned, but not entirely. Some flesh is still visible as are brown stains from the blood. The upper teeth are all visible, and the indication is that the skull is probably that of a teenager. I quietly point the skull out to Sergey, who is surprised, too. He says "strange people" and motions me to be quiet. Outside I ask him what that was. He smirks and says "tourist." Cute!

Before we leave in the car for our trip back to Irkutz, Antoni's wife takes two chickens from the yard, makes an excellent chicken soup plus pancakes, or blinis, a specialty of the area. They're plate-size, and we fold them in half, then in half again, and dip them in melted butter. Not bad, and the people themselves are very obliging.

I'm not looking forward to the ride back, but it goes OK. We pass a large collective farm that goes on for miles. Thousands of people work there. I'm told it's an especially good farm, run by a German-Russian man. We are now running low on gas for the car. The car actually performs well enough, except that the steering wheel locks up three times when we turn some corners, twice putting us in people's front yards and once in a field. We have to park on hills, too, because to get the car started we need to push it. Other than that, and searching for gas, the trip goes fine.

The search for gas has taken us to places most outsiders don't see. I'm told that outsiders aren't allowed in some of the areas we are travelling through. (This includes an oil field, where the land is covered with oil from leaking, rusty pipes and equipment. (Horrible!) Finally an official with a hammer and sickle insignia gives us permission to buy gas. It doesn't hurt that I am an American, my friends tell me. We got two buckets full. Of course there were several forms to be filled out first.

We pass groups of more dachas, sitting in the middle of nowhere it seems. They're built close as 20 feet apart. Vtali says if he had a dacha, he would prefer it be away from everyone. I agree. Though for these people, who live in cramped, dirty apartments, this must be literally a breath of fresh air. He tells me that the dacha dwellers all plant crops and pick berries but most do not make enough to sell when they return to Irkutsk.

Back at Eugene's apartment, I say thank you and goodbye to Sergey and Vtali - good guys. I shower and clean up while Eugene fetches Luba. When he returns, he brings me a small snack. We'll have dinner with Luba later. I grab some rubles to pay for dinner and we meet Luba at the Intourist Hotel. It's not bad, a little sterile, but people who stay there are not seeing the Soviet Union - whoops, pardon me, I mean Russia. The hotel food is OK and there are three liter bottles of vodka on the table. The bottles had been previously ordered by Luba, and she is drinking brandy. Eugene and I finish one bottle, he about 80 percent of it. The lights start going out. The dinner for the three of us, with the vodka was 200 rubles (about $6), which Luba pays. Sounds cheap, but here that's about half the average monthly wage.

We move to what I find out is a "dollars only" bar downstairs. I had offered to buy and now I realize I cannot pay in dollars. Eugene convinces the man that he will pay him tomorrow. I have two Miller beers. Luba orders something that she never touches. Eugene says he's had enough to drink but asks if I could buy him Kool cigarettes, which his girlfriend likes and cannot get anywhere else. Of course, I do. Obviously ordinary Russians do not come to this bar. Our bill is $16.40 - a bit different from the restaurant upstairs! "Stupid country," Eugene says. Luba agrees.

Earlier, on the way downstairs to the bar, Luba had taken my arm. I realize for the first time, she is potted (drunk). She tells me she will do anything for me if I can help her get to the United States. Uh huh. I have my beer. Soon she says she will wait for us upstairs - but doesn't. Eugene and I agree we should check on her, so we walk over to her apartment. After some knocking, she comes to the door. She's fine, just very drunk. We stop a car to get a ride back to his apartment.

Eugene had asked for some help with his conversational English. We spend the rest of the night going over five or six pages of examples, giving different comments and suggestions. Eugene is impressed, and I'm happy to help. We both end up laughing much of the time.

After a good night's sleep, it's off to the airport. Trouble awaits. Because of the fog, the plane that was supposed to take off yesterday hasn't left yet. Yoiks! What fog? There's some, perhaps, but I can see at least a mile. I suggest Eugene talk with some airport official. I wait in a room with Lenin's picture looking down at me. Eugene's back soon, with big smile. They're going to take off, and whoever he talked with got me on the first flight. Eugene thinks it's the North Korean plane that pulled up just a little while ago. We say goodbye, and I walk out past the North Korean plane to an Aeroflot one, which is much better. Off to Moscow!

The differences in flight prices are amazing. I pay about $200 for the trip. The Russian sitting next to me paid about 120 rubles, which at the official exchange rate is about $4. No wonder all the flights are full. Eugene had told me Luba and others sometimes pay someone at Aeroflot rubles for the ticket and pocket the rest. Nice spread. The Soviet-Russian economy is strange, and it's educational to be in the middle of it. Regular Russian people aren't paid much but really part of their pay is extremely cheap bread, housing, transportation and gas (4 to 5 cents for about a gallon).

The flight's fine. However, the treatment at the airport in Moscow, due to Aeroflot's admitted fault, is awful. Long and short of it is this: Because of Aeroflot's mistake, I am not allowed to go with a couple who have come to greet me and put me up for the night. It's unbelievable to me but not surprising to the couple. They're used to it, they say. A military guy was nice enough, though, and called the woman at Aeroflot who had made the mistake a quite obscene name - several times. At one point I thought of sneaking out, but thought the better of it. The officials at the airport actually put me up at a dacha not far from the airport. It had been the Communist Party headquarters for relaxation. I get a good night's sleep. A woman comes in and wakes me at 5:15 a.m. She soon returns as I'm taking a shower and says to hurry. Her voice a few feet away makes me jump. I hurry. The bus is waiting for me. I learn that the woman at the dacha was supposed to wake me earlier. "Stupid woman" is what the people at the airport would say - but not that nicely.

Getting on an Air France is a welcome luxury.

Second story boarding

Saman the monk - delightful guy

Thailand - 1992

Bangkok. Because the Grand Palace is a "must," it's first on my agenda. It's only about three blocks from my small hotel. On the way, women are selling a few sticks of gum or running a regular store. Lots of people standing around and whatever's done seems to take two or three to do it. For instance, at my hotel every floor has a desk with at least two women, seemingly for security. Everyone's nice - and nice looking, too. Both men and women are small, slim, with beautiful straight black hair. Politest country I have ever been in.

The palace is fabulous! Many buildings make up the Temple of the Jade Buddha. The carved Buddha itself is 66 centimeters tall, and exquisite. A gentleman, Mr. Troi, introduces himself. I hire him for a 150 baht – roughly six dollars - to give me a tour. His explanation brings the place alive and is well worth it.

Toward the end of the tour I mention wanting to see the Chao Phraya River, which is the main river in Bangkok and the center of much activity. Mr. Troi happily leaves the palace grounds and takes me to the river. For 400 baht I get my own 30-foot, high-bow Thai boat and driver. The sights along the river are fascinating, from large beautiful homes to the people living under the bridges and all the stages in between. On every property we pass there's a "spirit house" set on a post in the yard for the spirits who were displaced by building the home. The little houses remind me of our bird feeders and are about the same size. Many are tended each day by the homeowner and a little food is left for the spirits so they don't cause harm to the owners. Some even have fresh flowers.

After the river, a taxi takes me to the zoo. At one of the many food stalls, I'm served a good meal of rice, pork, scallions and sauce. Actually, it's very good, though it's too late now to wonder where the plates were washed. I did wipe off the fork with my shirt before eating. Hope I don't pay twice for this meal. The zoo has a surprising number of animals, but also many people and activities. The animals are just one part of the operation. There are people eating, sleeping and visiting. They can bring their own cars or motorbikes, so there are many parked right near the cages. Most of the cages are the old-fashioned cyclone fencing type and although the animals appear well-cared for, the cages are small and mostly concrete - a little sad.

Off to the teak mansion. This place is interesting, with lots of pictures of old Thailand and a small collection of old carriages. It was worth the short look.

Next I think it ought to be fun to visit a large shopping center on the Mah Boon Krung Canal. Maybe I can eat there or find a nice restaurant nearby. It's crowded - really crowded. Most Thai here are about 5- to 5½-foot tall, and my being a little taller lets me see ahead. Each seller rents a small stall. A little wonton soup tastes pretty good with lots of noodles and a few pork slices. I do purchase a camera bag for about $6 to replace mine, which is falling apart. I also buy some bracelets. I hope they don't turn the skin green. They weren't expensive.

Then it's back to the hotel for a good night's rest. Tomorrow morning, hopefully, a driver's picking me up at 5:45 for a run to the airport and my flight to Chiang Mai. After that, I'll be heading north to visit the Karen tribe (or Karin; it's spelled both ways).

The driver is there the next morning at 5:37. Great! Off we go. He tries to shift. No go. He jumps in and out several times, fiddling under the hood. Finally his frantic efforts at pulling something under the hood pay off and we're on the way. It's too early to perspire, but . . . He's the only driver I've had that goes slowly - most are crazy fast. Never thought I'd say "Mai cha-cha" (not slowly) but I do. He smiles and says "chai" (yes). On

the way to the airport he gets passed by everyone except a slow-moving bicyclist. Luckily, the traffic's not bad and we make it with time to spare.

After an hour-long flight, my new guide, Bun, meets me as I leave the terminal. While Bangkok is a very big, crowded, dirty city, Chiang Mai is more spread out, smaller and cleaner. Even the drivers seem saner here. Bun is only 20 but appears and acts much older, and his English is OK. We climb into his mother's car-truck and we're on the way to meet my hostess. The sights and sounds are wonderful. Thailand is 95 percent Buddhist, and along the way we pass hundreds of temples in various states of repair.

A short time later, we go off the main road and down a lane with walls of foliage, wood or concrete, and luckily miss all the chickens and dogs running to get out of the way. All of the homes are open below and have the living quarters above. They're beautifully built of teak and the rooms are large and open at the ceiling and windows. Shoes come off at the door. My hostess, Mrs. Nang, explains that mosquito netting will be put up at night for me. She rents the homes out for a living. They're charming and so is Mrs. Nang. She has a cook, yard boy and owns several houses. She gives me a short tour of the village, too, and shows me a home she recently built for her daughter for when the daughter visits from Bangkok. Because teak can no longer be cut, she bought several teak rice houses (storage) and brought them here. The cost with land, she explains, was about 300,000 baht ($12,000). The local prices are so reasonable that some of the newly rich in Bangkok have built second homes here.

Bun takes me to a temple not visited by tourists. He knows the man in charge and a monk lets us in. Male Buddhists are supposed to become monks after they are 20 and before they are married. They can remain a monk for a week, or longer. Some stay forever. Sometimes young boys are turned over to the monks when the parents cannot afford to take care of them. You often see monks standing outside in the morning with an empty bowl. It is considered good work to donate rice to the monks.

The Chiang Mai Zoo is a wonderful surprise, especially after Bangkok's. It does help, though, if the visitor is shaped like a mountain

goat. The very hilly terrain is charming and helps to separate the exhibits. Large, spread out and fairly clean, the zoo originated (I'm proud to find out) with an American who helped rescue hurt or abandoned animals. Nice legacy. Lunch is noodle soup, salad and a dozen or so flat pieces of pork on a stick dipped in a peanut sauce. Excellent! Bun of course knows the shop owner, who is a good friend of Bun's uncle.

Next on our list is the silk factory, which includes the baby silk worms, the mulberry bushes outside, and their cocoons. The tour and the accompanying explanations are fascinating. To make the silk we are familiar with, the cocoons are boiled to loosen the "glue" that binds the silk. After the silk is free, workers unwind thousands of feet and then bind it in ½-inch ropes tied at intervals. Finally, it's dyed. When the ties are removed, the silk is woven and a pattern appears.

Also engrossing was a visit to a carving factory that employs more than a thousand workers (but only 50 are where we visit). I do notice they have not picked the 50 ugliest girls to demonstrate to visitors or to help with sales.

Next Bun and I meet a friend of his who is a potter and co-owns a little shop with an artist friend. The artist explains he is working on a painting for the lobby of a new Holiday Inn and has nothing for sale. The potter has things for sale. Do you see a pattern here? Bun openly explains tour people get 20 percent and salesgirls get 1 percent of any purchase price. The silk jackets are from $16 to $60. The styles are not something I think would go over well here in the United States. Too bad.

Bun asks: "Would you like to go to a party tonight?"

"Sure."

He has been invited to the home of a Thai woman's home who has married an "English" man. "Many Europeans will be there," Bun tells me.

The party is at her impressive home located right on the river I was on just days before. The hostess is very gracious and welcoming, as is her husband. They have invited Germans, Chinese, a couple of Aussies, two from New Zealand, and assorted others that I don't get a chance to meet. I had told Bun I didn't have good clothes to wear and he said it wouldn't matter. It doesn't. There is a great range of clothing and I was comfortable in my traveling clothes. A wonderful selection of food was served. Several beers, much food, and several new acquaintances later, we call it a night. Bun quietly explains to me that his Thai friend, who is the bride, is much older than the man and she does not want him to know that. I hope they will be happy.

Up at about 8 a.m. the next day and we do more touring of the area, then off to see a special Karen village and another friend of Bun's. Hours later we arrive and it is special. A monk who is very well regarded has attracted about 3,000 people and more keep coming. He is building a modern city. Houses are still the stick-and-platform style but most are in the building stage, with few finished. There's huge open-air building where visitors can stay. The temple is very elaborate, and there's also an unfinished Olympic-size swimming pool and a helicopter landing pad. Talk about planning ahead! The monk is 75 years old and they've been building for 20 years. Nothing is finished.

For lunch we go to an outdoor market and Bun asks if I'd like to try something different. "Sure." We feast on fried ants, deep-fried bamboo worms and locusts. Actually, the ants just kind of disappear in the mouth with the first couple spoonfuls - there's not much to them and not much taste. The bamboo worms are my favorite - very similar to French fries. The locusts? I got through them, but they were not my favorite. I left the last leg on the table. These dishes are all very healthful, mostly protein!

The next morning at 7:30 I am to meet the new guide, Put, to take me by bus to the Karen tribe in the northern part of Thailand. Put is there but his English isn't. We'll do our best. We catch a tuk tuk (three-wheeled motorcycle-type vehicle) to the bus station and get on an Intermediate Bus. Whereas height was an advantage in the Thai crowds, this bus was not built for people with legs. The seat and legroom are so small that I take two seats and put my knees sideways. The Long Distance Bus is much better with A.C., built-in TV and stereo no less. I worry about the adequacy of Put. I wake him up early afternoon about 1:30 and ask him, "Is this where we get off?" He jumps up, grab our bags and we get off. We walk past a market with cuts of pork attracting hoards of the less discriminating flies. I think "Thank you God that we're not going to eat that." Wrong. Put buys it. It'll go well with the onions, garlic, cabbage, and bottled water.

Legs going numb

A pickup truck stops and the driver asks if we want a ride. Put negotiates him down to 300 baht ($12). The truck delivers ice, which is in the metal boxes in the back. We climb in. Put asks the driver to make a stop at a local Karen village to pick up a porter he's used before. We arrive about 6 in the early evening at our destination.

The villages remind me of the villages in Papua New Guinea or Borneo. The pigs, chickens (healthy looking), and the always-present dogs keep down the number of crawly things on the ground. The houses are all similar and consist of a raised platform with small logs or split bamboo forming the floor. Sandals are taken off as I climb the short ladder. Of course the ceiling and doorways are not built for anyone over 5-foot-6. The large inner room is about 20-by-20-foot, with a fire for cooking and warmth. I "get acquainted" by giving out a few balloons to the kids. Everyone stares at the tall white freak, and my beard probably makes the effect worse. Most Thai and Karen I've seen have beautiful hair, but only where it belongs - on the top of the head.

A loudspeaker disturbs the quiet. It's a Buddhist prayer from a monk who lives, and works, in the village. His house is on a little rise in the land overlooking the village. Although most Karen are Christian, these are Buddhist. Approximately 41 families and two elephants make up the population. The elephants were used for hauling the teak logs but now they have no work because cutting teak is illegal. They wander and mostly take care of themselves.

No'tat, the porter, prepares dinner, which is a plate of sticky rice (5 inches high and 10 across) plus a separate dish of pork and vegetables. It's good. We're sitting around an outdoor fire negotiating with the owner of the elephants to take us to the next village. It seems like they are just rambling on. Two hours pass and we go to bed. Negotiating is a long process and we don't know at the end of the night whether we have the elephants.

Going to sleep, the sounds are the occasional bark of a dog, grunts of the pigs, music from the loudspeaker and a little laughing. Waking up the next day, the sounds are the same, with the addition of roosters followed by women pounding rice. It's not 5 a.m. yet! I find that by having the cover of my sleeping bag over my head I can still hear everything.

Rice and a spicy fish make an enjoyable breakfast. Good news, Put says everything's okay for the elephants. The owner has gone to find them. The village is building a temple and we walk to see it. Again, everyone watches me, the younger very directly and the older pretend I'm the same old thing they've seen many times. I show pictures of my daughters and wife. Very interested. Very tolerant. The guy who owns the elephants comes back. He says he can't find them. Put knows my thoughts and suggests to the man he find them. We stay at the village two nights instead of one.

When we entered the village, one farmer was particularly outgoing and pleasant as we walked past the field where he was working. It turns out he's the monk! He invites me to sit with him in his shelter, which is a little different than the others. The floor is only about 3 feet above the ground and open to the village. We're also invited to sleep here tonight. As I look out, there's a little smoke, people cooking, cutting bush, planting, talking. I'm offered tea. There's a lot of standing, squatting, sitting, watching anything of interest. The pace of life is slow. The monk's name is Luong Saman. He's offered many dishes and invites Put and me to eat, so we do. He's very nice, down to earth, and has a great sense of humor.

Prayer time! The monk's loudspeaker comes on and the people start gathering. His platform becomes kind of a stage. I go down with the rest of the crowd. After everyone is assembled, he asks over the loudspeaker for me to come back and take a picture. I go up, shoes off, to the platform and take the picture. The elders and headman follow me and are on the platform and I can't get off. I'm trapped! He motions me to sit down. It's very rude to point your feet at anyone or a picture of the Buddha, but sitting on my legs begins to hurt. The monk's sermon, or whatever, is long. Afterward, I'm slow to get up. The monk laughs at me. I tell him

Our $8, thirty foot raft

after 50 years as a Catholic, now I'm a Buddhist for a half an hour and become a cripple! He laughs even more.

The next morning he asks if I would like to go for the blessing of a new house. When we get there, the family has all gathered. He instructs them to have string strung all around the house. He then wraps the ends around a bowl of water and says a prayer that everyone repeats line by line. The owner of the house is told to bring a lighted candle, which he does. Wax is dripped into the water. That's it.

Put beckons me. The guy with the elephants wants to go so we're off at 7:30 swaying on the back of an elephant. They have a great way of getting on the elephant: To mount, we simply enter the man's house, (it's open on the second floor) and get on the back of the elephant. They're the same height. Convenient! For those who have not been on an elephant, the gait is not even nor is it particularly comfortable. It's nothing like a horse. The owner rides on the elephant's neck and directs it with verbal and foot commands. We ride in a box on the back called a howdah (literally a bed on the back; it isn't), which sways and lurches. Some of the trails are so narrow that one might hesitate with a horse.

When we arrive at the next village, it's late and we go to the head man's home, as usual. We become quite comfortable in a short time. Now sitting across from me is a boy of about 15 who has been quietly watching me. He shows me two mashed fingers. I tell him in sign language to wash them. Minutes later, he comes back and we put ointment and bandages on both. Balloons are given out to some kids; the ones with a few grains of rice inside are especially big hits. There isn't any formal education as we know it but they seem to do fine. How long would I last here in the jungle? Different education.

The next day it's elephant time again. Soon we come to a large overhanging limb that we must find a way around. Down to the left there's only a 4- inch thick tree blocking the way. A short verbal command and the elephant's trunk and head easily push the tree down. A walking bulldozer! Now I see how this elephant could drag a huge teak log through the woods without much damage to the forest. A tractor would have to take out hundreds of trees just to get here.

At the next village, we're greeted by about 20 dogs and they're really coming after us. The elephant just strolls along with his 7-foot strides. The dogs are following us closely, all barking. All of a sudden I feel the elephant take a deep breath raising us up. Put and I grab the sides of the howdah. The elephant turns around so quickly that we hang on for our lives. The deep breath is shot out the trunk, creating a whirlwind of dust over the dogs. They yelp and scatter under a nearby home. The elephant calmly turns around and we move on. Some distance away, I hear one faint yelp from under the house. Goodbye to the elephants and the elephant man.

Last night Put had said he couldn't figure out why he coughs so much. He said it with a smile as he was starting his fifth pack of cigarettes for the day. Tobacco is raised all over, and it's the roll-your-own type.

If you looking for it, there's much to be repulsed by: the spitting and snorting; everything dirty - hands, hair, clothes, floor walls, ceiling, teeth; the dog and cat eating off my plate while I eat. But there's a lot of good, too: many genuine smiles; they don't hit their children ever - dogs, cats, pigs, yes - but never the children. Everyone seems to work, not hard, but helping.

Off to the river and the raft. The raft is about 30-foot long, made up of eight pieces of bamboo tied together at both ends with a raised platform about two-thirds of the way back for packages and passengers. The pilot poles from the bow. A brilliant iridescent kingfisher watches, a black butterfly with an extra-long tail flits. It's about 80 degrees, and sunny. I'm told the raft takes about a morning to build and costs about 200 baht ($8), and the pilot costs 100 baht a day for two days. Downstream they abandon the raft. On the way, the pilot makes a stop on the way at a small village. Notat and the pilot disappear. They are referred to as "the dead," Put says because they use opium. They have gone to spend the money they're earning. Put says the pilot tried it about three years ago and now he can't quit. Here they come. We're off. There's some booming in the distance. We are only about 5 kilometers from the Burmese border. The Burmese army is fighting the Karen. Put and the others tell me that we don't have to worry because the artillery is targeting a Karen village that has given the Burmese trouble. This village hasn't. The problem is they have to shoot over this village.

Thailand - you've been great!

Welcoming celebration

Borneo - 1993

As far as I can figure, it's been about 40 hours since leaving Milwaukee. We land at Balikpapan and after a screaming two-hour drive arrive at a hotel in Sarminda, another town in the Indonesian part of Borneo. The small but oil-rich Kingdom of Borneo and Malaysia make up the rest of the island, which is the third largest island in the world. A quick shower and four hours' sleep and off I go with Musa (my translator/guide) and Bus (the cook) to a local airport to grab a seat on a little one-engine plane.

Funny, there must have been a shorter way. Milwaukee to Los Angeles to Honolulu, to Biak in Irian Java (renamed Papua in 2002) to Denpasar (in Bali) to Jakarta to Balikpapan (both in Indonesia) and now landing on some dirt strip in the Indonesian highlands to visit the Dyak people. They don't get out much . . .

And that's why I'm here - to visit people and cultures that probably won't exist for much longer. A river is nearby and some Dyaks meet us, including the headman of a nearby village. Packing up doesn't take much time, and we head out to out to his village.

Most Dyaks live together in elevated longhouses but the one in this village burned down recently, so we stay with headman in a temporary

Arrival in the Highland of Borneo

one. This will be the first of several villages we experience. Typically the chief (headman) and his family stay in the middle, and as people get married they live in units on either side. The building is raised about 6 feet above the ground to keep the ground-loving creatures at bay. A shared open "veranda" in front is available to all and functions as a town square.

Some of these longhouses I visit are very substantial. One of the floor planks on the porch was 33 feet long, 3 feet wide and 4 inches thick. Impressive! When entering, your shoes come off at the doorway. The longhouses are elevated to lessen the invasion of insects, snakes and small animals. The chickens, dogs and pigs that live underneath help get rid of the pests. They also take care of the thrown garbage. The balloons I shared are a great icebreaker with the kids, as usual.

In the next village the headman is quite intelligent and engaging. He mentions he was in the army and is proud of it. We seem to have the bias that such people are uneducated and, therefore, not intelligent. The truth is they are as intelligent as anyone but educated in things they need to survive and live well. He knows that George Bush is president but was of the opinion that Europe was part of America.

Bathing and toilet facilities are the river, which appears quite clean. The chief's wife is pleasant and helpful. I'm told that a short time ago the girls here used to elongate their earlobes. The older women still have theirs elongated, of course. Now, though, if someone goes to town "everyone stares," so the younger women don't do it anymore.

First of Several Dyak Villages

Mosquito netting is put up for the night. My bed consists of a ⅛-inch mat on the floor. The sounds of the night include dogs yelping in fights, coughing, a baby in a nearby unit who awakens twice in the night crying and is nursed back to sleep. A rooster announces his presence at the first sign of light.

We are up early. (Remind me to never have a rooster!) New porters arrive. Each village has porters to go to the next and when they get to each village, they don't usually stay. They turn around and go back home. It's about an hour to Long Uro, then three hours to Long Sungei. Tough trek! Some hills are really steep, with wet slippery clay and all up and down. Not 20 feet of flat land. One hill is particularly steep and long. I am really puffing and so are Musa and Bus. The porters are ahead of us. I am quite relieved just to get to the top only to see the Dyaks sitting resting with their packs on the ground - sweating profusely - each enjoying a cigarette. We all have a lunch of some meat over cold rice. I ask what kind of meat it is. "Just meat," I am told. It was good.

While they are still resting, I leave and head down the path toward the next village. It isn't too far. I arrive about a half an hour before the rest. It is delightful - going at my own pace, stopping to see ants, butterflies, and more. After the others catch up, we enter the village. There are always lots of stares, especially at the white guy. We always go first to the headman's quarters, but it isn't a regular longhouse this time. The village is healthier, the dogs are better looking, the chickens fatter. The villagers have an acre-sized island where the pigs are kept. They've dammed a stream and made a 2-acre lake. I'm told these villagers use water in the rainy season to power a waterwheel to provide a little electricity and to mill rice! Easier than using 5-foot poles to pound rice in a two-holed kind of table like most other villages do.

Rest is welcome and sleep comes easily. Dawn comes early. Last night I had to go to the river, and fumbled with the latch on the door until the chief's daughter took mercy on me and quietly got me a flashlight and opened the latch. I silently patted her shoulder a big thank you. Soon everyone's stirring. Musa and Bus ask if I want to bathe, so we go back to the river to soap up. Kids are bringing their out the balloons I have given them, breakfast is cooking (tea, rice with hot peppers, bread with pineapple preserves). This village has about 300 people, of which 103 live in the longhouse. Later that afternoon all of the villagers plus a few from other villages an hour away show up for a welcoming ceremony - for me! All are milling around on the veranda for an hour or two before the show. Much excitement, jockeying around for a position, older ones acting cool, all of us just hanging out.

The headman's son starts the ceremony with the introduction of a "pastor" from one of the other villages. Evidently the party is a good opportunity to advertise, telling when services are, etc. The headman's son gets up again and announces all the dancers by names and introduces the dance to me at some length. Long, slow dance: one left foot step, one right foot step, ending with a stamp. The costumes are colorful and consist of basically a top and a sarong decorated with beads and sequins, each one different from the next. Musical instruments are homemade guitars and wooden xylophones. Another dance; same girls. And another, with two warriors and several others.

Then three girls come and get me amid much laughing (not mine)

and dress me in an odd, stiff fur-covered skin (boar?) and a shirt of tiger skin. An ornate machete and a helmet of goat's hair and feathers top it all off. My dance was a little less spectacular. A few rushes at the audience (learned in fencing years ago) with the machete drawn as a sword. It got the kids to scream and back up. Several dancers tried to imitate. Mine was an easy act to follow. After the welcoming celebration, we retire to the headman's quarters.

I had recently been told by a young Finnish couple I met that the Dyak people have a lot of lice. I asked Musa if it was true. "Yes, it's true," he said, pulling back his hair to show me many. I did have repellent but had only used it in the houses for the little flies that were bothersome.

Sitting there, minutes pass without words; there's nothing to hurry about. The headman's wife sits nearby. She coughs then expertly spits down the cracks between the floorboards.

I decide to lie down; sitting without a back support is killing my back. As I go about lying down, an old woman comes in and gets a rolled straw mat and a pillow. She motions for me to get up so she can make

Headman and wife - notice the tiger skin and steps behind

me comfortable. Wow! Nice. I lie down again. Smoke hazes up along the eaves, which must be 20 feet above me. Kids are running, talking, playing in other compartments.

There are just 7-foot walls, no ceilings to the rooms, and just the roof above. The adjoining compartments have open doorways to the veranda. Privacy when changing is done by simply turning sideways. Everyone politely pretends you're not there. The walls here are decorated with pictures of Jesus, Mary and Joseph, plus pictures from calendars. The floors usually have areas where sheets are laid over the rough boards and poles. They look like a cross between linoleum and shelf paper. There are areas that are kept very clean, including these floors. Everyone seems to take a bath every day to keep clean but living surrounded by jungle, it's difficult.

Dinner is ready. Light is provided by a kerosene lamp and the fire. I am served first, while Bus and Musa are cleaning up. I recognize a drumstick and take it along with an extra amount of rice. The other bowl has noodles, potatoes, some chicken parts, and who knows what. I can't see but I dig in. The rice is good. I bite into a drumstick and let it drop through the cracks in the floor. Maybe it was a bad piece.

Another bite, very tough. I don't want to be impolite, so I eat half. Musa and Bus now begin eating. Bus takes the flashlight and looks for the parts he wants. Why didn't I do that? Musa cleans my plate, discreetly putting the half-eaten drumstick back on the platter. Maybe I should have eaten it. They take some chicken and don't try more than one bite. Very old chicken, they joke. No good. They laugh. "You didn't eat that did you?" Cripes!

While we are still sitting around the fire, the headman's wife gets some white paste and crumbles some brown stuff on it over a green leaf. Musa says this for strong teeth. (I ask Bus later and he says it was cocaine and brown sugar). Later I see her red teeth - betel nut, not cocaine.

A little boy about a year old plays with his family, the headman's two daughters, son-in-laws, Musa and Bus. Kids come to stare at me from a distance. The headman's wife plays with her little grandson. He pushes her away but she continues. There's gentle chuckling by the few who notice. I remember these are the people, who until just a few years before had in their cemeteries statues of men with erections, for it was considered good luck. Having children is something sought after. The mortality of children and the life expectancy are not good. Different thoughts. There are now about 15 people in the headman's quarters watching me write, but when I look up they are doing something else.

In the morning we walk about 10 minutes to visit the headman's garden. Overlooking each garden is a little 'sleeping house." Someone's always there at night. If they hear something, they pull a string which is attached to a bag to scare the bears away. They also have a carved bird on a branch. There's a string tied to it that goes to the river. The current of the river makes the bird move slightly, enough to scare the other birds away. Ingenious.

The power of the eyes here is amazing. You can clear a 20-foot path just by looking at the villagers. Kids hide behind someone else if you look at them more than a half second.

I find an inch-long leech on my foot and another on my pants. Bus finds another and drops it down to the appreciative chickens. Returning back to the previous village, we find that the church service is just starting. Everyone here is Catholic because a priest from the United States came through a few years ago and shared the word. I slip into the back with the headman's son. The kids up front are singing to the accompaniment of a guitar. People turn and stare. Soon, the news I'm here travels forward. Up front the kids actually get up, turn around and stare. Singing almost stops. This is mildly embarrassing. I see the headman two pews ahead and we nod to each other. A dog walks back and takes a sniff of me. The dog returns and so does the singing.

After church we retire to the longhouse and I have a long discussion with the headman and Musa. After some time, the headman has a question. He has heard (only about a year before) that we Americans have been to the moon. "Is this true?" he asks. You have to remember, we went to the moon in 1969 and this is 1993 and he's just heard about it!

I answer him (somewhat proudly) that, "Yes it's true!"

"No, no", he says. "This is not good." I figure he has some superstition or thinks the moon is made of green cheese or something. I ask why he thinks this is not good. "You Americans are so rich and so smart, I worry that someday you will not believe in God."

Wow! I answer weakly that there are some in America who do not

Guide and porters

believe in God but most people do. And wasn't it the Americans that paid the expenses of the priest who came here and shared the good news? The chief seems happy and genuinely relieved - perhaps less than I am about his question . . . and his thought.

We're going downstream today by canoe to Long Nawang. It should take about two hours. Thank heavens the trekking is over. I'm getting tired of trying to prove I can keep up with a girl porter and a 12-year-old boy carrying 40-pound pack from the last village. I'm excited to see the canoe and river. Maybe I'll feel more at home.

The dugout is 30-foot long, and narrow but deep. This one is different than the dugouts in Papua New Guinea. These have half-inch wood strips nailed on the outside to help keep the waves out and provide more stability. There are three of us passengers, and three paddlers. The guy in the bow also takes a pole. The dugout is still cramped. Every half mile or so there are rapids - nothing real difficult but they certainly keep you active. Total cost is 15,000 rupiah (about $12 U.S.) to go downstream. Then the paddlers turn around and paddle and drag the canoe back.

I've see skins of the Sumatran tiger, three of the scaly anteater, various deer, squirrel and small cats, plus several I don't recognize and that Musa doesn't know either. The Malaysian border is only about a day's walk from where we are. It's about three more days travel to the airstrip.

When we finally arrive at the airstrip, we find many people selling deer meat, chickens, pineapples, birds, and more. Some chickens are alive and have their legs tied together. They're tagged, noting who's to pick them up in Samarinda. They're thrown in the luggage compartment over the bags. The plane from here to Jakarta is confirmed for the next morning. We arrive early in the morning to find the flight's been cancelled! No more flights to Jakarta. I talk with the supervisor and together we go talk with the station master who, after some time, puts me on another plane with only nine others. It's going to Jakarta but making one stop somewhere to pick up Muslims going to Mecca. We make the stop and disembark. Many Muslims are waiting to board. I get talking to one man who nice enough to share some food. He's a guy

Communal veranda

from Canada who's working here. We stay close to the boarding gate, and are the first ones to board.

Thanks station master (he bumped someone), and thanks to all the wonderful people I met in Borneo. God bless you all!

Senegal - 1995

It really isn't that Midwest Express Airlines is that good or caring (it is), maybe it's just the contrast. Air Afrique - you have to wonder when a name is pronounced like "A Freak." The boarding's OK. The plane's clean. It's just that after sitting on the runway (not the gate) at JFK International Airport in New York for 2½ hours, with no reason given (I asked twice) and more than a dozen trucks pulled under the plane out of sight, one begins to have some doubts! It's getting dark. Then there's the armored personnel carrier that pulls alongside, then backs up about 200 feet away facing us and turns its lights off. This is interesting. Hijacking? Bomb threat? With nothing else to do, your mind tends to wander.

Then the pilot strolls by. He explains, in answer to my question, "It's a simple matter about the cabin pressure. It ought to be fixed soon." Now at least I know what's going on.

After awhile, they serve dinner - while we're still on the runway. After dinner, they decide they need a new part. We find out that Air France has to fly the part over from Europe. (Air France does the maintenance and ticketing procedures for Air Afrique in the United States.) We've been here on the runway for more four hours when they decide to take us to a nearby Holiday Inn for the night. No one has any luggage, except a carry on. Luckily all my baggage is my pack.

By the time morning comes, seatmates are close friends and companions for breakfast, lunch and dinner. The bus back to the airport is supposed to leave at seven or eight in the morning, depending on what person you hear. It turns out to be seven. We spend the day at the airport and finally depart after midnight with no further explanations or apologies given. No Toto, we're not even near Kansas. At the airport, there was a considerable amount of fist shaking at one of the Air France agents. The agent was talking to about 20 very irate passengers who wanted to know what was going on. The comment that got the fists shaking was her response to some of them, "I don't know why you're so upset, we fed you didn't we?" And the French were the great diplomats?

I had gotten to the airport early, at the suggestion of one of the Air France agents, and rearranged the rest of my flights "direct" to Bangui (capital of the Central African Republic) from Dakar (the capital of Senegal). Yes, I remember the difference between "nonstop" and "direct."

When we finally arrive at Dakar, I'm met by Aquasi Aidoo, an employee and friend of Tim Bork, the brother of Lynn Dewing. Tom and Lynn Dewing are close friends of ours in Wisconsin. Aquasi picks me up and takes me to his home. His wife lets me know, by not stopping her work on the computer when I enter, that she has other things to do than entertain people to whom her husband feels obliged. Seems she is a feminist. We get along fine, however. I even kid her about it.

Aquasi is originally from Ghana and his wife from Nigeria. We have a good time at dinner, for which he insists on paying. They suggest they have a house guest who might like to accompany me to Goree Island the next day. The company sounds good. The infamous Goree Island is known for its role in the 15th- to 19th-century Atlantic slave trade. I want to see it.

Aquasi takes me to my hotel for the night. I can't believe someone is talking below my window during the middle of the night. Back to sleep for a couple hours and when I awake it's 10:30 in the morning. Well, it was the middle of the night somewhere. Aquasi had said his guest might want to go with me, but he hasn't called yet so off I go.

It's a short walk to the ferry, about five or six blocks. There's a big crowd coming – mostly French - so I hurry up. How many this boat holds I do not know but I don't want to wait another hour for the next one. No problem. The boat barely holds everyone. Ten minutes later we leave and within 20 minutes we're at the Goree Island dock. There are several persistent "guides" and "traders." Goree Island is part of Dakar, and in Dakar, everyone's a trader. Traders are anyone selling anything, and they do. They come by it naturally, for Dakar was a historic trading port, ideally situated by being the westernmost point of Africa.

The first stop is the northern fortification. It provided the defense of the Dakar harbor and that of the island itself. Most of the island's buildings were built in the 1700s, and many have been beautifully restored. The stucco walls and tile roofs stand amidst sand walkways, refuse and traders. Not one other American is here. Most of the visitors are speaking French.

On one of the main streets, which would be called an alley most anywhere else, is the slave museum. It's contained in a building that was the last stop for many before leaving the African continent. Rusted handcuffs are still bolted to the wall. There's a doorway open to the sea; nothing to be seen except water. I'm told it was the doorway to load ships . . . with slaves. It's frightening that we humans can be so unbelievably cruel and perverted. It doesn't help much to know that there was slavery in Africa (and still is) long before the Europeans, and that native Americans practiced it long before 1492.

On the southern cliffs at the opposite end of the island, a young man catches up to me and walks along. He introduces himself as Gora. He's interesting and knowledgeable. Gora points out where there was an attempt to build a causeway to the mainland at one time. You can still see some remnants of the stones. He asks if I'd seen the movie "The Guns of Navarone." Yes, I had. "This is where the cliff scenes were filmed," Gora says. I remember the cliffs being much taller. Well, maybe. I thank him for his time and head back to the hotel.

I pick up some French bread on the way. It's one of the good things the colonists left as a legacy. It's for sale at every little stand on the street, and is excellent.

There are two calls at the hotel. Aquasi says his house guest had wanted to go but was too late. Too bad, but my trip alone was fine. "How about a drink"" he asks. Sure, and let me buy dinner, I reply. Aquasi says he and his guest have made other plans for dinner. No problem.

They pick me up at the hotel and drive to one of their favorite places, which is open to the street. Three kids and one wheelchair-bound man ask for something. Aquasi explains most kids like these are given to a "holy man" to train. He gives them a place to sleep and feeds them, but they "work" the streets most of the day. All money goes to "the man." I suggest that's a version of a pimp. "Exactly," he says.

I give one of the girls a balloon. She tells another and another. All of a sudden, there are lots of kids. A big guy from the restaurant chases them with an ax handle. The girl falls in the street and lies there, crying. Big man "suggests" they leave but I grab his arm and explain I had invited them. "No problem then" he says with a smile.

I pay for the drinks - three freshly squeezed orange juices for Aquasi's wife, two gin and tonics for him, and two beers for me. The total is about $20. We talk on the short ride back. Nice people. I call his wife "Tory" and tell her why (a reference to one of my strong-willed and hard working daughters), and we get along fine. I tell her that she is not allowed to meet Tory - they'd take over the world! She loves it.

Back at the hotel, I eat in the little open-air dining room. Tonight there are two musicians with guitars and high falsetto voices making a pleasing background. The beet brochettes with a little onion, tomato and green pepper are good, as are the excellent French fries. Cost about $5, including another beer.

I'm packed. My ride should be here at midnight. My departure's scheduled for three in the morning. Because my "direct" flight has five stops along the way, arrival is supposed to be nine tomorrow night.

As I wait, I remember a well-dressed woman I saw yesterday. While she talked to those around her, she brushed her teeth with a "Masai toothbrush" - a wood stick with frayed ends. I'd seen it before; it's not uncommon. I also remember Aquasi mentioning that 40 percent of the people here die before reaching the age of the girl with the balloon, who was perhaps 8 or 9. Those who survive are strong. He says it's not just genetics - that helps - but it's their positive attitude. Interesting thoughts.

Olivier - French Guide

Central African Republic - 1995

Well, we've taken off and landed a few times and now I don't even know what country I'm in. From Dakar, Senegal, to Accra in Ghana, backtracking to Abidjan in the Ivory Coast, to Lomé in Togo, to Douala in Cameroon to N'Djamena in Chad, and finally we're off to Bangui in the Central African Republic. I feel like I ought to help load live chickens at every stop, except we're in an Airbus 300.

We finally arrive. Oliver has flown in from Paris to be my main guide. He picks me up at the airport and takes me to a little hotel right on a river. Across the river is the Democratic Republic of the Congo. The hotel has only about six rooms and a few tables for food and beverage. We sit down at one of the tables, and I ask if they have any dark beer.

"No sir. Sorry."

"No problem, just any beer then."

The waiter begins walking away, then turns around and says, "Well, we do have Guinness."

Oliver and I have two beers each as we watch the dugouts paddle by.

The next morning it's not a limo that picks me up but a "push-to-start" car. We pile an awful lot of stuff in, plus the driver, Oliver, Patient (a local guide) and me. There's also another guy in the back. I ask who he is. "He's the mechanic."

We bounce along. The transmission grinds and clunks. Can you feel sorry for a car? On the highway it's much better and now we're rolling.

After two hours, the highway turns to sand, then to red dust. We stop at a checkpoint. There are six people sitting at makeshift desks alongside the road. They are all trying very hard to look official. We're told we have to see "the man" in the little building. They all point to a little building 50 feet away. It seems like it's their only job other than that of one man who will pull the rope that raises the wooden pole barrier across the road. This man has on an old army cap.

The checkpoint building has two or three decrepit rooms, and there several people, including "the man," who sits behind a desk looking quite stern. It seems that with the slightest bit of authority comes the instruction manual that says you lord it over those below you. Oliver whispers what he had told me before: "He will definitely want some money." My real estate smile appears. The man takes down all information; where we're going, with whom, when we're returning. We talk a little. Next he wants our passport numbers. I fumble, find some Altoid mints and offer him one. He gently asks if he can have two. "Of course."

Oliver and I have each have a mint, also. "The man" takes down the passport numbers. I thank him and we leave. Oliver's astonished – the man didn't ask for money! I love it. Those 15 minutes were shot but it was a fun experience. The guys at the road wave goodbye. I feel sorry for them.

The next checkpoint's a minor one. This time "the man" is seated on the side of the road at a table. He raises the barrier with a big smile and waves us on after apologizing for "stopping the 'two presidents.' "

Soon we come to a river to cross and stop at the improvised ferry. We say goodbye to the driver and thank him. The awaiting dugout is the largest I've ever seen. It must be 30-foot long, 3-foot wide and 3-foot deep. We load our gear. Small waves wash over the edges as we go along. I hold the camera bag up, ready to swim with it above my head if necessary. We bail, paddle and float downstream for an hour or so when we reach our destination.

Tonight we're to camp at the home of a former guide, Augustin. Augustin went blind a few years ago. He's about 40, still runs the porter group, and is very agreeable. The local porters are Baka (or Ba'aka or Aka) Pygmies. Patient, the local guide, is a member of the Bantu tribe.

Blind Augustin

Later I hear the story of when Augustin became blind. When he went blind for no apparent reason, the authorities wanted to know why he went blind and what caused it. They hired an Aka Pygmy shaman (who I will stay with a few days from now). The Pygmies are not respected but many think they have some magic powers. (Incidentally, using the word "Pygmy" is not an insult here as some outsiders think. That's what they call themselves). Also thought to be magic are the forests in which they live. The forests are believed to be deep, dark and filled with many evil spirits. I find out that the Pygmies do little to dispel this belief. It serves them well.

The shaman hired by the authorities questioned everyone involved. He found out that Augustin and his brother had a argument. The brother moved to a town some distance away. The shaman actually testified in court that the brother had put on Augustin a curse that caused him to go blind. The court agreed. The police were instructed to go to that town and arrest the brother. They did (bet he was surprised). The brother was then sentenced to jail. This all happened several years ago. From what I am told, he's still in jail.

During my visit, I think how the world works. The Pygmies are the low group on the totem pole. No one speaks their language. When you are "below" another group, you learn to speak their language. Therefore, on this trip, I speak English (dominant) to the Frenchman, who speaks

French (dominant) to Patient the Bantu, who speaks Bantu (dominant) to the Pygmies. This language principle seems to be true in every country I've been in, and is probably universal. That's all the more reason all Americans should learn English. At this time it's the language of power in the United States and the world, too. Ethnicity doesn't hold one back here as much as the inability to speak the language of power. Yeah, I know, it's not fair. Politic Real. Expect fairness in the next world.

Before leaving the US, I was fortunate to meet two professors from Harvard who gave me a full sheet of paper with Pygmy (Aka) words on it. They had done their doctoral thesis on another Pygmy tribe (there are five distinct, separated groups of Pygmies in Africa). The five languages are different but mutually understandable and fairly easy to pronounce, unlike many other languages. I memorized many of the words, which really came in handy. It's a big hit when I talk directly to some of the Aka and we share a laugh about something Patient and Oliver don't understand. Of course, half the time, I don't either.

The next morning we're off to visit a village where one of our porters has a wife and father. It's an easy walk as far as ups and downs go. There are few hills. I have my own canteen, empty it twice and then finish off Oliver's extra one. It's 90 degrees and very humid. After 4½ hours, it's not quite as much fun. The path is difficult to find at times - the porters who are leading change their minds twice to where it is and we have to circle back. The trail constantly curves and is overgrown with small bush. Enough light gets through the canopy to allow plenty of ground cover to grow. Machetes have previously cut many branches at 45-degree angles. Hardened, the new spouts cover up the sharp points, as I quickly discover.

The Pygmies are as small, as I had imagined, but strong. Maybe the cigarettes help. Their big advantage seems to be that even though I am following all them, I collect all the cobwebs above 5½ feet. They also had asked Augustin for some palm wine before we left. Don't think they got it. Oliver, Patient and I take a five-minute break at a little encampment that's been deserted. The porters continue on. Later, our stopping will prove to be a big mistake.

We arrive at the first little grouping where each family has their own

Our tents, villagers' houses, and Pygmies

The Bantu Woman

hut. This is where we will sleep tonight. The little village is about 100 feet across and the middle of it is branch-brushed, hard-packed dirt. There about 30 people living here, including several Bantu people. One Bantu woman lives across the river but also has a house here to collect coca leaves which she sells. (Yes, that coca.) The villagers' homes are different from the Pygmies' huts. They are upright sticks covered with mud – technically, wattle construction. More work but more room.

Brown butterflies - 30 foot dugout

The Pygmies' huts are made by putting young saplings in the ground, bending the tops to a central point and layering banana leaves over the framework. The floor is dirt. They are really small, and I could not have stretched out inside in any that I saw. Patient and a couple of the porters put up tents, one for me and two for them. The Pygmies at first are quite shy. The adults glance, but quickly look away and pretend not to notice. Several children run into their huts when they see me. For most of them, I'm one of the first beings they've seen who are 6 feet tall, bald and - you guessed it - has this sickly white skin. Guess I'd run, too.

There's another Bantu living with the Pygmies. Isn't it fascinating how many ways there are to earn a living? This guy is a butterfly collector, and he's most excited to show me how's it's done. I find interesting to see the methods used to collect the butterflies.

One method: He puts an attractant on the ground in any clearing. Then he comes back daily with a butterfly net waving it over the stuff and catching them as they take off. The second method: He builds a cylinder of a cheesecloth-like material and hangs it from a tree in a clearing. The cylinder is about a foot and a half in diameter, 2 feet tall and is closed at the top. At the bottom, three strings suspend a 2-inch platform with more attractant on it. The butterfly flies in to snack, then flies up to leave and is trapped in the cylinder. Evidently it never dawns on them to fly down and

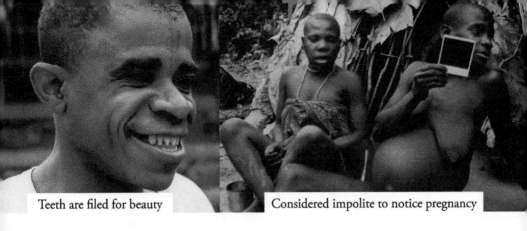

Teeth are filed for beauty

Considered impolite to notice pregnancy

away to freedom. Intriguing. Oh, the attractant? It's irresistible to them, he says: Ripe bananas mixed with human excrement. To each his own!

Each butterfly is carefully crushed and put in a paper container, which is folded in a triangle. When enough are collected, the man makes the long journey to Bangui to sell them to another collector. That collector uses all the colors of the wings to make beautiful, framed pictures that he sells. They're nice - I've seen them - but the colors looked even better, in my opinion, on the living butterfly. My new friend knows the price and name of each butterfly. One he just collected is worth about $10, because it is so rare. It's rarer now. He has hundreds of all types.

There's a little time to relax before dinner. Patient has discovered he's picked up many ticks. They appear as little specks of black, like a poppy seed. Oliver looks and has lots, too, as do I. The porters, who didn't stop at that deserted camp, don't have any.

The porters seem excited. They all pitch in and take the ticks off us. Each is taken off and pinched between the fingernails to kill it. My ticks appear to be fairly well organized. They're mostly on my ankles and uniformly arranged about one quarter of an inch apart - at least a hundred. Amazing! The back, neck and legs are not spared. They are easy to see on Oliver's white skin and mine, but more difficult on the others. Three of the friendliest Pygmies enthusiastically help me with my feet and legs. We all laugh when I suggest I'll take care of the ones on my upper thighs and beyond. Men's humor.

(An aside - after I get home I find three more ticks the size of rice grains under my toenails. The doctor who removed them actually wrote a paper on it. I'm famous somewhere).

Patient and Oliver are busy with other things. I'm alone at last with the

Pygmies. The balloons I give out are great. Even the shyest kid takes part. The Polaroids are excellent too. A picture's taken and they crowd around leaning against me watching the magic picture develop. None have ever seen this before. It was magic the first time I saw it, too. Before taking any picture, I ask "Da mo dinga?" (Do you want this?), pointing at the camera. The slightest nod signifies "Yes." An hour after taking a picture of a young couple and their baby in front of their hut, I glance back across the clearing at them. They are still there, still looking at their picture.

A bag shower is set up and though I never thought I'd be cold again, the cold water jolts comfort back. Feels good to get rid of the grime, if just for a half an hour. I certainly could have washed up in a stream, but after they had gone to the trouble of setting it all up, I can't refuse. Within 15 minutes, I'm sweating again.

As the night goes on, each family sits in front of their own hut, and gentle talking and laughter fill the twilight, along with the sound of chickens, crickets, and a bird here and there. Tired, I lie down in my tent. Soon there is singing. I look out and in the moonlight to see several Pygmies dancing and smiling at me. The butterfly collector and his wife are there, too. I can barely see. Accompanied by a drum, and banging on a Fanta bottle, the dancing goes on for an hour. It's in honor of me visiting them!

Sleep comes easily. It's raining, a little, then a lot for several more hours. The tent and the fly keep out 95 percent of the water, and I adjust the position of the camera and my pack to avoid the rest.

In the morning the soil is so sandy that there are no puddles left by all the rain. Voices, a few birds, someone singing some words, a call across the clearing, a cough. We're slow to get going and it's decided we need five porters instead of the four we had yesterday. They did too much. Porters get $2 a day, plus a gift and a little food.

It's 11 a.m. when we get on the way. The tea and hot multigrain cereal were just enough for breakfast. An orange along the way with plenty of water rounds out the intake. The color of your urine tells you if you are drinking enough. Too dark? Drink more. The bathroom is any place out of sight. The trail is so slight that if it weren't for the porters and Patient up front, I would have had to stop and search for it every 20 feet. If Oliver or I stop or slow down, Patient and one porter always notice and wait. If there's a fork in the trail, they'll drag a foot to mark which way we should go.

We only pass through a couple of streams but the cool water feels good on my feet. Several times Patient yells "Hunts!" or something like it and we all jump and run like the devil. It took me a couple of times before I realized he was saying "Ants!" They bite like the devil. Once you get past the area where they are, you stop and examine your legs and shoes, ridding yourself of the ones that made it onboard fighting to get to the bare flesh. I understand there are thousands of species of ants here.

After about 3½ hours, we arrive at the next Aka village. Neither Pygmy village was on a stream, but both had "sources" (dug holes where water is collected). We had gone on ahead a little and now the porters have arrived. The tents are being set up. About 15 people live here and there are eight huts, some typical Pygmy huts and a couple that had been built for the Bantu villagers but that are now occupied by Pygmy families. I bring out more balloons but there is only one child who shyly accepts it and only then with the encouragement of his mother. He puts it in his home and comes back out.

The Polaroid's better. A father and son portrait is shown to others when they return from gathering. We all laugh at the expressions caught by the camera. Several more pictures are given away. It's fun to see them develop and watch the expressions on the faces of the photo subjects. The kids love them almost as much as they love the balloons. It's also fun to see them not recognize one person in a group - themselves!

This place is called Wa Loon' Goo. The father of Antoine (another guide) is a villager and his mother is an Aka. I'm told he is treated as an Aka, with no special privileges or disdain (however he is not considered a villager). I meet his mother. It is not unusual for villager men to have an Aka wife, especially if they are already married and have not had any children. Village women, however, do not marry Aka men. The Aka are considered beneath them.

Antoine's mother has a headache, so she does not want her picture taken. Two aspirin and a little talk, and her headache is gone as is her reluctance to a picture. In fact, she and her wonderful, old wrinkled mother get to like it and willingly pose again and again. When the flash of the Polaroid goes off the first time, the old woman is really startled and makes a funny, squinting face. We laugh together at the expressions on the Polaroid picture. I notice later she's still looking at her picture. I walk past her and pretend to be startled and squint. She laughs. I have a new friend.

Someone is coming. A hunter and his friends are bringing in a monkey (bo'tee) they just killed. The tail is tied to the head and acts as a handle for slinging over the shoulder. Practical. We buy half of it for dinner. A duiker, a small forest antelope sometimes called a dik-dik, is roasting over a wood fire (or mee'ah). They are smoking it to sell to the villagers, so we can't buy any of it. Too bad; it smelled good. It is supposedly delicious and definitely a preferred meat. The monkey is a distant second. Gee - too bad.

The chickens look healthy here, especially compared with the walking cadaver of a dog. There are bees everywhere. The Aka keep some hives nearby. Honey is one of their favorite foods. The first man we see is an uncle to Antoine. He is very nice as are the others once the formalities and shyness are overcome. Clothing seems optional for the very young. Everyone else has a mixture of pubic aprons with "arse grass" behind, or an eclectic variety of hand-me-downs from somewhere. A hen and her three chicks are chased from a home.

The huts here are made a little differently, with the large banana leaves placed over smaller leaves and supported by a framework of saplings. The "furniture" is a log, a rock or two forked sticks stuck in the ground with a crosspiece for sitting. In one hut there were three sets of those with a dozen saplings to form a couch or bed. The height was about 6 inches.

The Aka cut their hair very short. The men have a considerable amount of hair on their lower legs. It's tufted and kinkier than most people in Africa I've seen. I look for more ticks. None, but Oliver points out my arms are covered with red botches, as are his. "It'll go away," he assures me. There's no itching, probably fleas or those little flies. Never felt them.

Lunch consists of a cracker-like bread, tea, liver pate, fish in a mustard sauce from a can, plus a small can of pudding. I have two candy bars and one high-fiber one. A chicken takes some of the bread off our floor-level "table" (which is a tarp), and is yelled at. The chicken drops the small loaf in the sand and the loaf is replaced on the table. I didn't care for it anyway; it was getting stale. It took the canned ham last night to make it taste good. Hungry? The chickens look good here, better than this morning. The hungrier you are the better the chickens look, I suppose. We had a chance to buy a chicken this morning and we didn't - "It was too expensive." Now I'm told that the monkey tastes better than dog. "Have you had dog?" "No, I haven't."

The Aka must have been occupying this village for a long time, or else the sites have been used many times before, because the middens (refuse heaps) that surround the village are 2-feet high and 12-feet across. Everything that is in the middle of the huts - extra food, excrement from the chickens and dogs, leaves, whatever - is swept around the back of the huts each day with brooms made of branches.

At dinner, a bite of monkey meat isn't bad at all. It's a very fine-grained, firm, dark meat with not a lot of flavor. I don't eat much; want to make sure the porters have enough. Time for bed. A lady in the hut to the left of mine calls out "Ooooooo" every 15 seconds or so - for an hour. Odd.

Up early, about 6:15. Today we're going to Mungo, which is about a three-hour walk. Near the end of the trek, we cross quite bit of water, at least a 200 feet. The good news is it's only 2-foot deep and no leeches. The bad news — there's a muddy bottom. The villagers have damned a small stream where they collect 1- 3-pound catfish. We're coming to a small village, and Oliver bargains like a trooper for some of the fish. He knows what the price they should be. Very hospitable people and we have good fun bargaining. They kill about six and we leave. Total cost: About $3.

Now we're coming into a large clearing with a huge 12-foot termite mound. This is the Aka village of Mungo. This village is more open and friendlier, with maybe eight small boys running around. Balloons are vigorously played with all afternoon. A nice woman agrees to a picture and I give her one. Taking pictures of anyone is not a problem after that. They all want one now.

This village was built by Bantu villagers but now is occupied exclusively by the Aka. The chickens look healthy and so do the three dogs. Everyone spends much of the day looking at pictures. An old man is making a kaka, a backpack. I use every Aka word I know in the next 10 minutes asking about it. He seems genuinely pleased to explain how he makes it. Fun! Hand gestures help. It's interesting how he does it: The wood is bent while it's soft and wet so that it hardens to the shape he wants. Everything is held together with small strings of vine, wrapped and knotted tightly.

Some delicious pineapple is served. A fiber candy bar is shared. Later, a cold shower feels good. Then we share what they call wheat that looks like what I would call rice. It's mixed with diced tomato, and is excellent. We pawn off the bread and canned fish to the porters, who love it.

Relations Lesson 101 from my wife: Ask a person something about themselves, something they really know, show interest, and watch them come alive. Everyone is friendly but reserved. The older kids are too cool to risk talking with me, for fear of being embarrassed. There is one small boy in particular who responds to my faces and gestures. I wave him over and ask him about a few words on my list. Soon all the kids are there, including the older ones. Soon they are trying to outdo each other with helpful answers. Aka Language Lesson 101 in progress, in earnest. Many corrections and suggestions are made in pronunciation, all clamoring to be first. They love it, and so do I! One of the helpful boys does an interesting thing proving we are all somehow alike: I have thanked him several times for helping with a word. I compliment another boy next to him for coming up with a word. Even though there is plenty of room, the first boy steps slightly in front him to intercept my attention. There are some traits we all share.

I see a man looking at the picture I have given him. No, he's looking at lots of pictures in a small album! Someone who had been through here before actually went to the trouble of sending these pictures back. How very nice! (At least he put mine in the beginning of the album.)

Unfortunately, distended stomachs on the kids here are quite common

— about half the children have them - but not the adults. Because they look healthy other than that, a biologist I mentioned it to later told me that it was probably caused by worms.

The toes of most of the people here are disfigured, likely a combination of ticks and cuts. Wearing any form of shoes or sandals is a sometime thing at best. One of the porters, Rambo (seriously, I politely asked twice when I was introduced), cut his foot and Oliver put a piece of tape on it. Rambo then put on a used sock of mine and walked that way. Of course the sock had no sole left after the first hour or so.

As I noted, the clothing here seems to consist of a simple pubic apron or hand-me-down shorts. Cleanliness does not appear to be terribly relevant. Feet and hands are seemingly never washed but faces and the rest do not appear dirty. Fingernails and toenails are left natural. Many toenails appear broken off. Small children are washed with a bucket over the head, and lots of love.

Yagbia is my special friend. He always stays back with Patient just in front of me on the trail. He points which way to go and what to look out for. He unobtrusively and gently shows me low branches, the way to go, and things to avoid. Yagbia is now asking an old woman if she would like her picture taken. She's properly embarrassed but agrees. It turns out that she's even more pleased with the results than the others. Over here it seems like everyone "freezes" when having their picture taken. Smile? Certainly not. For some reason you must look like expressionless at best, intimidating at worse. We have a lot of fun together seeing the pictures develop. I kid her about such a somber face. She loves the pictures - and the attention.

Holes in the ears are slightly bigger than is usual in America, but I do not see anyone with more than one hole per ear. I suppose they would think it barbaric. Also many have a hole in the upper lip right under the nose that is not used anymore; maybe it's out of fashion. Oliver says they used to use wood plugs, but now it is only for the older woman. Similar to Papua New Guinea, it is not the "thing to do" any longer.

The pecking order not only applies to chickens and dogs in the clearing, but to people as well. It's just more immediately evident with the

Pygmy ax and dog bell | $2 ax

chickens and dogs. When it comes to playing with the balloons, there are great differences not only in athletic ability but "who's who." Personalities emerge. I discuss with Patient the differences in giving directions in Africa and home. Here, the body language of the giver shows total disrespect (at least it appears to me) toward the one directed: A quick wave of the hand, the looking away, the brusque command. The lack of negative reactions tells me it is customary. I tell him I have found it in every country in West Africa. He smiles shyly.

Yagbia is back. The man with him has two axes, or zum'bee. I had asked if I could buy one. They are branches, including the fork where a piece of rough steel is fastened with strands of vine. They are very sharp. How much? He wants more but we end up at about $2. It is fair, Yagbia tells me. Later, I wonder how I am going to get an axe through airport security in a carry-on.

Several fires are going, and smoke is always part of the scene, as are the chickens. The chickens not only supply meat and eggs but also help keep the crawly things at bay. The dogs are used to hunt and keep the bigger animals out of the village. Shi means shoo to the dogs and chickens, and they all respond quickly. The butterflies and the lilt of language going back and forth complete the picture of this peaceful village.

The spoken word seems to be monotone then drops at the end of the sentence. A higher pitch or faster speaking means emphasis or argument. The variety of intonation seems to vary but these patterns are found in the back and forth across the compound.

In the last village, one of the village boys picked up a small dog and threw it, twice. Laughter followed.

It's morning again; tea and toast with jam start us off. We also treat more of the cloudy water we have for drinking. The kids have invented games with the balloons, but interestingly enough they all play individually, not in groups. Glancing at the sky, it looks like rain.

As usual, we say goodbye and I shake hands with every adult who has lined up to do so. "Au revoir" and "Merci." On the way out, I say "Au revoir" to one of the dogs sitting there and offer to shake. Big laugh. Everyone watches every move I make, but try not to appear to be doing so. I certainly don't mind. I am the oddity here. They have good senses of humor.

We're heading for Karawa which is only about two hours away. Typically I give away any clothing that has been worn. Today's fashion has all the porters proudly wearing my donated boxer shorts with plaids and stripes - very colorful. They laugh when they see my reaction.

The going is easy for a mile or so, and then we reach water. Oftentimes the trail is the waterway, where constant use of a machete is not necessary. A dry trail comes soon.

No rain yet. It poured last night, and even though it is the dry season, everything is wet. My shoes and socks start out dry after being left near the fire. The temperature is about 82 degrees (same as usual) and surprisingly the humidity isn't too uncomfortable. Breezes only are felt in the occasional clearings. The only insects that seem to be abundant are the billions of ants and butterflies - both in huge varieties.

We run through an ant area. Sometimes it's necessary to run a hundred meters, sometimes we just jump over a foot-wide column of the little creatures. We always stop to check our legs and shoes immediately afterward. (I miss one and discover it still fighting to get through my sock when we get to Karawa.)

Karawa was built by the villagers (Bantu) and has a cleanly swept area of hard sand in the center. There are several villagers still staying here with the Aka, including two visiting sisters looking for coca leaves. The older one wears nail polish, and is very friendly and a kind of a flirt. The differences between the Bantu villagers and the Pygmies are very evident. The Bantu are more forward, the Pygmies quite shy. With the Pygmies, a slight nod of the head upward to say "yes" to a picture or question is almost unnoticeable.

The flirt says she will cut some lettuce for us for dinner. Good. She sits down and eats with us, then asks for a balloon, then a bite of my candy bar. When she sees the picture of Alex, my granddaughter, she tells Oliver that she has three black babies and would like me to give her a white baby like this. I quickly surmise that she is not speaking of an adoption agency. Some pickup line!

Minutes later, a man dressed in shorts, what was an officer's cap, and matching khaki shirt comes over to us. He's the shaman, the one who was called by the government to determine what caused the blindness in the man we'd met earlier. He's very nice and hospitable, and interesting to talk with. No, I didn't ask him about the blind man.

Some other villagers pass by with loads of manioc and banana leaves. Picture? No problem.

Only one villager is nasty. I hadn't met her or talked with her, and certainly hadn't asked for her picture. She comes over and with her finger waving in my face tells me "No picture!" She didn't understand I was giving the pictures away. I tried to explain. She is still yelling at me as she goes away. We didn't understand each other's language, and that's probably a good thing thinking back. I don't know what she said but neither did she know I called her a bitch. She'll be back later. . .

The porters have the tents up, one for Patient, one for Oliver, and one for me, as usual. My shower is constructed of four or five fresh saplings holding up a curtain. Next, they fill up a black bag with a spigot on it. The sun warms the water. I try to tell them not to go through all this bother but I find it's a wasted effort. Constructing the shower is the way it's done, period. The black bag of water in the sunlight is hot in just an hour or two. It is a wonderful luxury.

I've read where we in the United States have about 20 percent of our time which we consider "free." These hunter-gathers have 80 percent free time. Hmmm. Life is so simple here. Food, shelter and what they consider necessities are kept simple, too. The Pygmies have a saying, "A hungry Pygmy is a lazy Pygmy." Boy could we learn from that!

The chickens look pretty healthy here. They are actually quite beautiful. Maybe it's time to think about coming home. As I told you earlier about what my wonderful wife said, "When the natives start looking good, come home."

The nasty villager is coming back. She's found out that I was taking pictures and giving them out. Now, with the nicest smile, she asks if she can have one. I know, I should give her one - it would be the nice thing to do - but I don't.

It's peaceful here, but certainly not perfect. Conflicts, sickness and other troubles abound, but they certainly seem happy in the same degree as we are. I'm sitting on a bench. There is a group of men about 50 feet away conversing in quiet voices.

I let my feet air out and then put on my dry shoes. The nylon exercise pants work well: light, allow sweat to get out, dry quickly and are some protection against the bugs and brush. Two of the porters are so shy that they still have not talked to me except to answer in a low grunt never looking at me directly, always looking down. Always subservient, always polite. Uncomfortable for me.

Time for dinner. Life centers around food and sleep. Not bad, huh? A couple of candy bars, ham, large crackers. Patient asks: "By the way, do you know what avocados are?" Sure! I tell Patient about guacamole and what's in it. He's excited. He gets some onions and peppers (no tomatoes, darn). We dice up them up, mash the avocado and presto – a sort of guacamole! Of course there are no tortilla chips but crackers provide a good substitute. He loves it. Oliver tries it and likes it too. The Pygmies, one by one, try it. They like anything besides manioc paste and bananas. They love this. Fun time!

Sliced fresh bananas in a canned milk pudding make a delicious dessert – sort of like banana cream pie. Pineapple here is always good too. After dinner, I head out for the "restroom," which remains any place out of sight. It's twilight, and as I head down a trail, a tree shakes. I take it that means someone else in using that spot. Twenty feet further becomes my spot.

On the way back the "tree" is walking in front of me toward the center area of the camp. I sit down and the tree is a bird dancing around with wings of branches! The dancer is so well covered that the only human thing you see, and darn little of that, are his legs. Drummers join in.

The Bird Dance

Small children start to dance with the tree and themselves. Pretty soon everyone is dancing, even the porters. Do I dare take a picture? I try. Flash! Everyone yells and jumps. It's the first time the tree has stopped. Then the music and the dancing resume. There are many dance steps. One favorite is someone hunched over with their arms between their legs, with a rhythmic bending of both knees, then pushing out the butt into the air - great with grass skirts!

There are two drums. One is a hollow log about a foot in diameter and maybe 4 feet long ending with uneven cut notches. The other is more normal shaped. A very talented boy beats two sticks over the open end. It's a very quick beat. Many of the songs are sung by the leader, and then repeated by a chorus by all. Fabulous! Am I here? I light a flashlight and everything stops again. I'm sitting with the headman (I know there isn't supposed to be one, but evidently they haven't read that book), and the other elders. I present him with a gift of a bottle of honey from home. Honey is a favorite treat here. At first he takes some and rubs it on his arm. He has never seen honey in a bottle. I indicate tasting would be better. He loves it! He gives a taste to the dancers on their fingertips.

The dancing and singing have now gone on for hours just 15 feet in front of my tent. It's dark except for the flickering of the dying fires. Occasionally the whine from air being released from a balloon adds the 20th century to a prehistoric scene. Patient has given out some alcohol. Age makes no difference here: there's a 6-year-old smoking. Shadowy silhouettes dance and walk and sit nearby. The moon shines on black skin and the trees are outlined against the gray sky. Sand reflects the moon's rays. The drums provide heavy beats.

The Pygmies look normal size until I stand next to them. Body odor is sometimes strong. Cigarettes provide their own dance in the darkness. There are babies sitting on shoulders, and others being nursed by their mothers. Everyone in the village has joined the gathering. As I sit in the entrance to my tent, some of the older people walk by to say goodbye and shake hands (very loose, more like grazing). I finally realize that this party is for me and that several people from other villages have come over to join in! If I ever thought the Pygmies were always shy, it's because I hadn't seen them at night, uninhibited, loud and unafraid to lead or join. The party is winding down. The drummer has retired, and now a harp is played gently, with the murmurs of a dozen conversations and hundreds of crickets part of the sound. It is a gentle release of the day.

The next morning at 6, the alarm clock chicken is going off. Breakfast is pineapple, tea and Country Store cereal. Coca leaves are being bundled for transport. They are sold as a flavoring for rice. An old man, blind in one eye, walks past. We helped him last night by putting a little antiseptic on a sore on the bottom of his foot. He didn't keep the bandage on it, and he is walking on that sore foot.

The headman – not as shy as most of the others - comes over to my tent, where a little present-giving ceremony takes place. I ask him if the honey was good: "Ee boo' ee, moy ango?"

It was, he says, and again we enjoy the memory of it and his popularity. "Au revoir" and handshakes for everyone.

On the walk back, sadness overwhelms me. I've been so lucky to have this experience. It is my last day is this beautiful forest with these beautiful people with a different way of life. How much longer will they have it?

The cry of "hunts" awakens me and we run on ahead. Then I walk slowly, extending my time here for a few more minutes, a few more pictures.

I had purchased a dog bell, or ee lay' boo, in Karawa. The Aka dogs don't bark, or they can't, and the bells are the way to keep track of them in the jungle when they go hunting. It is one of the few items that the Akas make, crafted from a hollowed out gourd, with a stick or bone as a clapper.

It's only a two-hour walk and no water to go through to get to Bozengunda. This village is not as picturesque as the others, and there's no shade. There's a woman in a bra - a French bra, Oliver says, approvingly. A newly built hut with dirt piled all around the base makes a good picture. The leaves are still green. We visit a hunter's house, but he's not home. We were hoping to taste antelope here. All of these homes are together. At Karawa, there were three small settlements about a quarter mile apart. They were made up of three different, but related, clans who intermarry but cannot live in the same encampment. The clans were the Bom boo loon goo, the Boz zam boo and the Boo za boo.

As is the custom, the porters always eat separately. Patient joins Oliver and me. The porters usually get anything we don't finish, but their main food is manioc, which they love. There are few people here and so we go into a vacant house to get out of the sun and have lunch. Guacamole and crackers. It's about 90 degrees, so we continue to drink a lot of water. Two women are coming - villagers. It's the flirt from last night. We are in her house. She sees the Polaroid and wants one. Sure. We help her and her sister put their heavy baskets back on and get a great picture of them for her. We talk, and she gets another idea. "Do we have a knife?" I let Oliver get his. She cuts coca leaves for our dinner. She shaves the leaves very finely and gives them to us, as a gift. "By the way, that's a nice knife. Can I have it?"

We use the leaves that night as flavoring for some rice. As we sit down to dinner, Oliver says he might have one of those ticks left in his foot, and three porters run over. They almost seem happy about it. The porter called Solocuy gets a stick and digs away at Oliver's toes. He finds three ticks! Then he tells one of the children to get a burning ember, not to sterilize it, I find out, but to harden it. Oliver is now using many colorful French words that I don't understand, but the English ones I do. Must hurt a lot! The porters seem to continue to enjoy it. They have been digging for about 15 minutes and have gotten one out, the biggest they've ever seen. Amid much laughter, they say the ticks grow well on white blood. I had taken my shoes off to be examined, but by now I am positive I don't have any, so put my shoes back on.

"No, no!" They demand to check. Oliver is now rubbing his hands in gleeful anticipation. He also says some very nasty words of disappointment when they don't find any. He doesn't seem the least bit happy at my good luck.

Morning. Darn chicken! I brush my teeth and can feel something in my palm- a tick. Oliver will be so pleased, but he is not out of his tent yet. One of the porters digs it out. It is the twin of Oliver's large one. At breakfast, Oliver thoroughly enjoys the fact that I was not spared, but is disappointed that he missed the operation.

Again, there's the chain of language that comes from the principle of power. I speak English to Oliver. Oliver speaks French to Patient. Patient speaks Songa, his language, to the Aka. No one speaks Babinga, the language of the Aka. The fact is, even some of the Aka gave up a separate language years ago, and now speak a dialect of the Bantu. The porter Yembo, one of the shy, quiet ones, speaks Babinga as do the others as their own language. Some of the porters, including Yagbia, speak enough French to get along well with the outside world. Few people in the country speak English. (Oliver lives outside of Paris and flew down to translate for me.)

The Akas' personal habits, with the exception of the unavoidable omnipresence of dirt, are quite clean in comparison with some other peoples I've visited who live close to nature. In front of almost every hut lie immaculate mounds of manioc and, occasionally, coffee beans drying. Their handling of food is no different than what we would do in the circumstances, and there is comfort in eating anything that is given. Oliver happens to mention during breakfast, "Did you ever notice that the pygmies never fart, burp or spit?" I had noticed they didn't spit.

There are other interesting – and practical customs. Yagbia's first wife died about two months ago and he's still collecting enough money to pay for a ceremony. By custom, he pays everyone who comes to the ceremony, just for coming. He is also responsible for feeding them, while they stay. The burial of the body is immediate, which is practical because of the constant heat and humidity. The ceremony takes place when the bereaved is financially able to do so.

There are also no areas that we would think of as cemeteries, so the custom is to bury the deceased anywhere. Where someone is buried is of no importance. Most likely, it is probably a carryover from the days of a more purely nomadic existence. This contrasts with the villagers, who many times bury the dead in a prominent place in front of their homes. The grave is topped with a concrete bunker, which protrudes about a foot above the ground.

It's time to say goodbye, and more gifts are given out, which seem to be appreciated. As we leave, several people walk along with us awhile. Just a few hours' walk brings us to the river. We are at one of the normal crossing points and discuss the trip as we wait for the ferry. The river is almost 500 feet wide here. Two small dugouts appear, and they are the "ferry." Everyone climbs in, and the freeboard varies between 1 to 2 inches, with water sloshing in. The woman who is paddling ours doesn't seem concerned. I lift my camera and film to keep them out of the water.

That Pygmy ax I bought? Got it all the way through the lax security to Paris. The security woman there was adamant that I could not take it onboard in my backpack. (I had called it a "Pygmy artifact" before she uncovered it fully). I suggested twice the pilot could take it. Upon landing in Chicago, there was the pilot holding the ax, saying goodbye to everyone. He was quite excited to see it: "It must be very valuable."

It is.

Aka language - some conversational words and phrases:

- And: moin
- Ant: ee' coo
- Back: m* beek' ay
- Bad: ee' bee
- Basker with strap: u' gwa
- Be quiet (for one): na ka' kay
- Beautiful: lain' gay
- Bed: boo tung' gee
- Big: m* ba' ee
- Bow and arrow: ban'goo moin yon'go
- Boy (young): mona pie' ay
- Butterfly: ee con gon' go
- Cap: ay ko'ti
- Cigarette: m* bon' ga
- Chicken: ko ko
- Children: bona bee' kay
- Children of the forest: mi' ki ba endur'a
- Come here: Ya' lo
- Dance: ee b
- Do you want this? Na mo ding'ga?
- Dog: bwan'dee
- Dog – "Go away": Too' kay
- Dog bell (for hunting): ee lay' boo
- Drum: mu kin'da
- Eat: zan do' ko
- Ears: ma lu' ee
- Eyes: mee' so
- Far away: eh ting' go
- Finger nails: ay la' dee
- Fire: kun' nay
- Wood on fire: mee' ah
- Food: n* do' ko
- Foot: ma' ku

- Forest: en dee' ma
- Friend: con guy'ee
- Girl (young): ban a bet'tu
- Girl (older): mona mwan'tu
- Good: muy an'go
- Goodbye: mana moo'shwa
- Gnat: mum bung'go
- Hair: bu' koo
- Hand: ma' bo
- Hat: eh ban'da
- Head: mo shu' l
- Heavy: yamo lee'ta
- Hello: la moo bal'an vey
- Honey: boo'ee
- Honey bucket: moo see kee
- House (square villager's type): a bo'ke
- House leaves (large): mon'go
- How are you? Ba boo'eh?
- How many children do you have? Abena bana bwey?
- Hunt: eh du'a dee' ma
- Hunting net: bo kee'a
- Hut (Aka's leaf-covered style):mp pee'ko
- I'm sorry: Ne mo kun' dwa
- Knife: ee ay tu' bu
- Language (language of these groups): Ki (Ki Batu)
- Love: bo ling gan ee na ku
- Leg: lun'ga
- Lips: moon'wa
- Man: pie' ay
- Manioc: man'nee och (also, yo kota)
- May I take your picture? Ne ti bouch a vay un?
- My name is . . . : Comb bu'mu . . .
- Monkey: bo' tee
- Mother: in'go

- Neck: mon gay' doo
- No: bo'eh
- Nose: m* nu (one syllable)
- OK: mee yon' go
- Of; ah
- Pack (narrow): m* band'da
- Papa: tay'ay
- People (Aka): ba Bing'ga
- People: ba Ba'tu
- People of the forest: ba Ba'tu ban endur'a
- Pepper: bo doin'go
- Porter: na mun'da kum'ba
- Puppy: bwandi bo'bo
- Rat: ee su' ru
- Sacred horn: mo lee' mo
- Sapling: moon mu' lay
- Shirt: ee a tu' bo
- Shoes: ba po'po
- Shorts: ki lo'tee
- Sing: lem'bo
- Skin: day kat'ah
- Small: mona lain' gay
- Socks; ba bed' ay lay
- Spear: lee kon'go
- Stomach: em' moy
- Sunglasses: ba ta tel'la
- Thank you: na mu bi aka merci
- Teeth: mee' new
- Tongue: ay lem' ee
- Travel (as in "I travel"): Na mu dwa ba' butu
- Trek: enzi ee lie' ee
- Tree: mor' lay
- Tribe (six nearby groups): Ba'tu
- Vine for net: n* ku' sa

- Voyage: anzie lay' ee
- Walk: cool' way
- Water: my
- Water from water-producing vine: mo zam' bee
- What's your name? Comb bu vey' onay?
- Where's Mama? En go wa'bay?
- Where's Papa? Tie ay tung'go?
- Woman: mo' tu
- Yes: ee
- You are bad: ah ben na cot'ee na' ku
- You are good (pretty): mo too (w) may angu
- You liar: bongo ya'ko

Numbers:
- One: m* mo' tee
- Two: ba' by
- Three: ma'sa too
- Four: o shoo'
- Five: o coo'

- The m and n sounds are pronounced as in humming. The mouth is closed with the m and with n the tongue is at the top of the mouth so that the sound is produced through the nose.

The Statue - 1995

We were proud to be the third generation to live in the old house. There were lots of good memories. That is what made it all the more difficult to move. An excellent job opportunity in Atlanta brought the decision to a head. We never realized that by cleaning out the attic, we'd come across the strangest story. I still don't know what to think of it. Under some old clothes at the bottom of an old trunk that was my grandfather's, was a very old metal box. In the box was a handwritten account of what happened in the summer of 1891. Here is what it said:

August 19, 1891, account of James F. Bruce, 13 years old.

My family lives in lower Canada in the town of Anders Crossing. My father and mother own the general store. I work there too, after school. Every Saturday in August, we take the train for an outing. The train drops us off about three hours out of town and picks us up Sunday night on its way back. We just stand on the side of the tracks and wave to make it stop. The brakes make a screaming sound and then a loud hissing when the train stops. There is a lot of noise and smoke when it starts up again too. It's always great fun and we all look forward to it. My mother and father, my two sisters, my uncle Nels, his wife and two children usually come, along with our neighbors, the Manegolds. We discovered a spot along a stream where lots of blueberries grow. We pick a lot of them to sell in the store, though we eat as many as we take home. It's our secret place. We bring along tents and set up our camp right at the edge of the stream.

This past weekend something happened that we were all told to never tell anyone, and I never have, but I want to write it all down so I won't forget a thing. As usual, we arrived at the stream late Saturday morning and immediately began picking blueberries. By noon we were all hungry for the big lunch that mother and Mrs. Manegold had packed. After lunch, we picked even more blueberries to take home so mother could make jam and a pie. It was just getting dark when two huge creatures came into our camp. (I was so scared I couldn't move. We all were.) They had to duck under an overhanging branch. (I measured how high the branch was later and it was eight and a half feet off the ground!) They were not only huge but were covered with what looked like fine hair. In the light of our campfire they appeared almost green. They walked right up to us and it was evident they only had covering for the lower part of their bodies. They appeared to be men, and sort of human, but none like I'd ever seen. One came up to me and asked me in English (but it was funny sounding) if I would like to have what appeared to be a ball with soft spikes. I didn't know what to do, but I took the ball. Whenever you touched or even held any of the spikes, they would change color! When he threw the ball it would change colors as it bounced along the ground. It was great. I stared at them. All of us were still a little afraid, but they seemed to be friendly. Then the strangest thing happened. One of them took out what appeared to be a gun of some sort and quickly pointed it at me and I felt a warmth go from the top of my head to my feet. I jumped and looked at my father. He didn't know what to do either, it happened so fast. Out of the gun the man took a blob of what appeared to be clay, or soft metal. I don't know how else to describe it. Then he put it in my hand. Then he squatted down next to me and pointed to the blob, which was warm and moving. It was growing! I almost dropped it. It started growing into a shape of a person. He kept saying "good, good." I remember laughing a little. Now everyone had crowded around to see the blob. We were all quite close and I realized the man's arm was next to mine, because I could feel the hair. He was strange, but the green tint wasn't as green as I first thought. He didn't seem as huge as before either, but that's maybe because he was squatting down next to me. We all watched the blob I was holding. It was forming more and more into a little statue. Then I realized it was a statue of me! It was perfect in every detail, even my cap. The man asked if I wanted it. I nodded "yes" and I was very grateful. He seemed very gentle but he was still a little scary because he was so big and different. Then almost as quickly as they had come, they were gone, ducking under the branch at the edge of camp. We didn't know what to think. I still had the spiked ball and the statue. We all talked about it far into the night. Father said he heard in early summer some hunters had told about three similar creatures that came into their camp, but no one really believed the hunters. Everyone said they had been drinking too much. It seemed the creatures they saw were different from the ones that visited us. They stared at the hunters and laughed among themselves. They spoke funny sounds, none of which made sense to the hunters. They towered over the hunters. Then they pointed their guns at them. The hunters felt a warmth go from their head to their feet like we did, but they were given nothing, not even a spiked ball. The hunters said if they ever saw the creatures again, they were going to yell at the creatures not to fire their guns at them, but father wondered if they really would. The creatures were awfully big and the guns didn't actually hurt, the hunters admitted. The hunters said they were glad when the awful things left. I was sorry to see them go. It was kind of scary, but fun."

Then I saw it. Under my grandfather's papers, there was a small statue of a boy, perfect in every detail, even a cap.

(Written upon my return from visiting the Aka, the Pygmies, in the Central African Republic. I gave away balloons and Polaroid pictures.)

Ivory Coast - 1995

A friend of a friend has invited me to make a stop in Abidjan, the capital of Ivory Coast, on the way back from Bangui in the Central African Republic. As soon as I get settled in my hotel, I'll call her. In planning the trip with an agent, I had asked for a local hotel, not the Holiday Inn type. This one's local. Seems like there are quite a few couples very much in love here (not the Christian type of love, more of the hourly type). I call Michelle and she picks me up.

Michelle's an Associated press reporter for 23 countries in Africa and works through stringers (local reporters). She's half Rhodesian, half French, and delightful. Screamingly liberal, she even has to turn over a magazine on her coffee table because it has a picture of Republican Speaker of the House Newt Gingrich on it. With my very Scottish last name, Michelle mentions that her sister is studying and teaching in Glasgow, Scotland.

We go to a congenial Vietnamese restaurant. Michelle insists on paying for dinner and strongly suggests I stay at her home the next night. I agree. She rents the house, a nice enough home next to the Ivory Coast minister of justice, who has a guardhouse out front. Michelle has a sentinel who sleeps on a piece of cardboard in the garage and watches the house for her. He also opens the gate to the sound of her truck-like car, which is outfitted with rhino bar bumpers. Makes her feel powerful, she says.

The next day I drop my bag at Michelle's and went to see the zoo. It's just OK, though it's supposed to be one of the best in Central Africa. Next I find the Natural History Museum is closed because the staff is setting up for some type of exhibition. After finding the curator, he sends for someone to let me in (everyone sends for someone). The museum is made up mostly of interesting old masks. It's just OK, too.

The Basilica of Our Lady of Peace is the biggest church in the world they tell me. It's located in Yamoussoukro, the administrative center of the Ivory Coast. In this country with a population of 24 million people, about one-third of the people are Muslim, a third practice traditional African religions and a third are Christian, mostly Catholic. Even though the Our Lady of Peace is 30,000 square meters and St. Peter's Basilica in Rome is only 21,000, the interior of St. Peter's is larger and holds 60,000 compared with 18,000 for Our Lady of Peace.

The $300 million cost of building it was very controversial at the time. It was dictated by the president, who happens to be represented in the Basilica as the only black-skinned figure in the colorful stained glass windows.

I find out that the drive to the Basilica would be an "estimated" two to four hours to the huge church in a very crowded bus. I'm concerned about getting delayed somewhere and not getting to my return flight on time. I had planned on seeing it and should have gone anyway.

Michelle and a few of her friends get together after work, and we all go out for drinks and dinner. They're fun and have varied backgrounds. They ask me about my visit to the Aka Pygmies. Somehow the mention of guacamole comes up. I tell the story of suggesting to the Aka to mix the avocado with some tomato and onion, how we used some Swedish crackers to dip into it, and that the Akas loved it. Michelle gets all excited. She says she is going to write a column about it and knows just the right headline: HE INTRODUCED GUACAMOLE TO THE PYGMIES.

Wonder if she ever did.

Sifaka

Madagascar - 1997

Madagascar is the fourth largest island in the world, located about 230 miles off the African coast. It's one of more than 50 countries in Africa, and is perhaps most famous for being the home to lemurs. It's the only place on earth that you can find lemurs except for a few on the nearby Comoros Islands.

Lemurs are primitive prosimians (pre-primates) belonging to the ape family. They've existed for many millions of years. The name comes from the Latin meaning "ghost." Lemurs were so named because of their huge eyes and the nighttime activity of some. There are many different kinds of lemurs on Madagascar and they may number over a hundred varieties, including all the subspecies. They range from the tiny pygmy mouse lemur up to the Indris, which might weigh up to 20 pounds and can leap a fantastic 30 feet.

Most lemurs are vegetarians, although a few small ones eat insects. The majority live in the trees but some, such as the ring-tailed lemurs, like to stay on the ground. The sifaka likes both trees and ground and has strangest way of moving. Standing up on its hind legs, it hops sideways, keeping its arms out to the side for balance. The ringtail lemurs walk with their tails straight up waving back and forth, signaling to the others their location.

The lemurs are the main reason for my trip here. All species are endangered. People eat them, sometimes kill them because of superstition,

Spiny forest

and continue to absorb their natural habitat for farming. The few that have survived so far were aided in the past by the fact that Madagascar is an island and, therefore, the lemurs had no additional competition or predation from other animals from the mainland of Africa.

Besides the lemurs, I'm also lucky to see some unusual snakes up to 6 feet long - none are poisonous, I am told. Chameleons are plentiful, too, when you know where to look. Half of the world's approximately 150 species of chameleons live on Madagascar. Their separately directed eyes and changing colors fascinate any observer.

The approximately 22 million Malagasy people are a combination of African, Malayo-Indonesian, and Arab ancestry. The land is mountainous and the strangest area on the island is called the Tsingy de Bemaraha National Park.

Two things set this area apart from any other area I've ever seen. One is the so-called Spiny Forest. A great many trees in the park have large, 1- to 3-inch-long sharp spines. Some have spines covering every inch or two on their trunks, and some have these spines 6 inches apart. The second thing is that the trees grow in between the oddest looking pointed towers of stone. There are mountains of these towers, some small, some hundreds of feet high. Their surfaces have been worn away by rain, leaving sharp cutting edges of stone.

My delightful guide, Goulan, and his wife, Manitah, take me to a "trail," from which, if I want, we can climb to the top. He has climbed to the top once before, he says. The "trail" is more of where growth and debris has filled up the crevices between the stone towers, less of what anyone would call a trail. "Let's go," I say.

Along the way brown lemurs swing ahead of us. How they negotiate between the trees is unbelievable. How they grab the tree trunks or branches without getting stabbed by the spikes is impressive, to say the least. Most of the "ground" we're walking on is leaf and branch litter, and only 6 to 12 inches wide. Finding handholds on trees that don't have those 3- inch needles is needed nearly every step to negotiate the climb. Progress is slow.

Pretty soon my confidence grows and I pick up the pace a little. Mistake! My foot slips a bit and instinctively I grab for a branch, realizing instantly that the tree is one with needle-sharp spikes. Pulling my hand back twists me and I fall down a good 7 feet and land on my back. Luckily the spot where I land is the only semi-flat spot on our entire climb. Many scratches, a few impaled needles, and a nasty gouge in my right arm are the only injuries. My hand and arm are bleeding. The rest of the climb is tough but the view from the top of the Tsingy cliff is awesome and, of course, all the more so because it was a lot of work to get there.

Goulan's wife, Manitah, is good company, but at this point it's obvious she didn't know what she was getting into. She looks beat. I don't look so good either.

When we descend sometime later, we visit some caves, and in one we explore hundreds of feet back underground. There are combinations of large "rooms" and narrow and low passages. Everything is spotted with dung from the two species of bats that make their home here. Many of them screech out their welcome as we move through. Beautiful little creatures!

Alright, I admit it. I was getting quite confident in my rock-climbing ability even though my legs have lost their youthful springs. When I fell, it was embarrassing. Goulan and Manitah kept asking me if I was OK. "I'm fine, I'm fine," I told them. Washing up later at camp helps a little. I don't realize until the next morning that my butt's sore and I cut my knee too.

On the drive back, Goulan stops to show me a "sacred" tree where the villagers have left offerings for different intentions. A coin and part of a paper bill are there. Of course there is the accompanying horror story of what happened to a man who took the spirit's money. Short version: he died.

From the way Goulan talks, it's obvious that he doesn't believe in it, but I do notice he leaves a small coin as we leave. He's Christian and his wife is Muslim (which in most places is not common). In the Islamic faith, it's traditionally acceptable for a Muslim man to marry a Christian woman but not vice versa. It's obvious that neither lets any religion get in their way. In fact, she not only takes me to dinner one night when her husband went out with the guys, but it's quite evident she's not encumbered by a head covering or bra.

Some places we visit by plane and motor launch. When we get out of the boat in wildlife preserves, we come across semi-tame lemurs. At one, a lemur jumps on my shoulder to get a bit of banana. At another, there are 20 French tourists, the only travelers we've seen on this trip so far. Oh well, there goes the neighborhood! But I also realize the only way the lemurs are going to survive is when they become a recognized, profit-making asset. Twenty-five cents buys a small bunch of bananas, which doesn't last long.

Food here, even for humans, costs next to nothing - even in the nicer restaurants. A chateaubriand that night is $5. It consists of a zebu steak with fries. The zebu looks like our Brahman cattle but about half the size. The Brahmans were first bred in the United States from cattle breeds imported from India and are descendents of the zebu. The chateaubriand is tasty!

I sit and watch the people and surroundings. There are intriguing African-style sarongs mixed with Goodwill sale items, and bare feet, sandals and shoes. Beautiful trees and flowers squeeze past the junk and filth. Some of the cars are so old they must have been here before cars

were invented. It appears the French got a good start in building an infrastructure, but no one's kept it up. The roofs on many of the nicely built buildings are rusting corrugated metal.

A zebu drawn cart goes by. Ducks walk down the middle of the street. A radio is playing. Two girls walk by with baskets of greens balanced on their heads; the youngest cannot be more than 6. Surprisingly, there are few motorbikes here. Taxis consist of pick-up trucks with seats in the back. I look down and notice my otherwise clean pants have lemur prints from this morning. Cool!

A couple of nights ago, a German woman who spoke fluent French told me disdainfully that the Malagasy still speak a very stilted, basic French: "Not fluent at all." She'd been here for two weeks and knew not a single word of Malagasy. She didn't appear to see the irony.

One night at dinner, I look out over the grass and see an upright tail swaying back and forth and imagined the ring-tail lemur walking beneath it. If there was ever an animal that appears to have an attitude, it's the ringed-tail lemur. I know, anthropomorphic.

Another fascinating thing in Madagascar was at a museum inside the zoo. The extensive displays included the actual bones of the extinct elephant bird, a 10-foot tall monster. The display had the skeleton of an ostrich next to it for comparison. Never had heard of the elephant bird or saw one before. The leg bones were not only longer but much heavier than those of the ostrich. There were even eggs of both. The elephant bird's egg was several times the size of the ostrich, maybe 14 inches long.

In Madagascar, poverty is all around but, at the same time, most people seem fairly healthy. One exception: Right next to where my guide,

Neighbor with sick baby | Neighbor dressed for picture

cook and I are camping, there's a shack with sounds of a baby crying. After dinner we invite some local kids over to share some popcorn made in its own pan over our fire. Lots of fun - they love it! The mystery is what is cooking in the covered pan and the eating of a new treat. It's a big hit with everyone.

But that poor baby is still crying. I inquire about the baby and am invited into the shack. The home is about 7-by-10 foot with a low fire burning in a rusty piece of old metal roofing at one end. The baby's next to the fire. The mother explains that the baby always wants more water but she tries to limit the amount she gives it. The baby has a fever and doesn't look good at all. I gently suggest that maybe the baby should be moved away from the fire and given all the water she wants. And how about some wet cloths to help cool her? It just seems to be common sense. Maybe a half an aspirin would help, too.

They quickly agree as if I'm a doctor. We get the aspirin. The fever goes down quickly and all seems quiet that night. The next morning the baby is better but is getting a fever again, they say. The mother and her husband are leaving to go to the nearby village. We ask why. They are going to ask the villagers for money so they can get a bus to the nearby town and to pay the hospital.

"How much will it cost?"

"About three dollars."

Wow! Easy decision. They seem very excited to get the $5 dollars we

141

give them, and we are excited to help. We wish them well and off they go. God bless them! (Of course, when I get home I'm told that babies should not be given aspirin. Evidently I was not the only one who was ignorant about such things.)

Interestingly, I found out later that they believed the reason the baby got sick was because she had wandered outside with a knife and had hacked at a sacred tree. The parents were instructed to take the child to the tree, apologize to the tree and leave a little money as an offering to the offended spirit.

The Air Madagascar planes I've flown on, even the intra-country ones, have been excellent - Big Boeing 737s. Last night's flight from Diego to Tana, with one stop, had only 20 passengers on the first leg. This morning's flight to Fort Dauphin is 20 percent full, at best. Security at the airport is next to non-existent.

The land stretches out below, revealing patches of green rice paddies, semi-barren hills, and small mountains. Only 5 percent of Madagascar is untouched forest and none of it is visible from here. The lemurs are viewed with distain by most Malagasy and some view the chameleons as bad luck, especially if one comes into the room. They are so slow and harmless, but I suppose their strange looks started the myth. From the air, the country doesn't appear crowded. However, the fertile areas are the valleys, and as Roland my guide says, he never saw a valley without a rice field. For a family to claim land as their own, all they have to do is live on it for five years.

That night the moon and every star in the heavens are visible.

The air here is clean, even with all the cooking fires and diesel powered vehicles. The clouds come and go and feed the omnipresent streams from every hill and mountain. Even the poorest people seem to have enough rice, vegetables, fruit and zebu. Again, the cost of food, especially the meat, is surprisingly inexpensive. A good meal of zebu and a potato with bread is less than $3. Everyone looks in good condition and healthy. However the traffic makes we fazas (foreigners) cringe. Trucks and cars are obviously bigger and more important, and they have the right of way. The drivers, including mine, come within a foot of pedestrians, zebu and other cars - often at considerable speed. All seem to know the rules- even the animals. Quick learning through natural selection?

Zebu carts are common, and carry produce and people at a leisurely pace. One- and two-hitches are most common, though I've seen four zebus pulling a large cart.

The Malagasy automatically speak French to me thinking correctly that whites are almost all French. A few know some words in English and some - a guard here, a desk clerk there - are happy to strike up a conversation to practice and learn. Many of them seem to think that English will be more important than French in the future.

From the plane, the views through the clouds shows large forested areas - maybe some lemurs make their home there in peace. Oft times the reason for the name Red Island comes to mind. Especially in the north, the many rich tones of red clay are barren of vegetation. All of a sudden I feel terribly privileged, certainly uneasy, and perhaps a little guilty as I travel through these lands knowing a hot shower tonight and a luxurious America eventually await. If a faza wants to feel wanted, this is the place. The white skin is a target to be close to, to know, to be seen with. A balloon becomes "a gift from the faza to me!" A woman has it made if she's with a faza. Henry Kissinger was right: "The greatest aphrodisiac is power."

The forests give way to some deserts of the south. There are sparse grasses with what looks like a golfer's nightmare - millions of sand traps. A river runs a ribbon of life through a lifeless land. The green looks friendly; the rest does not. Four people meet me at the airport. They're holding up a sign with my names reversed. They put me in a car to go to Berenty. The driver speaks as much English as I do Malagasy but is very nice and we make it work.

Strange changes in vegetation come into view. We pass through woods, a desert and a cactus mix. Over a hill there is an abrupt change - a huge plantation of sisal, the stuff that used to make rope. Guards raise a bar for our car to enter the Berenty Reserve. The reserve consists of the remnant of the original forest along a river and the growing sisal.

I'm told the owner's father started planting sisal in 1928. His son, French also but born here in Madagascar, has continued the sisal but also started this 600-acre reserve, which contains four species of lemurs: the ringtail, brown, lepi and mouse (the latter being mostly nocturnal). He then introduced sifaka lemurs. There are an estimated 900 lemurs, not counting the nocturnal ones.

My guide meets me as does the hostess and I'm shown four bungalows that are very well made and comfortable. These are guest houses. I throw my stuff in one and take off with my guide, Andreus.

The ringtail lemurs are the most numerous here, and one group's territory includes my bungalow. It's obvious some people break the rule and feed them. Some of the lemurs actually approach and certainly aren't afraid. I find them absolutely priceless! My grandchildren would go nuts. Although the reserve does provide supplemental water (in little concrete pools) and the occasional food in the hard season, the lemurs generally stay because the surroundings are prime habitat for them. I'm taking too many pictures of lemurs, I know, but the opportunity won't come again.

Lunch is wonderful - some crabmeat something stuffed in a zucchini thing. How's that for a description? The whole creation is breaded and deep fried. That's just the starter. Add to that slices of sautéed pork with potatoes and carrots, and flan for desert. (Dinner later turns out to be two crabmeat eggrolls, beet slices and a mixture of vegetables, with banana flambé for desert. Are we living, or what? All so nice, yet a Coke or bottled water is extra.)

After lunch, Andreus is invaluable as to information and locating some of the more elusive sifakas. We also see a little bit of posturing between the sifakas and the ringtails guarding their territories. They're not much different in size and a little jumping toward and then away each seems to settle the matter - until next time. All the trails we go on are wide enough for the small truck that occasionally deposits water at the little pools. The whole place is great, and maybe it's the best way possible to preserve a tiny bit of what's left. Will the small gene pool be a problem for the future? Who knows!

The rest of Berenty is impressive, too. There are quarters for guides and drivers. At the opposite end of the complex, there's a restaurant, dry moats for tortoises, a place for a couple of crocodiles, and an airstrip.

Later I sit near some ringtails. It appears that I am sitting on the border between two ringtail groups. The other group approaches. It is an odd feeling, and fun, when the posturing takes place right around me. Many lemurs use scent marking to stake out territories and to have so-called "stink fights." This is such a fight. The lemurs pay no attention to me. They rub their long tails over a gland that produces a strong smell. That produces a powerful weapon to be waved in the direction of your enemy. It would appear to be an advantage to be upwind in this fight. I find out that I'm not.

Just before dinner, a short drive takes us to the Spiny Forest area. It's easier to see the mouse and lepilemurs here because the foliage is not so high. The torches bring back an occasional red glow and there they are! The mouse lemurs are not much bigger than their namesakes, and are very shy. They move very slowly or stay quite still.

We see a lepilemur but it's too hidden to get a good camera shot. The next morning I meet Andreus at eight and we see the usual lemurs. (Would you believe it, they're already the usual?) Then, though, he takes me to a special spot on the river where the villagers are allowed to bring their zebus for water. He says he sometimes sits here alone with the lemurs. He says he loves it here and loves the lemurs but has no affection for the Frenchman who owns all this. The Frenchman certainly has done a lot of good here, but from the stories Andreus has told, he still has a colonial attitude. Also, perhaps the storyteller is biased. I take several nice shots of birds.

Next we visit the small museum that is really quite nice - partly the Frenchman's work aided by an American, Sarah Fee, who wrote the English notes and explanations.

Lunch was two Cokes, strips of breaded deep-fried fish as the first course, then half a small chicken, rice and a side container of white gravy. Dessert? Chocolate mousse with chocolate curls on top. Wow! The waiters, Desiree and Clement, and waitress, Elan, do an excellent job.

After a long walk, I meet Desiree with his wife (who works in the kitchen) and give them a Polaroid portrait. Nice people. Afterward Andreus takes me to the sisal factory. Basically, what the workers here do is feed the sisal leaves through a large machine that separates the long fibers. Next, the long fibers are dried on outdoor racks for about two days. Finally, the result is baled and sent to Fort Dauphin, where it is made into rope. The shorter fiber is dried and used as stuffing for mattresses.

As the driver pulls up to the sisal factory, there are about 10 guys hanging out in front. The big machine is down. They give me that knowing look which is a mixture of yeah, a faza, a rich guy, and faked boredom. I go over and ask if I can give them a picture. The place livens up. Everyone mills around laughing. I give several more. I catch the eye of the foreman, who is wearing a hat and acting "foreman-like." I give him a wink and he's my friend. Machine's fixed, back to work and everyone waves. Yeah, you're right - I love it!

Dinner that evening is garlic shrimp, squiggles of beef over spaghetti, and a tangerine and orange for desert. I pop for a liter of Coke. Desiree says there's a Catholic church down the road, and we arrange to meet at 7:30 in the morning at breakfast. He said he would go with me, though just 10 minutes before he had said he was Protestant. Tonight the stars are intense bits of light, the Milky Way is clearly visible, and all those stars between the other stars we don't normally see are there, too.

At breakfast it's still odd to look out over the grass and see an upright tail, ringed, swaying back and forth. Here and there, the lemurs sit eating or simply looking around -tame yet really wild. There's a minor skirmish on the roof nearby and one comes down near me. The cook schusses it away. I guess they leave calling cards, which don't make the cook's job any easier. The lemur moves away and is now sitting just out of sight of the cook, then is at my table. Cook sees it and moves right, lemur moves left. Cook takes the jam off the table, lemur loses interest.

Desiree shows up and we walk toward the church. It's 8 o'clock, but no one's there yet. Soon a guy rings a bell vigorously. The service obviously starts when the bell rings. People start coming and we all have fun taking and giving pictures. I ask Desiree to take the pictures, and he takes to the job like a general. I realize we're actually delaying church, so I signal that's all the film we have (which it is) and we all move inside. I ask Desiree to explain and apologize that I will have to leave early. Everyone nods their understanding.

There's much singing but not with nearly the gusto of the church in Tana. The bell ringer is also the deacon, and he does a good job for a semi-attentive audience. Desiree and his wife, Ninah, and their daughter have left to go to the Protestant church nearby. I try to leave quietly by the back door to be inconspicuous but it isn't missed by anyone including the deacon who waves goodbye.

Goodbye, and thank you God for letting me visit this wonderful island and wonderful people.

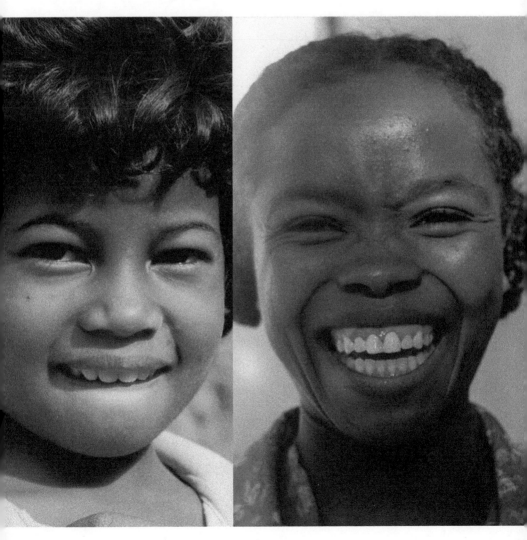

Driver in Amman · The Magnificent Treasury · Entrance to Petra

Jordan - 1998

Of course the pyramids in Egypt are fabulous, but there are other ancient treasures in the Middle East, too. The legendary Petra - the ancient capital of the Nabataean Arabs and one of the most famous archaeological sites in the world - is one. I must see it, but Petra is not as simple to visit as the great pyramids. The Egyptian pyramids are a short walk right outside Cairo. Petra is about a three-hour drive through the desert from Jordan's capital, Amman.

Coming out of the Crown Hotel in Amann, I find that the wonderful air-conditioned JETT buses that go to Petra are off today. "Bukra" (tomorrow), I'm told. Someone runs to find a man who speaks English. The man says for 100 DH ($142), he'll find a taxi to drive me. I look aghast, of course.

"How much do you want to spend?" he asks. No answer.

He shrugs. He can do if for $70. He finds Mohmed Ali, a pleasant young man who takes me to his "taxi." Mohamed warns me his not actually licensed, but it runs well. The poor old Opel doesn't look like it will run at all. I briefly have second thoughts.

The divided highway to Petra is in decent shape. Along the way there are a lot of sheep and goat herds, and the occasional donkey carrying their owners. Here and there, fine-looking Arabian horses appear, but with the landscape so barren for as far as one can see, it's a mystery as to what any of them have to eat.

We stop along the way, and Mohamed buys me breakfast. It consists of a spinach turnover and a turnover with a bit of lamb. In addition, we scoop hummus with pieces of flat bread. Pickles, tomatoes, and something tasting of apple finish off a great meal. It's more than I need, and all of is good.

Petra is about two miles off the highway. The regular entry fee is 7 DH ($10). Mohamed explains how he will talk his way in and get me in, too. He doesn't. On top of that, the police want to talk with him – something about not being licensed to drive visitors. I pay the 7 DH. Mohamed is enthusiastic and optimistic, I'll give him that. He disappears, after saying he'll meet me later.

There are guides, horses, glorified goat carts and camels for hire. Most visitors walk, as I do. The walk takes me through a winding gorge with 600-foot walls, carved many thousands of years ago by an ancient stream. The whole area is now surrounded by desert, but flash floods still do occur, they tell me.

The Treasury (Al-Khazneh) is where scenes in the movie "Indiana Jones and the Last Crusade" were filmed and is the first thing you see after coming through the narrow, easily defended gorge. The structure is 80 feet wide and 127 feet high, but has only three large rooms inside. There are many other buildings to see, as well. It's estimated that more than 20,000 people lived in Petra at the height of Nabataean power.

Everything at Petra is cut out of rock. We're used to cutting stone and then using the cut stone to construct buildings. What the Nabataeans did here is different. They "built" by cutting away what was not necessary, and what was left was the building – inside a mountain. Another difference: we build from the bottom up; they cut and chipped from the top down. Glorified caves – but what glory, especially knowing how long ago they were made.

Archeologists say the nearby ruins indicate a civilization and the domestication of grains occurred here about 8,000 years ago. Petra was successful because of its location on the spice trade route. Oddly, almost all of the unusual construction was completed in only 100 years or so – about 2,000 years ago. The main buildings were "discovered" fairly recently - in 1958. Remarkable!

All of the Petra dwellings are essentially big or small holes in the walls of stone. Some of the "low-income housing" is essentially the proverbial hole in the wall. Many are impressive, large and ornate. Some have still-visible paintings on the walls and ceilings. In addition, leaking moisture over the many years has brought out the natural colors of the minerals in the stone. Beautiful!

Despite the number of visitors, Petra is unique and compelling. The combination of the naturally carved shapes of the stone walls and the colors of the manmade "buildings" is awe-inspiring. Almost as amazing is the water system: Water was bought in from 5 miles away, delivered via a manmade clay pipe. Gravity supplied the power at a constant 4-degree pitch. At the peak of Petra's power in 300 AD, it must have been impressive to see.

As I return through the gorge, I see Mohamed waving at me from behind a bus. It seems the officials at Petra are on the lookout for him. It's time to leave anyway, and we do.

Back in Amman, waiting for a Chinese restaurant to open, I venture into a small store nearby. The shopkeeper had once been an engineer for an American company, he said. The company had asked him to work in Iraq. Shortly after he arrived there, the Iraqi government jailed him for spying. Three other Americans got out, he said, but he did not – until 19 years later. The man does not like Iraq.

The next day, I have a wonderful middle-age driver. He tells me about the time he was stopped at a traffic light in Amman and gazed at the beautiful wheels of the Mercedes Benz next to him. He looked and looked, thinking how happy he'd be to own them. Then he looked at the driver, who was smiling at him – King Hussein himself! The king asked him if he liked the car, but he was so flustered he couldn't speak. The king laughed and the light turned green. "The king is a very good person," he says.

You can picture customs as a challenge – and an opportunity. What a job – horribly boring, probably. At the airport leaving Amman, an officer asks what my Polaroid camera is. I take his picture. The picture develops as we and a couple of others watch. This is their first experience with a Polaroid. I give him the picture. He and his friends love it. I pass with no problem, leaving smiling customs officials.

Egypt - 1998

A tout in Cairo at the airport is quite helpful and after a little negotiating we come to a price, including that I will pay afterward, not now. No, not even a down payment. The tout arranges a driver, who agrees to meet me in the morning at my hotel at 8:30 "American time." I suggest I will have to get someone else if he is not there. He's there, waiting and smiling, at 8:30.

Cairo has the worst drivers and the worst traffic I have ever seen in any country. After suggesting twice, loudly, that he slow down, we get along fine. Doing a hundred kilometers an hour (about 62 mph) in the city is not smart in any county. No seatbelts, of course. In spite of my request to go slower, we have two accidents in two days. One's his fault, one's not. No one stops. Drivers throw their hands up in disgust at the other and drive on. You don't want to involve the police. They would not help and would want a bribe, I'm told. "Might makes right" in driving here. A donkey cart has rights over a pedestrian, a car over a cart, and a truck over everything else.

As a game, I try to find just one car without a dent. In two days of driving, I cannot. The horn seems to be as essential as the steering wheel. Cairo also has more military than any other city I've been in. Sometimes there are six to eight on every main corner, all armed with automatics. The army is good, I'm told. The police are not – they're just looking to locals for bribe money. Cairo's great for sightseeing, though. There's an abundance of sights and people to discover.

Much wheat is grown in Egypt, and generally food is not expensive unless you go to one of the high-end tourist places. About $3 or $4 (American money) for an excellent meal at one of the nicer local places, plus whatever you drink, is typical. There always seems to be two or three people to do a job where one would be enough.

My driver speaks a fair amount of English. We are getting along so well after awhile that he invites me to dinner and to see his home and meet his family. I reluctantly accept. His wife and three daughters are all very gracious, and, of course, very surprised to see me as we enter his apartment. No phones to call ahead. His wife and daughters are all dressed in what appears to me to be nightgowns, and make no attempt to change. Immediately, they start to prepare dinner for us.

The living room is maybe 7-by-8 foot. There is a kitchen, a bath and two small bedrooms. Five people, plus a 6-month-old live here. Cozy.

Some practicing Islam require women to be covered from head to toe. I learn more Arabic. We all laugh and talk. Dinner's ready, so the driver and I eat. The women eat after. Obviously, they are accustomed to waiting and willingly run to fetch anything needed.

The older daughter, maybe 20 and who speaks a little English, asks me what I would like to drink.

"Whatever you have is fine," I answer.

"What would you like?"

"Do you have a Pepsi?"

"Yes."

I notice that instead of going to the closet-sized kitchen, she is putting on all her garb. Out the door she goes - to the market to buy me Pepsi. I am the honored guest and am treated like one.

Funny, here I am, a strange man in their apartment home, and the women are modest enough but certainly not overly so. To go to the market or anywhere else outside, though, they really cover up. We have good fun – they're a nice family. They like me. I suppose it's easy to be popular when their entertainment is so limited.

The next day I plan to see the Valley of the Kings. Thousands of years ago, when the pharaohs figured out that even the pyramids were being broken into and treasures being taken, they opted for a different strategy. The Valley of the Kings is about 300 miles south of Cairo just outside the city of Luxor. (Oddly, the Luxor Hotel in Las Vegas is in the shape of a pyramid but there are no pyramids in Luxor). The trip to Luxor involves an overnight train. The ticket office is closed so I have to buy a ticket on board. I opt for the luxury of the sleeping car instead of sitting up all night.

"Is this the president's cabin?"

"Yes, yes," says the conductor, with a smile (of course, it's the only one left and the same as all the others). We have a little small talk. The man turns out to be the train manager. He later tells me that he only charged me for a single and it should have been for a cabin. It's about $40 less this way.

Later he stops by to ask me to join him in his cabin for tea. There we have time to settle most of the world's problems. Delightful interlude with a nice man! He tells me the train is the only one in the world that serves meals in the cabins. I noticed later there wasn't anywhere else to serve meals. The food is included in the price of the ticket. It's a little better than airplane food, but not much.

Luxor, with the Valley of the Kings and all the history, is most interesting. This is where the royalty were buried in the "New Kingdom." Instead of using pyramids as had their predecessors, these leaders thought their tombs would be safer from the robbers and subsequent rulers if they were burrowed in the stone mountains with the entrances concealed. Their strategy worked - for some of them.

The Valley of the Kings is on the west bank of the River Nile, while the people in the area live on the east bank. The reason for this is that the sun rises in the east each morning, symbolizing the renewal of life, and sets in the west, which symbolizes death. The Nile is Egypt. Docked along the banks of the Nile are hundreds of unused large boats, smaller feluccas (smaller traditional wooden sailing boats), and many other vessels. A huge number of horse-drawn carriages and donkey-drawn carts go past every minute - empty. Business is not good. Later I will find out why.

We've all heard of King Tut (or Tutankhamun, a pharaoh of the Eighteenth Dynasty), who was actually quite young and a minor king.

He's only famous because his tomb, when finally discovered, was intact and, therefore, he became well-known from all that was left behind. The tomb wasn't disturbed because it's located right next to another one that was discovered earlier and looted. The tomb robbers didn't think anyone would be buried so close to another pharaoh, so its intact discovery wasn't made until 1922 by Howard Carter.

Across the way and down just a bit is the grand burial tomb of Ramses III. At the entrance there is a sign with some information including who discovered it and when. Would you believe it was discovered by "J. Bruce" in 1768? James Bruce was the famous, 6-foot-5 red-haired explorer from Scotland. He was famous for finding Lake Tana, which was thought at the time to be the source of the Nile. Much later it turned out he had discovered the source of the Blue Nile, a major tributary leading from Lake Tana in Ethiopia.

Finding the source of the Nile was the great quest of Europe in the 1700s. Thousands with huge entourages had embarked on that quest, many dying after encountering warring tribes and disease. Bruce reportedly saved a queen's life and therefore was given safe passage. When Bruce returned to Scotland after three years of traveling, he wrote a book recalling his adventures. The true stories were so fantastic that few in Europe believed him. Oddly enough, as I remember, the book doesn't even mention the finding of Ramses III tomb.

Time for some ancient humor. Luxor is also home to the Temple of Luxor and the Temple of Karnak. On one of the temple walls, a pictorial story tells of a Nubian king and his wife. There is an unflattering picture of his wife, who is quite a large woman, riding a donkey. The ancient comment on the picture is, "Poor donkey." Nothing changes.

Across a bridge on the east side of the Nile is my hotel. Up on the rooftop is a pool. I have no suit. The attendant says no problem when I point to my boxers. There are two other men sunning in one corner. The view of the Nile and Luxor with all the activity is fabulous. Wow.

Luxor is a city of about 150,000 people and it seems all the men are out and about - drinking coffee, walking somewhere, selling something from the late afternoon 'til well after dark. Few tourists venture to the backstreets, which is too bad. They are missing a much better experience than the light shows at the mortuary temples. After several miles, each street lined with tiny stores and shops, I see one of the little corner restaurant that looks fairly clean. The owner and I have a long discussion over his preparation of fried potatoes and beef shish kebab, which are very good. On the way back I spy a slice of 2-inch-high honey cake. I ask how much. "Five." (That's about $1.50).

I look at the vendor as if I didn't hear.

"Two," he says.

Excellent cake. All along the route back, I'm greeted, stopped and cajoled. "French?" No.

"German?" No.

"American?" Yes. Their favorite, I'm told by the guide.

1998 is the perfect time for me to visit Egypt. There are few tourists. There haven't been many Japanese visitors since the Gulf War earlier in the decade. It's because of what everyone calls "the accident," which it wasn't. In 1997, 58 foreign tourists (including 36 Swiss and 10 Japanese) visiting Deir el-Bahari, an archeological site near Luxor, were among 62 people massacred by Egyptian anti-government extremists thought to be tied to an Islamic terrorist group. The massacre put a chill on the number of visitors for a while. I'm told tourism is about a third of what it was. Sad; it's hurting many of the locals.

Negotiating expected. When I returned from Luxor, "my man" awaits me. Off in the direction of the hotel, but soon we are going down side streets. "First, Mr. 'Whatever-his-name-is' wants to see you," my driver says. He runs up to an apartment while I wait in the car. He comes back and says that "Mr." will see me. Offers of Pepsi and tea are refused. No softening up here. The man and I finally agree, again, on $50 for today - total. We talk a bit and he says another $10 is for the airport. He sees my unhappiness. No ten. Oh, he had forgotten to mention I owed him some dollars from the other day? I had already told his driver, "Too bad."

He brings it up but then shrugs. We stay at $50, which is what we had originally agreed to at the airport when I arrived. (The driver has been very nice; I gave him an extra $30.)

Another hit from the attendant at the mosque. Shoes are normally taken off at the door and set nearby. The attendant says he'll watch them for $3. "I'll carry them." He takes them for nothing like he does for everyone else. All these people are very polite and nice, just trying to get as much as possible. The driver insists he and his family want me to come for dinner again. I refuse at least ten times. (I should have gone).

It's Saturday afternoon, and following a lunch of chicken, rice, vegetables and that excellent flatbread, I'm dropped at the Shepherd Hotel. The hotel is right next to the Nile and boat captains constantly ask if I want to go for a ride. Only $50 - but they will settle for $5.

Paperwork here is omnipresent. There also seem to be two, three or four people to do any work type of work, where one would be sufficient.

Also abundant are the signs for long life and other well-known ones for stability, for dominion or prosperity, and the crook and flail and the crook symbols used in ancient Egyptian society that accompany the pharoahs' statues. (The shepherd's crook stood for kingship and the flail for the fertility of the land.) There must have been at least four women that ruled. One kept her son out of the limelight until he was 22 years old. In return, he erased all symbols of her that had been created.

Today is a "Coptic day" for me. Coptic is the Greek word for Egyptian Christians, and it dates from the first century AD. St. Mark the Evangelist is said to have brought Christianity to this area. Saint Virgin Mary's Coptic Orthodox Church, known as the Hanging Church - so-called because it was built in the third century AD above some remaining arches of the Roman fortress - is interesting, as is the rather extensive Coptic Museum nearby. I overhear an English-speaking guide and decide to splurge, hiring him for $3. He's very knowledgeable and able to answer my numerous questions.

At the Museum of Cairo (or Museum of Egyptian Antiquities), I also hire a guide who is very informative and shares many details I would never have known. When I leave the museum, my driver is arguing with five policemen. They want to give him a ticket for not having his readable sign on his car. It's faded, they say. (It's not). And his license plate is dirty. (It's not). The driver is not angry at the bribe attempt (such attempts are usual). He's angry that he has to trouble a friend of his in the government to fix the ticket. The police go out of their way to inform me it has nothing to do with me and that I am most welcome.

Hotel's Social Room - men only

Sultan Hotel - my $11 room

Yemen - 1998

Even though the flight took off a little late, we arrive early. I grab a taxi (or vice versa), ask for the Sultan Palace Hotel, and off we go into the night. Fifteen minutes later we turn down a narrow dark alley in old Sana'a in the southern part of Yemen. Most of the buildings are three- to five-stories high and all masonry. The hotel is a converted 500-year-old home. I hope they have a room. They give me room 405 on the top floor. There are four beds, or rather mattresses on the floor. The room is very clean; no one else there. Cost is $11 - just right. The bath down the hall is shared and the squat toilet is common.

I talk to the owner-manager, who has a car and driver to take me to some of the mountain villages tomorrow. He also invites me to chew qat (or khat; the leaves and buds of a shrub chewed or used as tea as a stimulant) with him and his friends later tomorrow. I accept both. The car and driver costs $60.

The drive takes us through scenery that reminds me of Colorado; the architecture definitely not. The valleys are green but everything else is stone. The homes are stone, too, some multistory and built for defense. The ones on the mountains - with cisterns for water – only were overcome with the advent of aviation.

As I talk to a friendly man during a stop, a boy slaps his siblings to stop their persistence. A woman objects, and the boy grabs her roughly and tells her off. The man I'm talking with makes peace with them and explains

Sana Architecture (and forbidden picture of a woman)

A Janbiye - every man has one

to me that it's OK – the woman his mother. Respect for women? All the women here are fully covered; many have the face veiled, including over the eyes. No pictures are allowed except of children and men. I get one picture of a young girl (not woman yet) without a veil. Beautiful face. It strikes me that maybe the Virgin Mary could have looked like this.

Lunch at the top of a mountain was delicious: meat, rice, flatbread and seven bowls of stuff to dip the bread in. It's twice what the driver and I needed, plus a liter of water each. Less than $4.

The owner of the hotel had told me that until 1953, Saudi Arabia footed the whole bill here in Yemen. Now the Yemeni have to work. Much better now, he says. The water is piped to villages to get people to stay there. The population of Sana'a is about 100,000. I buy a jambiya, a curved dagger, and belt for it. For most of the men here, the jambiya and belt is part of their attire, along with the traditional loose ankle-length garment and a suit coat. Most wear the twisted head covering and have beards and moustaches.

When I return to the hotel, the owner-manager and five of his friends have gathered and ask me to join them. We talk and chew qat from about 5:30 to 7 p.m. When you chew, you are to keep the result in your cheek, simply adding to it. After chewing a bit, the manager smiles at me and says, "You don't like it, do you?"

I slightly shake my head no, and he indicates how to get rid of it. The friends are very nice, the conversation good; friendly of them to invite me to join their gathering.

A long walk after dinner (it's safe) brings an invitation from a man to visit his home to meet his family. I foolishly don't accept. All the shops are open but way outnumbered by the raft of people selling from setups on the sidewalk.

The next morning, the call to prayer drones out from dozens of minarets. I wonder how many people will go. None that I see do, and yet their faith seems deep when I talk with people. Not reasoned faith from those I talk with, just very sure and learned by rote.

Old men in their traditional costumes, women clothed head to toe, the chattering noise of the marketplace, children laughing, pushing and

Pre-puberty: allowed to show a little hair and the face

talking – these are my impressions. Many younger people try their English out with me. "Hello" is frequent and even "I love you" several times from 7- 10-year-old girls with giggles. "Welcome my friend" and "Where are you from?" are common. When I tell them "very good" or 'A mare' a kay" (America) with a thumbs up, the reaction is always enthusiastic.

Cats, a donkey, bulls, one camel, goats, sheep and a few dogs and chickens are all right here in town. The place is a somewhat of a garbage pit, though I see people sweeping and picking up almost as much as they discard. No litter law here.

A group of local boys and men invite me to have lunch with them. It's in the same room at the hotel where "we" chewed and talked. Yesterday the gathering was made up of a judge, a hospital administrator and the hotel owner-manager. Today it's the help. Most enjoyable: no charge, good talk and fun. Breakfast earlier, I find out, had been included with the $11 charge for the room.

Thanks, Yemen, for your hospitality on my short visit!

United Arab Emirates - Abu Dhabi – 1998

There could not be a greater contrast than leaving Yemen and arriving in Abu Dhabi, the capital of the United Arab Emirates. I think the reason for me making a stop here is the name. Abu Dhabi: It just sounds exotic and interesting.

The airport is immaculate. The taxis are waiting. No well-used taxis here - they are all newer Mercedes. The driver is nice but has no idea where my destination, Dana Plaza, is. The airport is some 15 miles from the city on a three-lane highway. It's an absolutely straight 15 miles. It's absolutely flat. It's absolutely clean and absolutely smooth. The highway is lined on both sides with palms, so it's impossible to see beyond them. Oil money - big oil money. It's oddly sterile.

When we get to Abu Dhabi - which sits off the Arabian Peninsula on an island in the Persian Gulf - the driver stops and asks several people how to get to Dana Plaza. After some time, we find it. Everyone here is from someplace else, including the taxi driver. Ten years ago there was nothing here. Now the city is populated by people from India, Pakistan, and from other Arab countries. The first impression of Abu Dhabi is that somebody has cleared out Chicago and replaced everything more than 10 years old with a sleek skyscraper or apartment building, and are keeping it so clean that you'd swear no one lives here.

A little background: When a friend of mine heard I was going to Abu Dhabi, he introduced me to a pilot who flies for the Emirates. The pilot and I only spoke by phone. It turns out that the pilot flies for one of the emirs on his private 747. During our phone conversations, he revealed that he wouldn't even change the oil on the plane except in Paris or New York; doesn't trust anyone here. He lives in Abu Dhabi. Unfortunately he's not going to be here while I am. Very graciously, he has suggested I stay with his wife in his apartment on the 16th floor overlooking the Persian Gulf. What's to decide?

The pilot is amazingly candid and tells me his story. He had been hired to fly for the Emirates and among the benefits is his beautiful apartment. Once moving there, he hired a cleaning woman. She got pregnant. The authorities said he would have to leave his job if they were not married. He liked his job. He married her. He says when the job is over he'll divorce her. Can't believe he's telling me all this. And now you know why I'm not telling you his name.

The apartment is impressive, as is the view. The rooms are filled with expensive Oriental rugs and antiques. The pilot's wife is very nice. Their year-and-half-old child is cute - for 10 minutes. The whole city seems soulless. I make some calls and get an earlier flight out.

The pilot's wife insists we go out to dinner to the El Sombrero restaurant. Perhaps there will at least be some good Mexican food. The restaurant is sterile but the food is good. She insists on paying as she had been asked to by her husband. Their little daughter is with us. She's . . . active. The woman says her husband doesn't like going out with the child. Later, I write the pilot a thank you note. He's still married to the woman. I wish him the best. Still haven't met him, years later.

Most places I've visited are interesting. Meeting people and enjoying the different cultures is great. I'm sorry to say I don't give UAE a real chance. There are probably many interesting people here. Leaving early eliminated visiting neighboring Oman, too. Foolish on my part.

Bhutan - 1999

Situated between the Tibet Autonomous Region of China and India on the edge of the southern Himalayas, Bhutan is spectacularly beautiful. Picture Wyoming without as much human intervention. The air is crystal clear. A few roads that do cut through this idyllic landscape are blacktopped but most are only wide enough for one lane of traffic. For two oncoming cars to pass each other, one has to pull off. Trucks even have "Honk to Pass" signs on the back. They move over as soon as they can. Politeness is part of the culture.

The small country of Nepal next door has about 600,000 visitors a year, including 30,000 who hike to the base camp of Mount Everest. To compare, Bhutan has only about 6,000 outsiders a year and most of them are traders or farmers from India. With a total population of about 650,000 and a very old, mostly unchanged culture, this gem is something to experience. A surprising 95 percent of the families own their homes, but by law the homes have to be built in the national style. Tradition is all important.

Bhutan just had its first television program aired this year. It remains a constitutional monarchy. There have been four kings including the present one, who married four women on the same day and - would you believe it - they're all sisters! (What was he thinking?)

I was fortunate to get a solitary visa. Normally, visitors are only permitted to visit Bhutan with a small tour group. Luckily, the travel agency in Seattle, Wash., that I worked with is owned by a woman whose uncle, Mr. Rinzing, has an agency and a hotel in Bhutan - and some influence. Because of very few visitors (and even these not particularly encouraged), the charge of $240 a day includes a hotel, meals, a driver and car. I didn't really want to stay in a hotel so the accommodating Mr. Rinzing arranged for me to stay for part of the time in a farmhouse and a private home with families he knew.

The present king's father wanted to have the people educated, and in English, so in 1962 he asked a Canadian-born Jesuit priest, Father William Mackey, for help. The king knew him from India, where Bhutanese royalty have traditionally been sent to be educated. At the time, there were no schools in Bhutan other than the monks teaching Buddhism. Father Mackey not only agreed to come but spent the rest of his life in Buddhist Bhutan, setting up the school system for the entire country.

English is the medium of instruction in schools and is widely spoken. (The official language of Bhutan is Dzongkha, which is derived from Tibetan, but documents and road signs are written in both Dzongkha and English.)

A few other things to note about Bhutanese culture:
- All things have spirits and are respected. Some spirits are evil. For instance, they are not sure of the existence of the Yeti, so the Bhutanese have set aside a huge mountain sanctuary for it, just to be safe. Not even citizens can go there.
- There are many symbols of good luck but the ones that stand out to most any foreigner are the small male genitalia replicas hanging down from the corner of many homes. One – measuring 6-foot-long - was painted over a door.
- I am told that many Bhutanese believe in God. (Buddhism is typically viewed as more of a philosophy than a religion).
- The traditional national attire for men is a robe called a gho and for women it's a long dress called a kira.

My guide, Palden, is fun. He says a monk told him he was a bird in a previous life. (Buddhists believe in reincarnation). I ask what kind of bird? He doesn't know: "The lama didn't say."

164

Cow downstairs

Palden has picked me up at the international airport in Paro, and after a short drive around this small valley city, we begin the three-hour trip to Thimphu, which has a population of about 40,000, is Bhutan's largest city and its capital. On the outskirts of Thimphu is where we'll find the farmhouse where we'll stay for a couple nights. It's late afternoon and after asking directions a few times, we see a black man (the only one I saw in the country) on the side of the road. He's pointing to a house. Here we are!

We stop and climb up and down ladders to scale the fence that keeps the cow in. The cow lives on the first floor. Another ladder leads to the second floor where the family lives. A steep ladder is also in keeping with a belief that bad spirits can't get up steep stairs or ladders. The second floor contains two large rooms. One has been prepared for us.

There's only a candle for light, so I don't immediately notice the family sitting along both walls. Tea is ready and is good. I greet the shy family - a balloon and pencil help warm things up. Later, I try to go to the outhouse in the dark and that steep ladder almost makes me a spirit.

That helpful black gentleman turns out to be my cook! His name is Oca and he was born here in Bhutan. Dinner is filling and good:

Downtown Thimpu

scrambled eggs with chilies, French bread, and tea. After dinner, I meet Mr. Rinsing, the travel agency owner, who could not be nicer. A wonderful walk through town completes the evening.

The next day I go down to the communal water pump to wash up. A girl from the family, wearing blue jeans (very unusual) tags along and watches. Shirt off, I do the basics. She's very nice, offers me soap and asks if I'm cold. We have a nice talk, but the situation feels a little weird.

Palden and I want to see one of three festivals, called tshechu, that are held every year at this time. The tshechu held at the dzongs, which act as monasteries, forts and administration complexes all in one. Only during the three-day festival are non-Bhutanese allowed on the grounds. The pageantry is slow and non-stop. Only 10 percent of the audience is watching. The other 90 percent of the people are watching, greeting and talking.

I'm told this is one of the few ways boys and girls from the surrounding areas can meet. Some of the monks are dressed as clowns and act as coaches to help the younger ones get their dancing and acts right. As clowns, they can also do all the things you aren't supposed to do, such as point at people. They wear hats with phallic symbols - rods of colored cloth coming out of their hats.

As I watch, I notice curious people watching me. A group of about 10 girls, maybe in their early teens, are surrounding me. We're all looking

166

Dzong Festival

at the performing monks. All of a sudden someone strokes my forearm. I look down and see one of the girls has just touched the hair on my arm. They don't have hair on their arms. The girl is a little embarrassed, so I stroke her hairless arm to make us even. Lots of laughter!

The other girls soon follow up with each feeling the hair on my arm, accompanied by more giggling. We visit; a delightful way to spend an afternoon. I give away few Polaroid pictures. The ensuing disturbance soon stops the show, so we quickly stop the Polaroids. A monk comes up and asks if he can have a picture of himself. Of course! With a smile and thanks, he gives me his apple. Tastes extra good.

Thimpu is friendly, poor and clean. It's filled with the wonderful Bhutanese architecture. The roofs of the buildings are corrugated metal or wood shakes painted silver, red or blue, and held down with stones. There's even an occasional roof of slate. The buildings are brick, mortared over, and then painted all white. The 6-inch timbers are painted, too, and provide the form for the windows. All of the buildings appear to be substantial.

The king has most the power but appoints a minister to run the country. One law requires all men to wear the national attire, the gho. It's looks comfortable and is tailored like a bathrobe. "No, there's nothing underneath," Palden says. "It gives you freedom to move." These people would make good Scots.

Some time ago in Bangkok, I met a Swedish engineer who designed hydroelectric plants. He explained that the Bhutanese don't completely dam the streams to produce power. That way the water keeps flowing and the ecology is not harmed. They're very forward thinking, he said. Ninety percent of the power generated here is sold to India. India also provides some aid to Bhutan. China is not thought of as a good friend but the Bhutanese want to keep things neutral, to the point where even the official time in Bhutan is halfway between the official times of India and China. If it's 9 o'clock in India and 10 in China, it's 9:30 in Bhutan!

One of the reasons for my trip to Bhutan is to explore the possibility of having a medical mission visit. I meet with the medical superintendent of the National Referral Hospital in Thimphu. He is a little formal at first. Then we have tea. The superintendent wants me to know medical missions were not new to Bhutan. Interplast Holland (a charitable organization that performs reconstructive surgery for people in developing countries) had been here - twice. The last time was in 1996. The organization's team was not invited back. (It seemed their attitude hurt relations.)

After he feels I have been put in the right frame of mind, he warms up. He tells me to write a short letter to Bhutan's director of health with the specifics. It probably helped that the superintendent's wife was Mr. Rinzing's niece. Then he invited me to visit the "ward" with him and we

168

had a great meeting with Dr. Sonam, the surgeon for everything and who has done some cleft lips and simple cleft palates surgeries. Dr. Sonam studied in Boston. We get along very well. Good meeting both of them.

Now Palden and I are headed to the old capital of Punakha in the Himalayas. On the way we pass rice fields, apple orchards, and even some banana trees. We have a driver and after about an hour, Palden says the driver isn't feeling well so he's going to drive. I offer to drive instead and surprisingly, he wholeheartedly accepts. Now I'm paying attention to not hitting dogs, cattle, oncoming cars and potholes - say nothing of staying on the left to miss oncoming traffic.

Eventually we see – across a river - the dzong we are going to visit. It was built in 1637 and is magnificent. The problem is we're still a half hour away because there are so few bridges. The dzong is located on a stretch of land at the meeting of the Pho Chhu (Male River) and Mo Chhu (Female River), and I'm told it's the only one on water.

I'm fortunate the dzong is in the process of a complete makeover, otherwise, I would not be allowed inside. They've been working on it for five years and have another four to go. Huge wooden columns support a second floor. Many statues of Buddha look down with their painted eyes from the high walls. There are saffron-robed monks, boys of 8 to 10 years old, and other men around. All are very welcoming. No cameras in the dzong, so the army guards nicely keep mine for me.

There are many people here and I tower over most. They are all dressed in their finest. Here and there I spy a perfect face, and when I ask, am almost always granted permission to take a picture. After lunch the Polaroids and talk make me some friends. We stop at a little stand and I have a national favorite, momos (dumplings, some filled with pork, some with cheese). They're excellent.

After watching some dancers, we decide to go to the secondary school for a variety show that evening instead of going back to the farmhouse. Palden asks the girl at the restaurant if we can use the "washroom" in back. It doesn't have any running water, soap or paper. You flush the toilet by dumping a bucketful of water from the large barrel of water nearby.

Everyone is pushing to get in for the show. It's friendly, but almost a dangerous stampede. Then we all have to leave. Now everyone goes back in. There are no lights, so we stumble over benches and people to find a bench to sit on. Now they've decided to show a locally made movie first. Palden knows both stars. Actually, it's not bad but the pace is excruciatingly slow. We leave after about half an hour.

As we drive along the next day, headed back to Thimphu, each mile seems more spectacular than the last. The pine forests have numerous small and large falls tumbling down from above. This road makes the hundreds of twists and turns on the famed route from Kahului to Hana on Maui in Hawaii look like a superhighway.

We honk at the sharpest corners. Luckily the traffic is very light. I've been driving for about two hours. At any time mention from the driver of a bad stomach, I am encouraged to drive. It's more fun for me, too. The hired driver falls asleep at the summit of Gangkhar Puensum, which is 7,570 meters high (nearly 25,000 feet) and is still sleeping a little later at Mount Masagang (about 7,000 meters).

As we're having lunch at the little Drukyul Hotel in Thimphu, Palden asks why I spoon the rice toward the outside of the curved plate. I tell him the truth - in order not to spill and to get more on my plate. He laughs. He says in Bhutan you spoon toward the center, the outside is for the devils. I make sure to spoon toward the center.

We visit an athletic field nearby, where there's a volleyball game going on. A Bhutanese team is playing an Indian team. It's the championships! Some parts of the game are good. Some, such as frequent underhand serving, indicate a lack of training. These college teams would likely lose to any of my daughters' teams. (Sorry, but they would.)

There's also a fair of sorts, with booths selling games of chance run by insistent students. Also there are booths promoting condoms, heating units that use sawdust, a health clinic for children, and a variety of other products and services.

The house I'm staying in tonight doesn't look great from the outside but the inside's fine. There's a sitting room, kitchen, four or five bedrooms, one of which is quite large, maybe 10-by-14-foot, and open to

Hostess

A little advertising

a 6-by-8-foot chapel with Buddhist furnishings. This turns out to be my bedroom, complete with sliding shutters! Actual windows are rare here.

Much of the surrounding land is planted with apple trees, which are individually rented by Indian merchants who come each year to harvest the apples. Looking around, I also see acorn, asparagus, beans, walnuts, chilies, and several other fruits with which I'm not familiar.

There's an odor in my room that's not pleasant. I discover that yak meat is drying just below my windows, which overlook the outhouse. Water comes from a hose outside, which is stopped with a wooden plug. The other end of the hose is stuck in a stream way up the hill. It works. Each morning pine needles are burned to purify the air, which from what I can tell doesn't need purifying except for near my window.

The next night I stay at a guesthouse. There are several Bhutanese doctors here, too. They are very cordial and we talk over dinner. They're convinced a medical mission would be very welcome and certainly useful, although one says their Bhutanese pride might get in the way. Another relates how a few years ago German man gave the government a check for $800,000 to help with the medical facilities. It took the officials three years to cash it because they didn't know if they wanted to be influenced that much by outsiders!

The doctors tell me there's a lot of bureaucracy here. Even the monks have dozens of ranks, signified by their many different colored robes and sashes. Another example they share is that most of the construction here is done by laborers from India because there are so few Bhutanese.

Building takes so long because only 10 Indian laborers are allowed in the country for each building project.

Later, I visit a small temple, one of the few in which I am allowed. There are eight monks in the back facing the various altars in the inner sanctum. No women. There are also monks playing long horns, symbols and bells near where I entered. Wonderful chanting!

They are all very relaxed, as am I, sitting cross-legged on the floor taking it all in. Another monk enters, sees me and motions to hold my hands out. Water trickles out of a teapot into my outstretched hands. I figure it's a ritual cleansing, so I rub it over my hands to wash them. Palden arrives shortly thereafter and the monk pours some water into his hands. Palden sips the water out of his hands. I look over at the sitting musicians, who are laughing as they chant and play. Live and learn.

Goodbye to Palden and to Bhutan. A good guy, and a wonderful, fascinating country!

The flights to Kathmandu, Nepal, are always overbooked, so being number one on a waiting list ensures a seat, I'm told. However, no one cancels. Pasco, the driver hired by Mr. Rinzing, will get me to small town at the border of India where I can get a ride through India to Nepal and on my flight to Tibet.

It's about two days of driving five hours a day. The road was put in by India in 1960 as a military safeguard against a possible incursion by China. It's rough gravel, with many turns and no guardrails. To get the road, the king had wisely bargained for a few free schools and hospitals. India agreed. It is one of the most scenic drives I have ever been on.

The driver, while very nice, is frankly not a great driver. He had asked if he could bring his girlfriend along. I agreed. The route is all mountain roads. After a short distance, I suggest I drive. He readily agrees and sits in the back with his girlfriend. There are some cattle on the road in the more level areas. They placidly stand as we go by. I could pet their noses without reaching very far.

Reportedly, there are 24 washouts on the way to India. This must be in reference to the major ones, because I have counted more than a hundred. At one point I followed an earthmover for several miles.

Switchbacks are used to climb and descend, but rain-soaked slides wipe out at least three sections of the road on the way down. My driver and his girlfriend don't seem to be overly worried. They're cuddling in the backseat.

We stop at a rather pleasant place for a needed rest from the braking, accelerating, dodging, honking (always honk) race across the mountains. Soon fog and darkness have set in. We have slowed to walking speed and are hanging out the window to see our way. With all the bulldozers and trucks, I notice our car is one of the very few. Surprisingly, there are a few scooters. We see no homes for miles and miles. Makeshift shacks and shops are there for the Indian workers who maintain the road.

The hours of slow, grinding driving stretch into more than six. It's 10 p.m. when I fall into bed thinking this has to be one of the most scenic routes I've ever been on. With time, a large SUV, and all daylight, it might have been much more pleasant.

The medical mission? I wrote the letter and we received permission to have a mission visit Bhutan.

Bhutan - some words
- Hemadatsi: National dish - chilies
- Kule: Buckwheat pancakes
- Buta: Noodles
- Datsi: Soft cheese spread
- Churpi: Hard cheese rings
- Phagsnapa: Pork fat
- Gondomaru: Eggs
- Kabze: Dried fritters
- Ara: traditional beverage with 20% alcohol
- Nadsa: Tea with milk
- Seudja: Tea with salt and butter
- Momos: Raviolis or dumplings
- Thukpa: Noodle soup
- Shabale: Fried dumpling
- Geong: Ordained monks
- Gup: Village headman
- Lhakhang: Temple
- Gompas: Monasteries
- Thangkas: Prayer banners
- Katas: White ceremonial scarves

Nepal - 1999

There are lots of delays coming from Bhutan. It starts with the auntie of one of the Bhutanese king's wives taking our vehicle because she wants to go the hairdresser. We are driving to Nepal in the first place because of the overbooking of the small plane that will take us to Tibet. "We should get started in the morning" becomes noon, and "He should be here any minute" gets old quickly. We finally drive off at four in the afternoon.

The road has been challenging but the views are spectacular. All around us we see all green pine forests and thousands of feet in elevation changes. We're heading to an airport in India. From there I'll catch a flight to Kathmandu in Nepal for a brief visit and then a plane to Tibet. Would you believe it - I actually am having fun! Really!

The morning after the long drive, I'm up at 5:45. A shower's going to feel great. Well, not as great as I hoped. The water trickles, but does the job. After eggs, toast and tea, Pasco picks me up. (Everyone has nicknames and his, Pasco, means "peace and cooperation" because in school he was always stopping fights.) About a mile out of town, the car stops, and Pasco fiddles with the distributor. A small van pulls up. The three people in the van are with the same company and we take over their vehicle, which is new. Yeah! And it's only 7 in the morning.

There are permit fees between districts and passport checks between countries. The driver argues with the official at each checkpoint. I mention that the straight road we're on must be the best in Bhutan. Pasco laughs: "We're in India."

Should have known; the scenery is different too. Rice paddies, forests, river, cattle, ducks, lots of people and trucks and bicycles (never saw a bicycle in Bhutan), goats, three-wheeled transports, motor or not, and oxen pulling carts with modern rubber tires or old steel wheels.

We pull into the airport at about 4 in the afternoon. Plane's "going to be on time." The counter opens at 5. Pasco's girlfriend, who I agreed could come along, is there too, and we all share a snack before I leave. They're nice people; I wish them well.

I have to go to Nepal first and that's fine. Things to see there, too. The flight to Kathmandu, Nepal, is uneventful, and upon landing there's a guide to meet me. He's already met three or four planes because the agency wasn't sure which one I was on. It's late and the guide and a driver take me to the Tibet Hotel, which is really quite nice. I ask the guide to pick me up at 8 and he says that is not possible and neither are most of the places I want to see.

Thank heavens a different guide that shows up the next morning. He seems much more positive and I see everything I want to, including several stupas (Buddhist religious monuments) and temples - several with chanting monks. There are many more visitors here: Germans, Dutch, and some Americans. Kathmandu is a winding, dirty, noisy, charming jumble of about 600,000 set in the Kathmandu Valley, which I understand was a lake many years ago.

I had called Father Bill Robins at St. Xavier School, so he's expecting me. It turns out that my guide's son attends St. Xavier's and he proudly points out that only 30 out of 600 applicants are accepted. Others, too, have told me the school is well-respected. Father Robins is very nice. I learn that his background is in physics and though he still teaches, he now runs Nepal Jesuit Social Service Center. This involves taking care of the "the throwaway kids, handicapped," he says.

I visit with some of the kids. He's doing good work. We rattle along talking and end up discussing where I should go for lunch. He'd like to join but cannot. The place he recommends has delightful little alcoves and good food; a quiet oasis. I meet an American from Virginia who's attached to the U.S. Embassy here. His specialty is antiterrorism. We have a long, interesting talk.

On my way to Tibet . . .

Tibet - 1999

Before coming, I had called four agencies that specialized in trips to Tibet. The answer was the same: The Chinese government requires going with a group. I prefer to travel alone because you're more likely to meet and interact with regular people this way. I make one last call. The very nice woman says she can get me into Tibet - alone. What? Great! Then she explains she helped a group of five go last year. Pardon me? "Four didn't show up." Aha! I went with a group of four. Three didn't show up.

The morning I leave Kathmandu, the guide picks me up at 7 in the morning for the short ride to the airport. Then I find out the border guard when I entered Nepal from India did not give me the required visa. After some discussion with several pleasant people, it's decided that I should pay a 25 percent penalty. It turns out to be about $7. Everyone is so nice and apologetic about it. They just weren't sure of what to do. I have five good friends by the time I leave.

I have some concern about the flight because four Americans with confirmed tickets just got bumped. The plane was supposed to leave at 9:50. It's a little after 10 when I am lucky enough to get on board. We sit on the plane another hour. At least it's a Boeing 757. Several announcements are made, and now the ground crew wants another head count. Finally we're off . . . and I'm on.

You have to love it! It's an hour flight to Lhasa and they show a Harrison Ford film but fast-forward it through many parts. Even with all the fast-forwarding, no one gets to see the end. I'm the first one out of the terminal because of no checked bag. The guide who meets me also has to take three others: a German woman who talks a lot and a couple from New Jersey.

When we get to the hotel, the Jersey couple keeps complaining that they had booked a better room. They decide to move to the Holiday Inn. The guide understands how I feel. He says he sometimes hates tourists, too. Now he's over with the manager angling to work with me. The people at the hotel are very accommodating. A glass of tea is served as I check in. It's not a great place but they're trying, and it's Tibetan.

My guide says the Chinese restaurants are cleaner than the Tibetan ones, so we end up at an Indian one. Go figure! The German woman is there and the guide is talking to the hostess and motioning toward us. I'll talk to him tomorrow about commission sales. Maybe the Chinese restaurants are cleaner but we're in Tibet. We agree to get together later and I leave.

Wandering around the square is fun and I find a Tibetan restaurant! There are no other outsiders here but they seem both surprised and pleased to have me. I point to a big bowl of noodles on the table next to me, where there were five friendly girls about 16 years old. They can speak a few words of English. With a lot of motions and hand waving, they seem to enjoy helping this ignorant man and practicing their English. Good dinner. Good entertainment - both ways.

The next day my guide pulls up in a rickshaw and off we go to see temples. Each one is spectacular in its own terribly cluttered, butter burning, dark way. (Butter is used for the candle wicks.) Sometimes a small fee, sometimes more, to take pictures. It appears that a portion of the monk's life is either taking fees or making you wait . . . to take fees. The fees and the wait are well worth it. The temples and sights are incredible!

We finally get to the fabulous Potala Palace, which overlooks the city in an imposing way. It is truly huge. Construction was started in 1645. It boasts 5-meter-thick walls, is 13 stories high and has more than 1,000 rooms. Did I say impressive? (Its colorful history is another story).

It's Sunday morning, so we'll have to wait until 10 a.m. to enter but I'm allowed to begin the long climb up because of being alone. There were warnings about altitude sickness being common for visitors - Lhasa is about 12,500 feet above sea level. A little headache persists, even with pills. There's a short wait at the big wooden doors at the entrance, and again inside for different rooms.

Rituals seem very important as do the many mythical stories that accompany each of thousands of statues, each intriguing. Many are leafed in gold and, interestingly, many are behind protective screens and chains. There are TV monitors everywhere! This is unexpected. There have been thefts, supposedly by Chinese soldiers. There's uneasiness beneath the current calm relations between the Chinese and the Tibetans. So many Chinese have moved to Lhasa that it's estimated they now account for 60 percent of the population.

With the number of cars, motorcycles and other vehicles, there appears to be quite a bit of prosperity here. The streets are lined with myriad little shops with two or three people manning each. It seems like everybody in town is a shopkeeper! Many just have little stalls in the courtyards. Some just walk along with their store on their arms. Western dress dominates, except in the temple areas, where more traditional clothing takes over.

There are numerous temples and a convent where a hundred nuns live. My guide and I get along well and he even invites me to his apartment, which is nearby. He's 26 and I get to meet his mother, father and three younger sisters. It's intriguing to see this family side of things. He tells me that his grandfather was in prison for 10 years during the Cultural Revolution, which began in 1966. At the time, he sent the family to India to live.

Lots more temples; one can get templed out. It's about 5 p.m. so I head back to the hotel and then to the square where there is lots of activity. I order potato-vegetable momos. They're quite good but unlike the ones I had in Bhutan; these are deep fried. I also have a Carlsberg beer. The food is quite reasonable here, and even the poorest people seem well fed. Now it's 6:30 and the sun is setting. There's one table of foreigners and the rest are locals. The golden roofs and spires of a temple are in front of me, the starkly bare mountains to the right.

The evening is filled with many beeping horns, much chatter, and lots

Where we meet the Boy Lama

Steep steps keep evil spirits out

of smells. Buildings appear to be well constructed and well decorated, only to be left to the elements with little upkeep. Many windows are draped with decorated cloths. From their appearance the cloths have been there for years. Most Tibetans and Chinese here are small in stature. Interestingly, many of the younger women wear platform shoes. Across from me three monks share some tea, and together we enjoy the bustle and the views.

Prayer flags are often part of the view. Tibetan prayer flags are different from the ones I have seen in Nepal or Bhutan. Here the poles are short and there are many coming from a central spot - mainly on roofs. Other places have towering 25-foot poles which carry many flags called "wind horses." These are placed separately in the ground.

The next morning, at about 9:30, we start driving north to visit a small monastery where a living Buddha (chosen by the Chinese) resides. The first hour seems a little rough, and we're still climbing. The mountains and the views are better with each turn of the road. The construction of some parts of the road is most unusual. They've used 2-foot squares of stone with mortar in between for the base.

It gets rougher as we climb higher. Barren hills and mountains surround us, scattered with cows and goats, and even a few pigs, donkeys and horses. The last hour of the drive is gruesome. Did you ever feel sorry for your vehicle? Most of the time we travel in first gear, propelled over a road made of small boulders. The Toyota Land Cruiser we have must have been outfitted to carry 10 tons. It has no springs to speak of, though anything less rugged probably wouldn't make it. Tiny settlements and squat single farmhouses, not particularly attractive, sit here and there.

We have arrived! There are quite a few yaks grazing in the area, so I try to get a picture but they're a little shy even though they're domesticated. The monastery is not large but pretty. A picturesque mountain stream flows down from even higher altitudes. Over the pristine stream is a building - concrete but not unattractive. I need to visit it. It's what we call basic. Inside there are six rectangular holes in the floor, each about 6-by-12 inches. No stalls. the holes are about 4-foot apart. It's a communal squat toilet. Looking through the holes one sees that pristine stream down below.

We're at 14,000 feet above sea level here, and I don't feel great.

The living Buddha who is about 13- or 14- years-old, is to give his audience at 1 p.m. The background story: When the well-known Dalai Lama, the spiritual leader of Tibetan Buddhism and one of its most revered living Buddhas, escaped Tibet after a failed uprising in 1959, the Chinese government decided they would need a replacement. They chose this young man (among others, over the years). He did not have a choice. He lives here as a figurehead.

Everyone is body searched. Cameras are not allowed. I don't know how someone with disabilities would make it through security. The last steep stairway is meant to keep evil spirits out but unfortunately it would also be an effective barrier for the disabled.

We and several other visitors, including a nice couple and the noisy German woman, file up a stairs. There are about two dozen others, all properly intimidated, who also plod along. I have read the bad English translation on the instructions, which include the proper way to "worship" the living Buddha.

My guide has gotten me a long white scarf. I present it and say

Sacred scarf and prayer wheel

"Hello" (certainly not bowing - idol worship, or worse). The young living Buddha takes the scarf and nods to my salutation without changing his expression. The German woman, after her emotional greeting, is standing aside savoring a few more moments in his sight before she gets pushed along. Hope she found what she was looking for. She tells me later that on her first trip here, she felt something for two small girls. When she asked a monk why, she was told that in a previous life they had done something for her. She now sends them money and visits them, and has converted to Buddhism.

If I sound cynical, maybe it's because it's toward the end of the trip and I think of all the personality cults - whether it's the Dalai Lama, the living Buddha, the king of Bhutan, the different worshipped saints of Buddhism or communism or democracy. I see them as false gods. Usually, the reverence given them is based on emotion, and non-thinking performance of rituals and retelling of myths. Intimidation, in the form of steps up to an elevated position, or surrounding of the "revered one" with splendor, are not directed to God, but to His servants. It sets the scene for disapproval by an educated and thinking audience of all religions . . . and God.

(Shortly after returning home, I read where the young man, the living Buddha, has escaped with his sister hundreds of miles by various means to India, which has given him refuge).

The long ride back to Lhasa gives me a chance to think of what it's all about. The altitude is exhausting and I head for the bed at about 3:30 in the afternoon and within an hour I am feeling better.

Soon I'm off to see the stalls across from the Potala Palace. Scouting for a restaurant takes me back to the area near the hotel and a little place overlooking all the activity. Dinner's tea and mushrooms and chicken with white rice. Even the chicken didn't know it had some of these parts and some remain on the plate. The juice, tea and mushrooms are very good. Dessert consists of some bakery goods found on the way back to the hotel. There are many shops selling clothes, including lots specializing in man's suits. I've even noticed farmers wearing suit coats in the field. The women go more for the traditional garb and make better pictures.

Waving is kind of fun. The varied reactions are also fun - some surprise, some bafflement. Today when I waved at some ditch diggers

Portalo Palace

who enthusiastically waved back, my guide asked me why I would wave at Chinese. Of course he's Tibetan and Tibetans ignore the Chinese. I waved at a girl this morning and she stuck her tongue out at me with a smile! Good thing I had read a little about Tibetan culture. Her gesture was a sign of respect and affection in the traditional Tibetan way. I returned the greeting. She smiled.

In some countries, people don't nod their head up and down to indicate "Yes." They wag it to one side the way we mean "Maybe." I learned that after asking people if I could take pictures and their nods meant "Yes" but I took them to mean "No." I thanked them and walked away. It must have been as confusing for them as for me. Missed several good photo opportunities, too.

Back in front of the Potala there are a lot of military personnel. The area has been sealed off by soldiers placed every 10 feet. There's a show going on, for only high dignitaries it seems. The monastery is lit up beautifully and now there are even fireworks. No one speaks any English so I don't know what is going on, but it's colorful and exciting.

It's been very interesting and well worth the trip but I won't miss the hacking, smoking and spitting everywhere (even by the monks inside the temples), nor the constant beeping of horns, the filthy conditions, questionable food, or rats (one in the temple and one in my room last night - at least they're smaller than the ones in the States).

On the good side, most people are polite, always move over when honked at, and of course the scenery is fabulous.

The plane is overbooked and some with confirmed seats don't make it. I do. It's a quick flight back to Kathmandu and just as we pass the greatest peaks in the Himalayas, the clouds break and Everest and other peaks watch us pass by. Wow! Without any reference points, it's difficult to appreciate the heights, yet the solid mass of clouds thousands of feet below the peaks gives an idea of the majesty. Awesome!

At Kathmandu airport I befriend several workers - security people and a custodian. I help mop the floors while the custodian and others sit and laugh.

Then I'm off to Bangkok, Thailand, which has a large, nice airport with lots to do. Next, it's off to Seoul, South Korea, for the third leg of five. Total trip time: about 47 hours. Already Lhasa seems like a distant memory; Bhutan even more so. I have time in Seoul to explore a little, visit the cathedral, have a bit of lunch then be on my way.

Angor Wat

Cambodia - 2001

As long as Cambodia is on the way to Bhutan, why not stop? Well, at least on the map it's on the way. I wanted to see Angkor Wat, the famous temple area.

We had received permission and an invitation to visit Bhutan with a medical mission. Dr. Ruedi Gingrass and his wife, Julie, are heading up the mission. When they heard that I was thinking of going to Ankgor Wat, they wanted to join in.

The flights from Milwaukee to Detroit, and then Detroit to Narita International Airport in Tokyo take a little more than 13 hours; from Tokyo to Bangkok, Thailand, is another six. We arrive at 11 at night and the Quality Inn near the airport is convenient. The plane for Siem Reap in Cambodia doesn't leave until 11:30 tomorrow morning. We'll have to come back through Bangkok after Cambodia, so I'll leave my suitcase here at the hotel.

The plane the next day is only about 20 percent full. Several forms are required for Cambodia, and a line of six uniformed men approve the paperwork when we arrive. It's hot, sticky. Because I have carried just a change of clothes, I'm the first one outside to look for transportation. Ruedi and Julie wait for their bags. On the way out, a man from the guide association tells me they charge $5 for a taxi to get to town. Outside, there are many offering assistance, some for a dollar.

I ask the guide association guy what's the difference? It seems there is none, so I start back outside and he says one of his will do it for a dollar. I

find out that the driver usually pays the association $2, plus something to the owner of the cab and an airport fee. Everything's a bet that the driver can get more work by guiding for us.

We ask about guesthouses and hotels. The one he suggests is OK but Julie would like to look a little more. Second one is much better and it's only $40 for the night. Ruedi points out a very plain guesthouse next door and laughs that I might stay there. I'm curious and wander next door. The upstairs has a room with four beds on 4-foot high platforms. The gentleman there starts saying beds are $3, then changes it to 4$. Three blind girls are there and I notice later that the place is an association for the blind, who also give massages. The "beds" during the day are actually the massage tables. Back to next door.

The three of us are anxious to see Angkor Wat, and we've agreed with Ta, the driver, to hire him for the day: $20 for him, $20 for the car. The temple is as fabulous as its reputation. The moats surrounding the temple grounds are two football fields wide. The temple tower, we're told, is the height of the Notre-Dame Cathedral and yet the main actual temple is smaller than my living room.

Despite the claimed 500,000 square feet of walls and towers, the

temple was only for the high priests and, therefore, small. The walls cover two miles. Bas-reliefs cover the inside of the walls. The walls actually are made up of two walls, with a peaked roof between them. All is built of stone. The ceiling used to be wood but is now gone. The bas-reliefs describe battles, foes, friends, demons, monkeys and common folk. After an hour, we need relief. I meet several younger monks, many of whom speak English and love to practice it.

Ta, our guide, has been excellent. He tries very hard and is knowledgeable to the point of boredom. We invite him to go with us to dinner. A blessed shower revives my spirits. The excellent dinner with tablecloths, three waiters, two beers and a bottle of wine is $44 dollars for the four of us. The wine and the beer were three quarters of the cost. The meals were only $2.50 to $3.50! I had wonderful chicken with cashews and Ruedi and Julie had something "amok" (a curry dish) and a fish soup. The rice was shared by all.

Interesting: At the hotel each room has a place near the door where at night you put the keys to allow the air conditioning and the lights to work. Of course it's always hot and humid when you walk in.

Today is April 2, and my birthday, but no one knows it. Ta takes us

to several more temple areas. On the main road to the temples, there is a kind of toll booth on the side of the road. The locals keep on the road, but we must stop and have our picture IDs checked. The areas around Angkor Wat are the only safe places in the country.

More temples - there are hundreds, as I understand, from the massive Ankgor Wat to 12 more across from the so-called Terrace of the Elephants (a platform at one temple from which a long ago king viewed the victorious returning army). All are fabulous. Not only are the details interesting, but imagining the backbreaking labor in this climate is impressive, too. I'm trying to picture what it would have been like a thousand years ago.

Some temple areas are nicknamed the "jungle temples" because the giant roots and trees have been allowed to overgrow everything. It gives an idea of what they must have looked like when they were discovered years ago. French, Chinese and Japanese organizations are restoring some of these. There are locals who keep the "lawn" cut with machetes. Also, there are workers, mostly women, spreading gravel along the shoulders of the road by hand. Each has a flat basket filled with one shovelful of gravel, then carried and dumped along the road. Much smiling, no rush.

What's my worst problem today? Nothin' Lord, nothin'.

Motorbikes are the main transportation it seems, and one to five people ride on each. Bikes and cars are plentiful, too. There are taxis made up of a motorbike with a trailer bigger than the motorbike itself. Many of the locals are out sitting at the little open-air cafes that line some of the roadways.

We stop at a very nice restaurant and then head back to the room for a shower. Back out mid-afternoon for a little more extended trip. I get several good portraits of some kids and buy a t-shirt for $4. Every temple has its group of vendors, including many children who seem to know a little English. Some practice "Good morning" and "How are you?" as you pass by. Back to the room for another shower - what a luxury!

Ta asks if he can pick the restaurant for tonight and, surprisingly, Ruedi and Julie quickly agree. Maybe they're tired. Ta picks us up about 7 p.m. and we bounce along to an open-air place right across from Angkor Wat. What a view! The café looks OK. Hope it's good enough for Julie and Ruedi. There's a large group of extended family of the owners here but few others.

Julie then brings out a bottle of dark Berghoff beer and says "Happy birthday!" Can't believe it - she brought it all the way from Milwaukee for me! Then out come balloons, sparklers, goofy glasses, party hats for all, and a cake with a greeting to me in Cambodian, for my "61st Anniversary"! We sample the cake and eat another great dinner. Julie tells me that in the bottom of my suitcase there's a birthday card from my family back home. And I had just brought a bag with a change of clothes; my suitcase is still in Bangkok. Wow - what fun!

Ruedi, Julie and Ta had gone out after we got back this afternoon to prepare all this. I take all the party things and leftover cake to the extended family and we all have a great time laughing together. They are clapping, and one points out that the laughing older boy sitting next to me is clapping with a hand and a stump. His hand had been amputated. I got one of the party hats and put it on the stump, then over his nose. He was obviously well-liked and they all went wild in their shy, self depreciating way. Nice people, simple life.

I thank them all for a very memorable birthday.

Bhutan - 2001

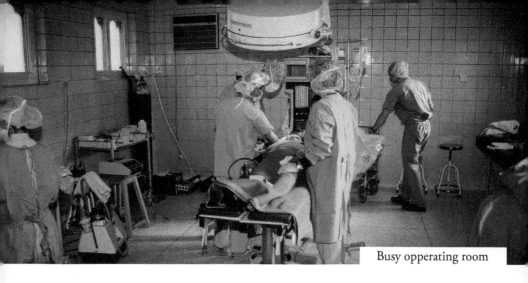

Busy opperating room

Bhutan - 2001

We were an odd group really, only seven of us, and unlike the few other visitors who visit this Himalayan kingdom of Bhutan. We're here on a medical mission. We're from Germany, West Virginia, Seattle, and four of us from Milwaukee. We think of ourselves as fortunate. While 600,000 people visit neighboring Nepal each year - 30,000 of those visiting the base camp of Mount Everest - this tiny country squeezed between India and China sees only about 6,000 outsiders a year. Most are traders and farmers from India. The farmers rent a few trees and pick the fruit at harvest time.

The Bhutanese don't really encourage visitors - or change. It's said they possess the most preserved culture in the world. It was my second time here. The first was my naive attempt to set up this medical mission. I thought the officials would love to have doctors and nurses come to help people. The medical official here in Thimphu was skeptical. He told me there'd been a medical mission visit some years ago. They were from Europe, and the local reaction hadn't been good. He wouldn't say exactly why, but their attitude seemed to play a part. It took some convincing to get him to agree to this mission. I found out later that he was married to the niece of Mr. Rinzing, the local travel agent and also the uncle of woman in the U.S. who had helped me. Much here depends on your connection.

On most medical missions, the surgeries performed are the type where follow-up is minimal - cleft lips, burns, etc. With one-week

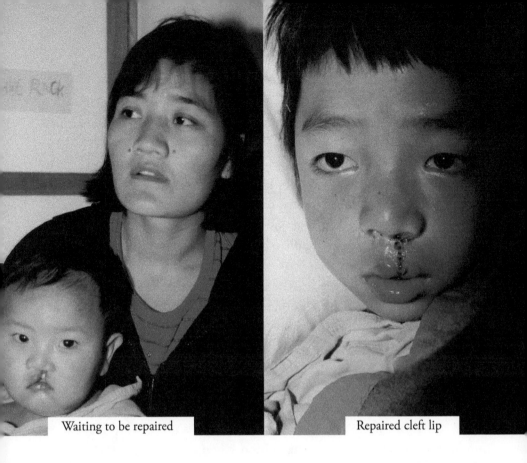

Waiting to be repaired

Repaired cleft lip

visits, there aren't any second chances to get it right. The differences the surgeons make is magical in countries with little real magic. More than one surgeon has told me they also just like helping people and not being concerned with lawyers and insurance forms.

Cleft lips are especially rewarding, but in an unexpected way. In some countries, the superstition exists that if a pregnant mother merely sees someone with a cleft lip, then the baby in her womb will have a cleft lip, too. Naturally, kids with cleft lips aren't very welcome where they can be seen. The magic comes after the surgery. Those same kids, who had cleft lips and were once relegated to back rooms for life, are now free to join in and be productive in their society. That's nothing less than magic. (Sadly, but realistically, doctors many times won't operate on any patient who has a chance of dying. No matter how much good the doctors do or how much they explain, they'll be blamed for any death and the missions will not be invited back.)

It's late in the third day and "we" have spent the time diagnosing patients. Everyone's tired. The next three days are full of scheduled operations. On the way back to the beautiful home the government has graciously provided for our stay, our guide asks if we would like to see what a typical Bhutanese house looks like. Great! The architecture of all homes in Bhutan must be in the Bhutanese style, by law. Most have a similar design, with huge, overly engineered beams, wide-planked floors and traditionally painted designs on the exterior. Often they have a phallic symbol over the door or hanging in the corner of the building for good luck. Yet, also typical, there's little furniture, insulation or heat.

When we make our unannounced stop at a nearby Bhutanese home, our guide tells the surprised – and very nice - owners the purpose of our trip. He explains that the doctors are going to operate on people and train the local doctors in plastic surgery. While we sit and enjoy the always offered tea, our hostess mentions she thinks the girl next door has a cleft lip. Few in Bhutan had been told of our visit so as to not disappoint all those for whom there simply is not time. Even so, the word has gotten our and too many operations have been scheduled for a normal day. Yet the reason we have come to Bhutan, this reclusive Buddhist stronghold, is exactly to help these unfortunate children and the occasional adult. We venture next door.

There we met 15-year-old Pemaa (which means lotus), who was born with a bilateral cleft lip and palate. This means that most of her upper lip is split up into her nose, making her teeth appear to stick out at a repulsive angle. The roof of her mouth has never closed, leaving a hole into her sinus cavity. When she eats, some food invariably comes out her nose. Understandably, she is thin.

These fabulous doctors schedule her for early the next day. Pemaa's operation is a complete success. With the lip closed, her looks have improved dramatically. Her palate would be closed on the mission's return trips in the fall. Not only has Pemaa's appearance changed, but her attitude seems to experience a revolution. Pemaa watches me take Polaroid pictures of her and others for the "before and after" shots for their files.

I ask her if she would like to try to take a picture. She takes the

Pemaa can now smile - sent by Her Majesty

camera and with no more instruction, produces pictures of her brother, mother and father. She is obviously bright. And she no longer covers her mouth in shame. Pemaa then spies a hesitant older man who has come to see the doctors about an eye problem. She takes him by the hand and shows him into the physicians. Although the doctors are unable to help the poor man, everyone is quite taken with the way she has acquired the nerve to take charge. Pemaa is discharged a while later with instructions to return in three days to have the stitches taken out.

Three days later, we find ourselves watching for her to come down the hallway. She has an unusual stride for a 15-year-old girl, somewhat akin to a stevedore with lots of seniority. Her confident walk can't help but be noticed. Her clothes look newer and are most likely borrowed. She stoically endures having the stitches removed. Physically, she is well on the road to recovery. She still can't smile yet, of course, but looks at us and squints her eyes, thanking us.

The medical mission has been for the physical well-being of the patients and all that will mean for their lives. That part is certainly successful. It bothers me, however, that Pema's physical deformity, now mostly gone, is still going to keep this bright girl from ever getting an education because of her age. She has never even been in a school.

During a break, we visit the Traditional Medicine Institute, commonly known as the Indigenous Hospital. Every cure here involves herbal medicines, poking with needles, or slight burning of skin. We're told mostly older people come here. All costs are paid by the government.

A man demonstrates how some of the cures work and most sound pretty reasonable. I asked what the little "rods" of metal with wood handles are for. There were about six different sizes. He tells me they cure many problems and it involves heating a rod until it is very hot and then holding it on the forearm of the patient. The resulting burn heals within a few weeks he says. I ask whether it works. "They don't usually come back," he answered with a shrug of the shoulders.

There's a young doctor in our group who's not a surgeon. He and I decide to travel east to visit Jakar, which is supposedly a seven- or eight-hour drive. We have a driver, Ogin. The scenery on the way is beautiful. Maybe halfway, we find the road has been taken out by a landslide. There's a bulldozer and backhoe working to clear it. We climb up and take pictures. Half an hour later they've cleared enough of it so we can get through.

We stop for lunch at a little café, where we ask three monks to join us. They're going south for a funeral and to have their radio fixed. I look at the old radio and wonder. We buy each an orange drink, and then I excuse myself and, when outside, ask someone where I can buy a radio. I'm directed to a shop down the street, where I find one. Returning, I tell the monks I want to buy their radio. We trade. They are very appreciative. After exchanging addresses, we're on our way again.

About 12 hours after leaving Thimpu, we arrive at a guesthouse in Jakar. There are individual units, each with wood-burning stoves and "Don't flush the toilet paper" signs. All knotty pine - they could have been in northern Wisconsin. Nice.

A doctor runs a small hospital here. Essentially, most of the hospitals in Bhutan are what Americans would call clinics. If they can't help you at the small hospital, you are sometimes transferred to the National Referral Hospital in Thimpu, the capital. If they can't help you there, you may be transferred to India. We receive a tour of the clinic, which doesn't take long, then get an invitation to visit a patient after lunch. Of course we accept.

We use a large Toyota pickup and several others come along. An hour on the main roads and half an hour on a lane brings us to a tiny village of attractive homes. Attractive or not, they still have an outdoor spigot for water and a communal outhouse. There's also a bucket of water and a dipper provided in the outhouse for cleaning your left hand afterward. (Eat and shake hands with right hand only . . .) With little or no furniture available, everyone sits on the floor and sleeps on floor mats in large rooms.

The patient is an 85-year-old man. It has been determined he has cancer, and after much discussion the decision is made by the son that he should not be transported to Thimpu to be operated on. The son thinks the operation would probably kill his father (and in my opinion, the trip to get there would kill him). The doctor is asked to see another patient. He agrees. He's a good person, and earns about $150 a month.

This scene repeats itself many times in the next five to six hours, with many apologies to us, but we really don't mind. The next person has pneumonia. At each house we have tea and ara, the traditional alcoholic homebrew - milky stuff. The tea's good. Every time my friend turns his head, I pour some of my ara in his cup. He seems to be enjoying himself and gets more talkative as the day goes by.

At one point during the afternoon, I mention to the doctor we're visiting that a group I'm with in Milwaukee sometimes ship medical equipment to countries, and asked him if there was anything that he could use. He explains that if he had the equipment to test for diabetes he could save several people a month. No promises, but I tell him we would see what we could do. (A very generous friend of mine with whom I help has already sent two 40 foot containers that haven't arrived yet).

On our way back, impressions fill my mind: women breaking up stones for gravel for the road; people everywhere wearing the colorful national costumes; Bhutanese architecture; that clean clothes don't seem to be a priority; lots of people walking, standing and sitting; group picnics; cows and yaks; children and dogs; and no guardrails with thousands of feet of elevation up and down. As we drive along, a girl of about 20 asks for a ride to Thimpu. She sleeps most of the way.

On returning to Thimpu and the hospital, the health minister tells me that giving the doctor the machine to detect diabetes isn't a good idea. Why? If it broke, the people would expect us to provide another one and we couldn't.

The next day the first patient to be seen has been mauled by a bear. One eye is completely gone. You can see right back into the poor man's head. His story is astonishing: Some people were driving past a mountain village and saw this 60-year-old man tied to a tree just outside the village. He had tried to protect his garden from a Himalayan black bear. The bear attacked him. The first swipe took out his eye and the second took his national costume, his gho. His fellow villagers thought he had bad karma. They didn't want that bad karma coming into their village so they tied him to the tree to die. The passersby cut him down and brought him to the hospital.

Bear mauling

Ruedi Gingrass and Dave Foraty (the surgeons) go to work and everyone is amazingly efficient. After the wound has been cleaned, Ruedi cuts a flap of the man's scalp and, leaving some still attached, swings the perfectly cut piece down over the man's eye. He even cuts the piece so as to leave a small strip of hair that would serve as the man's eyebrow. Then they take a piece from the man's thigh to cover the missing area on his head.

When he comes to, he seems pleased, but what he seems the most concerned about is the loss of his gho. He seems very uncomfortable in the ward without a shirt or gho. Hah! Easy fix. Off comes my shirt. The patient is pleased. Someone brings me some scrubs to wear.

A couple of days prior, the doctors had operated on a young boy who had severe burns down his leg, from his thigh to below his knee. The surgeons cut off the inch-thick scar tissue that had formed. It was so thick it had prevented him from even bending his knee. After the successful operation, they need something to place over his legs so the sheets will not rub while he heals. I was assigned the task. We find a clean box and simply cut a "tunnel" through it. It works.

The "bear man" has a similar need. It might be more sanitary to have

Dzong

plastic. A little swimming pool – the kind children use in the summer - might work. I run out and find one, about 3 feet in diameter, at a hardware store type of place. One of the men in the lobby has a large knife that he gladly lends me to cut the tunnel, and soon the bear man had his covering. One of the people at the hospital is laughing and shaking his head.

"What?" I ask.

"You Americans," he says. "You just do things. We would have taken months to do that."

I was kind of proud of that. And, oh, by the way, because the bear man could not return to his village, the hospital gave him a maintenance job for his remaining years.

Bhutan, which recently became a partial democracy by the wishes of the king, still has royal family. As was mentioned in an earlier chapter, the current king had married four women, all on the same day, and all sisters. Each wife has a separate home and the king visits periodically.

The most important queen - most important because she is the mother of the oldest son, the crown prince, who someday will become king – has invited us to lunch at one of the dzongs. Dzongs have multiple purposes as administration centers, forts and, at one time, royal residences. When the time comes, we are shown into a large room where there is a chair and small separate table for each of us. We join the queen, two of her close relatives and Bhutan's secretary of state, who motions for me to sit next to the queen. Obviously he thought I was important, and, as you might suspect, I thought it best not to correct the man.

The Queen Ashi Tshering Yangdon Wangchuck

After formal introductions, the queen thanks us all for coming and all the work we have done. Presently, we all get down to small talk. Because she was next to me, she talked mostly to me. During our conversation, I talk about this intelligent girl, Pema, and what a great transformation has taken place. She is a good example of how the doctors are helping. It is disappointing that I will probably never see her smile. The queen, a most gracious lady, says she will have a picture taken of her and have it sent to me.

Delighted and emboldened by her offer, I remark that it is sad she can no longer be formally educated because she has never started school. The queen agrees. She promises to make sure that Pema gets the education she so rightly deserves and instructs the secretary of state to take care of this. I am elated.

Later that afternoon, my own bias is brought to light by our head surgeon. I tell him how excited I am about Pema's future prospects and how she has helped around the hospital. "Wouldn't it be wonderful if she ended up helping people in that hospital as a nurse?"

He smiles at me and says:"And why shouldn't she be a surgeon?"

Yes, of course. Why not?

The queen has promised to send me news and a picture of Pema. Shortly after I return home, Major Sonam Tobgay sends several pictures of Pema, with this note: "Please find enclosed herewith the photographs, of Miss Pemaa from Paro that you asked HM The Queen Ashi Tshering Yangdon Wangchuck."

Pema looked pretty in the pictures.

Thank you, Your Majesty. And thank you for a most memorable lunch.

Welcoming Party

Guatemala and Honduras - 2002

It's called the "Land of the Eternal Spring." Guatemala is a beautiful country - rolling hills, some mountains and lots of water.

Dan Meehan invited me to go with him to visit a school on the outskirts of Guatemala City. It's run by Catholic nuns of the Missionaries of Charity order, founded by Mother Teresa. Many of the nuns are from the Philippines and South Korea. Dan has been very generous in helping them build the school. There's a girls' school and a separate boys' school, each with more than 500 kids. The kids are between 12 and 17. They're chosen from the poorest areas, and go home only two weeks each year.

The girls' school was built over an old dump but you sure can't tell. A guard opens the large security gate. The buildings are beautiful. Girls run over from every direction and surround our van. They're obviously expecting us. Several have guitars and other instruments, and they all serenade us. What fun! The nuns stay in the background. Seems they have told the girls they're in charge and are they ever!

After the welcome songs, two girls take each of our hands and lead us off to see their dormitory. The dormitory's immaculate and very crowded. In some rooms the stacked three-high bunk beds are so close to each other that some of the girls have to climb three and over a bed to get to theirs.

Then we're taken to their workroom. A Japanese company has outfitted it with modern sewing machines. There's a computer room, too. The company also gives the school its excess cloth so the girls make all their own clothes. When they graduate, the company immediately offers them a job. A win for both, it seems.

Next is a two-hour show they've prepared for us. There's even a big "Happy Father's Day!" sign on the stage for Dan and me. We're seated on two chairs in the middle of the 500-plus girl audience, which is seated in rows on the floor. There's singing, dancing, skits and even a kickboxing demonstration! Afterward, each girl comes up and gives us a hug as a thank you for coming. I think to myself, what a wonderful lesson for the girls in marketing, self-confidence and interpersonal relations. Wow - definitely impressive.

Sister Tirasita
Teacher & Kick Boxer

Finally, over lunch, we talk with Sister Genna, who is the Mother Superior, and Sister Teracita, who teaches kickboxing, among other things. We're given the background of the school and their thoughts on helping the girls. The sisters interview 200 kids a year, plus their parents and parish priest. Of those, 150 girls - who are poor enough and committed enough - are accepted.

We're told that without some skills and increased self-confidence (especially for girls here), their future prospects are limited. There are very few dropouts. The visit to the

A Happy Father's Day Show

boys' school was good, too. The boys are taught auto mechanics and other "men" occupations with the same idea: to prepare them to make a living and be independent.

The sisters have a total of nine sites in Guatemala for serving the mentally ill and the promotion of women, plus a children's daycare center, an orphanage, a center for the spiritual healing of victims of torture and for natural medicines. In addition, they work in local parishes with religious education. They receive no government aid.

Two other people we visit impress me. One is a guy who visited Guatemala and decided to stay. To reach his land and school, we travel by van to the end of a road and then by motorboat maybe a mile upstream. The school is being partly built by the students themselves and it's only a few years old. Even the smallest child carries a brick or some material up the hill every day to where the buildings are. Some of those buildings are for sleeping, some for eating, and some for both.

We visit one circular building that is for sleeping and work. About 10 hooks on the outer wall and 10 more on a central pillar support sleeping bags at night. The place is immaculate except for one thing: Under each place where a bag would hang, there were blackish stains on the floor. I ask

200+ homes for unwed mothers

what caused the stains. I am told me that sometimes the bats bother the kids when they're sleeping. "Vampire bats?" "Yeah, we've got to close up some of the holes in the roof."

Again, what's my problem today? Nothin' Lord, nothing.'

And speaking of no problems - a visit with Dan to a Catholic hospital gives me a little insight. We enter a room about 20-by-15 feet where, in cribs, are children – infants to about maybe the age of 6 - with deformities. Sad. My training in body language makes me recognize my outward revulsion, shown by my crossing my arms and standing back. Dan has his arms wide open, greeting one of the kids. Yoiks! Come on, get with it, Jim. I cross over near a crib with a tiny girl who couldn't be much more than 6. Arms lowered. The label on the bed says "Susanna." I ask the nun next to me how old Susanna is. She answers: "Oh Susanna is sixteen." Arms quickly cross again. It takes me awhile.

The next day we drive to neighboring Honduras for a short visit with someone else Dan has helped. This delightful, impressive nun organizes young people, especially those in trouble, to be self-sufficient. As we enter the main building, there are three women making food to sell and out back four men making bricks to sell. In addition, several run a hair salon and a bakery shop. All are profitable enterprises. With some of the proceeds, they've built over 200 one-room homes for unwed mothers! And each of those has its own little yard where the home dwellers are taught how to grow their own food.

There are so many good people in the world. God bless them and their work.

Brother, Mother, and Asmae

Morocco - 2002

It starts out easily enough. Dr. Don Laub calls me. I haven't talked to Don in years.

"Hi Jim, Don Laub, you ever been to Morocco?"

"Don! Hi, no I haven't, why?"

"Wanna go?"

"Sure. What's up?"

Don's parents and mine had been friends for many years. They'd even owned a horse trailer together. Don has been the head of plastic surgery at Stanford University for 20 years. The story comes out that there's a very persistent girl in Morocco who has written the United Nations for years asking for help. She's in her early twenties and had been hit by a car when she was about 3. The result was severe head and facial damage. Don says the U.N. got tired of dealing with her and dumped it on his lap. He probably regretted saying it exactly that way because now he is calling me with a request - go and see her.

That's how I end up on a plane to Casablanca. I convince Dr. Bill

Dzinski to come along. We're going to assess whether the local hospital is good enough for her operation and to see the girl, Asmae El Akil. She lives in Fez Medina, a short flight away from Casablanca, but as long as we're in Morocco, exploring and learning should be part of any trip.

The Hassan II Mosque, or Grand Mosque, in Casablanca is truly unique. It's the third largest in the world and the most complex, my research tells me. Not only large, but the minaret is 564 feet tall, the "tallest religious monument in the world," it's claimed. As you enter, your shoes go in white plastic bags and are carried with you. The heated marble floors are a surprise. There's a water-filled trough down the center aisle, but it's only filled when the king comes through the huge main doors, and the doors are only opened for him. However, two sections of the roof slide back on sunny days for the enjoyment of everyone.

Looking down, glass sections of the floor reveal the absolution rooms below where one washes before praying. The men's area is on the main floor. Women are sheltered behind screens on two huge balconies that are parallel to the center aisle. The main floor holds up to 25,000 people, and there's room for an additional 80,000 in the courtyard. The place is big but those figures are still difficult to believe. The laser light from the tower is visible for hundreds of miles. The ocean on three sides completes the spectacular impression.

The next day, Doctor Bill and I fly to Fez Medina, which was founded in 789 AD. Fez is the city and Medina means old city. It's a fabulous rabbit warren of people, shops and buildings, with a total population of about a million. The amount of smells, trash, donkeys, and friendly and curious people seem to increase the farther in we go. We see no other travelers, much less tourists.

Asmae and her family live in the oldest part of Fez. After some confusion, we find their home. Her family consists of her mother, her 16-year-old brother Anear and two mentally challenged older siblings. They live in a small three-room basement apartment with no windows. They do have a sink and shower, which use the same drain as the squat toilet.

Everyone's very friendly. However, our first encounter with Asmae quickly becomes uncomfortable. Doctor Bill immediately determines that her jaw was broken and it didn't heal properly. The scar on her forehead would be fairly easy to fix, he says, but not the jaw. What to tell her? She's expecting a miracle cure. We're Americans, after all. He tells her we will have to get back to her when we get back to the United States. We learn her chances of getting married in this land are nil if she looks anything less than perfect - and perfect she's not.

Asmae knows we want to see the hospital to determine whether the facilities are suitable for a future medical mission trip to help her, and others. Even though we have described what we want to see in much correspondence with Asmae, perhaps something has been lost in translation. We find the hospital is closed because of a festival. Also, many have gone to Mecca for Hajj, the Muslim pilgrimage. A closed hospital? "The best laid plans . . ."

Everywhere we go there are sheep, being lead, dragged and carted, one even goes by riding in a wheelbarrow. The festival celebrates the story of Ibrahim in the Quran (or Abraham, first in the Bible) where he is requested by God to sacrifice (kill) his son. At the last second, an angel stops him. A nearby sheep meets his maker instead.

Asmae's family, poor as they are, has somehow bought a sheep. It's being kept right in the apartment. I hadn't noticed at first, but the sheep is in a closet just off the 6-by-6-foot kitchen. We're invited back for dinner. No, it's not the sheep - thank you, God. We sit on well-worn couches lining the walls in a small room. The couches double as beds at night. We have a Moroccan dish - tajine. Couscous, carrots, squash, and olives are cooked together with a small amount of meat in the center. I try a bite of meat which is delicious. The whole meal is excellent, though I notice that Bill saves the meat for the others.

Everywhere we go, there are men with men, women with women. We decide the cafes are for men only. They can make a cup of coffee or tea last for hours as they sit watching people and talking. Restaurants are for food; still, seemingly only for men. I hear the five calls to prayer every day but it doesn't appear many heed the call.

On the last night with Asmae and her brother Anear, we insist on taking them to dinner. It's a mile or more through crowds, shops and donkeys (donkeys are used to haul goods and trash through the narrow alleyways). We move quickly and both of them watch out for us like hawks, making sure the occasional "bumps" aren't an excuse to lift a wallet. Neither is really happy to accept our invitation to dinner and now I see why. Moroccans here do not go out to dinner, and only when we near the gate at the far end do we come upon two little restaurants. They're more for visitors, not so much for the locals.

While we're eating, two black-jacketed men ask Anear to step over and speak with them. I think nothing of it until it gets a little heated. Asmae notices, and joins in. She's not shy. It's gets louder, so I walk over and shake hands, introduce myself and ask what the problem is. "No problem for you, sir," one politely answers.

They're policemen. He explains that they're here for my protection to guard against anyone using an unlicensed guide. I thank him for that but explain that these are my friends and Anear is not my guide. His politeness emboldens me to push it a little more and tell his partner, who was quite obnoxious: "You owe him an apology," pointing at Anear. At 16, Anear is a little shaken. Asmae isn't.

Probably good that cop didn't speak English. We are not believed, but it's obvious they don't want to make trouble for the visitor. They tell Anear that next time he better pay the license fee. Read bribe, maybe. They leave.

The next day Bill and I go exploring. Two funeral processions go by. The corpses are simply wrapped in blankets and carried on planks to the cemetery by little groups of mourners. We respectfully stand aside, waiting until they pass.

We pass a barber shop, and one of the men greets us in reasonable English. I respond: "You speak English well." "No, no," he says, "but I learn a little." Of course we stop. I start talking with another man, the barber, who very pleasant. We cover religion and philosophy in short order. He suddenly asks if we would like to visit a home where the family sheep is about to be slaughtered. Away we go.

When we arrive the sheep is already groggy. A girl is pushing some white pasty stuff into its mouth. The knife is out, several hold onto its legs, the thick hair at the throat is carefully parted. This is all taking place on the tile floor of their living room, but I do notice there's a drain

Kids in the street got to eat the head

at the corner. With a baaa and a few death kicks, it's all over and we thank everyone for the experience.

We head back to the barber shop, where more good conversations take place. The shop is not only for barbering but obviously a local meeting place, too. One gentleman politely tells me how horrible America is, then – honestly - within a minute asks if there is any way I could help him get a green card to come to America.

I ask another man if they can speak freely in Morocco. He adamantly replies he is free to say anything he wants. As he wanders away a little, the man next to me leans over and quietly says, "Yes, he is free to say anything he wants, but he is smart enough not to," and gives me a knowing look.

A few years later, we brought Asmae to the United States. We meet her flight in Chicago. Our car is the first car she had ever ridden in! She stays with us for almost three months. A plastic surgeon friend, Dr. Chip Mixter, performed surgery at no charge. The cost of the hospital was lowered to $15,000. A call to Chris Doerr and even that cost magically went away. God bless them both!

Marquette University Dental School saw her eight times. They took 17 teeth out on the first day! Eventually Asmae was fitted with a completely new set of teeth. Again, no charge. She was so thankful and never complained. She considered herself fortunate; she'd been waiting for years for help.

Asmae would go to Mass at Lumen Christi Catholic Church with me every Sunday and I would take her to mosque every Friday. She would sit with my family at church but, of course, we would have to be in separate areas at mosque. She told me she believed if you are a good person and try to live a good life, then you'll go to heaven.

We always invited her go with us and our friends to dinner, and she really enjoyed it. After a while, instead of ordering, Asmae would eat a little off my plate. One night at our favorite Mexican restaurant, I noticed she is particularly enjoying the meat. It was too late - didn't get a chance to tell her it was pork.

Honestly, because of the difference in cultures and habits, she was not the easiest guest, but she tried very hard. God bless my wife, for at times it was difficult. Asmae went back to Morocco a new young woman. Within six months she was proposed to - twice. The first proposal for marriage was from a zealot and she thought better of it. The second man was already married, had two daughters but he wanted a son. If Asmae wanted, he would divorce his wife. Again, she asked me what to do. I ask: "What happens if you can't give him a son? Will he divorce you?" Years later, she's still not married, but she's happy.

Although most of the cost was borne by others, Asmae still emails us her love every few months or so. God bless you, Asmae.

On the way to Asmae's apartment

Ethiopia - 2003

Spectacularly beautiful country

Ethiopia - 2003

After 26 hours' travel, my plane lands at Addis Ababa and I am met by Tsegaye. Local time is 3 in the morning. I'm tired. Tsegaye takes me to a hotel and says he'll pick me up "in a couple hours." Yeah, right. He's serious. The wake-up call is at five-fifteen. Off we go.

Ethiopia is beautiful, all green hills and mountains. The roads are challenging, especially so because of all the animals. There are the donkeys that carry everything, zebu (a variety of cattle with a Brahma-like hump and long horns), goats, sheep, and a few camels. And there are many

Market Day in Kombolcha

people. All – people and animals - move over at the sound of the horn.

This is one of the poorest countries on earth. The average income, I'm told, is about $110 a person per year, although 92 percent of the people are subsistent farmers, which helps (they have food, just not countable income). They rent the land from the government. In the northern part of the country, it seems, every tillable square inch grows something. Common are sorghum, corn, tef (an Ethiopian wheat-like grass) and beans. The rest is rocky pasture.

Axum - St. Mary of Zion and Ark of the Covenant Chapel

Endemic Gelrado Baboons

We arrive at Debre Berhen, a small town known for its morning market. This is the reason we had to leave so early. Lots of animals for sale stand beside sellers of honey, butter, colorful cloth, various grains, chickens, and everything else someone wants to sell. I have the "help" of about 10 boys who want to practice their English and perhaps pick up a coin. Even though I've not seen another white face, every kid has their hand out. All are friendly and well-behaved. I see that almost no one smokes here.

We stop at a local Ethiopian Orthodox church and listen to the priest sing. The priests perform the service and then go home and support themselves with some sort of enterprise, mostly farming like everyone else. They receive only a small amount for being a priest.

We pass through parts of the Great Rift Valley (where, through DNA testing, I found my ancestors had come from 50,000 years ago). I try to get a

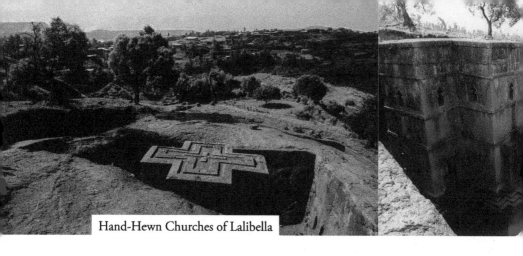

Hand-Hewn Churches of Lalibella

good picture of a gelada baboon. There are maybe a hundred in front of us but they don't let me get close enough. The leaders have a distinctive mane and a bare chest that flares blue and red when aroused. They'd make a great picture. And in my mind a better picture than the swollen red behind of some of the other African baboons. Anthropomorphic again, I know.

We have dinner at a little restaurant (certain of my friends wouldn't want the car to even slow down). After a meal of a tasty, thin steak with an egg over the top, we visit some of my guide's relatives in Lalibela. The mother and father (he was just promoted to head Lailibela's communications system) and their three daughters greet me. They arrange grass and flowers on the floor and give me a comfortable place to sit. Delightful!

The oldest daughter goes through the Ethiopian tea ceremony. The coffee beans are baked, and then ground. Tiny cups, plenty of sugar, and then a surprise - popcorn is traditionally served first. All is quite formal, and the family warm and most handsome. The daughters are 9, 15 and 17. They each in turn tell me about their school. All speak some English and are obviously eager to practice it.

Lalibela boasts an unusual church, actually several. The first one is a hundred feet away and you can't see it because it's carved out of the rock...in the ground. Nothing's above ground. The roof is the same rock and the same level as the rock 20 feet away. Amazing! Stone steps lead down to the entrance.

Although these churches are unique, all Ethiopian churches have a replica of the Ark of the Covenant. The replicas are paraded around town during the feast of Timkat Orthodox Tewahedo celebration of Epiphany, which is going to take place soon. The Ethiopians claim they also have the original Ark. Yes, the same one that held the Ten Commandments.

The short version is this: The original was built at the foot of Mount Sinai by King David, according to the Bible. King Solomon placed the Ark into the Holy of Holies in the First Temple in Jerusalem. The Queen of Sheba visited Jerusalem to meet Solomon. They got along well. She returned to Ethiopia and shortly thereafter bore their son, Menelik. Twenty years later, Menelik traveled to meet his father. When he and his party left, members of his party stole the Ark and took it to Elephantine Island where it stayed for 200 years.

It then was secreted to Tana Kirkos (an island in Lake Tana in Ethiopia) for 800 more years. Haile Selassie, longtime ruler of Ethiopia, built the Church of Saint Mary the Mother of Christ in Axum in 1965, and the special chapel next door. The Ark is kept in the chapel. No one except the monk who lives within is allowed on the grounds of the fenced-in sanctuary - and he never leaves.

Before dinner I go down to the corner where there is a small restaurant. Next door there's a pool table. It's the only one in town and it was delivered just a week before! No one's very good at pool yet. Someone asks if I play. "A little." I set up a three bank shot to a corner and luckily make it. Show off! I'm asked a lot about pool in the next hour. My reputation's established.

Later I have to come back to pay for a Coke that I hadn't paid for. The place with the pool table is now crowded. I meet the owner's son, who invites me to play. "Loser pays." Shark? He can play. However, toward the end I put two in and have a rail shot at the eight for the game. Before the game, we had talked about not leaning on the table while others shoot and being quiet. Just as I aim, he leans over and starts talking to me with a smile. I look at him, tell him to be quiet and take the shot without back looking at the ball. Cheers from everyone as the ball goes in. I pay the 4 birr (about 50 cents) anyway. I have some new friends. Much fun.

Driving along in the car, nearly everyone, especially children, bursts into smiles and waves when I do. Some walk seven miles or more just to sell two or three chickens for 2 to 3 birr apiece, (about 25 to 37 cents).

My smiling muscles actually get sore. Occasionally, there are rusted out hulks of tanks and other military equipment left over from World War II, and some from 1991 when the president was forcefully deposed. We're passing through a short tunnel when Wondu, my guide, points out a sign over our heads, which says "Mussolini." Wow, history!

My hotel is on the shore of Lake Tana, the largest lake in Ethiopia. After a muddy walk to the Blue Nile Falls in the morning, we take a boat in the afternoon to visit three of the 37 islands in the lake. Several contain monasteries. Churches are opened for me at each. There are familiar painted themes of St. George killing the dragon, Jesus and Mary, the crucifixion, the beheadings of many, the devil below, etc. Some of the paintings are from the 16th century and a few from the 13th, I'm told. Wonderful.

The last island is a "men only" island, and a monk comes down to the dock and to check us out. Wondu tells him I am James Bruce. The monk looks at me with that "Yeah, right" look. "Show him your passport." I do. Big change - big smile and a warm welcome. (More on why later).

The monk walks us up to meet one of the priests. The priest graciously shows me the "museum," which is about 12-by-12 foot. It's chock full of kings' crowns, silver, copper, and painted wooden crosses - beautiful things. One old manuscript is from the 1300s. Another, on goatskin, must weigh 35 pounds and was written in Ge'ez, one of the ancient languages of Ethiopia. He translates a portion. Fascinating.

Some of the timbers of the buildings here are huge. One of the main double doors of the church is more than 4 feet wide and 15 feet tall. Most of the buildings have tin roofs, though they used to be thatched and a few still are. The priest speaks fairly good English and we share many good thoughts on the Bible. He says Catholics are almost as good as Orthodox Ethiopians but that Muslims are no good. He scrapes his foot on the ground to emphasize his point. Protestants don't fare much better. Nothing politically correct here! We get along well.

He then invites me to have a beer with him and I readily accept. As we sit down, he gets out an old water bottle that's past use seems to have included holding diesel, and pours a generous amount into a plastic glass. The beer is mostly clear but appeals to a different taste - not mine. He also brings out some heavy, crusty bread made from corn and wheat, which was excellent.

When Wondu and I return to the hotel, I talk with people outside the gate, particularly two guards. One assists a cop when a minibus runs a red light. I head over to observe. The cop slaps the driver! The guards and I have a nice talk after. One says he was with the Special Forces and they are there to guard against terrorists, who they suspect are in the country. Their English is good but sometimes the niceties are lost in the translation. When we say goodbye, he wishes me "Goodnight and sweet dreams."

Gondar is next. This city is well-known and appears a little more prosperous than most here. The people there refer to the "castle," which is really six castles within a 75,000-square-foot compound. The best one is that of Empress Mentewab. She was the daughter of the queen who was cured of a disease by a famous Scottish explorer. In appreciation, he was allowed to travel in the area with some degree of safety.

The explorer's quest was a common one for Europeans at that time - to find the source of the Nile. Hundreds had tried and were unsuccessful. He was successful (although it was actually the Blue Nile) and his name is still recognized and respected here. That's the reason the priest at the island was so friendly. Who was the famous Scot that made his discovery in 1768? His name was James Bruce!

That night, we go to a bar and experience a wonderful tradition. It's a crowded little place of six bar stools and six tables. We get a beer and talk. A female singer accompanied by a male musician enters. (Gondar is famous for its singers.) The woman sings about Gondar and everything else, including singing to and about the customers. She asks Wondu my name and includes it in descriptions of me in her song. She's very personable. I tip her the customary four birr (about 50cents). They tell me the beat of the clapping or the drum is distinctive to each city. The singing, along with the shaking of everything, is tasteful, yet seductive. Delightful time, and very Ethiopian - energetic and modest.

The next day we stop for lunch at a little hotel. As we enter, the smell

Priests Celebrating Meskal

Holy Day of Meskal

The rush to get charcoal

of diesel is strong. I again wonder why they don't keep the doors closed from the street to keep the diesel smell out. Then I'm told many people here use diesel to wash the floors and walls to lessen the number of flies. Now I understand why the floor in the Lalibela was so slippery you could skate across it! This hotel is newer, so they don't use as much (and I don't notice any flies).

We arrive in Axum, where a huge amount of wood has been collected for a celebration of the Ethiopian Orthodox holy day of Meskel. The wood is piled 15 feet high. Hoards of people walk to the Church of Our Lady Mary of Zion, where many of the clergy talk about the gospel, AIDS, and the progress of the city. I follow along. The pile is lighted at 10 in the morning and it explodes into flames, which sends people running.

As the flames subside a little, the people rush back to get a bit of burning ember to use the ash on their faces and to take home. Each priest carries his own cross on a pole, and the garments are colorful - although some are quite threadbare. One talks with me and helps explain what's going on. It's a beautiful ceremony.

Nearby, a museum has coins from 400 AD with a cross one side showing the change to Christianity. I hear the celebrating drums, a trumpet, deep horn blasts, and notes from a stringed instrument. A hawk swoops down and lands on top of one of the stele. A Bible passage comes to mind: "Not Solomon arrayed in all his glory . . ." How pompous, silly and fun we humans are. Is this exciting? Oh, yeah.

Wondu is busy siphoning diesel from the four jerry cans on the roof of our vehicle. We have about a seven-hour drive ahead of us and there are no filling stations. The roads are all gravel; actually rock and mud would be a better description. I've seen more cattle, goats, sheep, and donkeys that I ever knew existed in the entire world. Also, I think we pass nearly all 55 million Ethiopians and wave to at least half.

Birdlife is abundant - white pelicans on Lake Tana, along with Egyptian geese, white-collared crows, doves, finches, spectacular yellow and black grosbeak-size birds, rollers, marabou storks, weavers, and bright blue starling-like beauties with vermillion bodies and black wings. Flowers are numerous, too.

Most fields here are plowed with oxen, the farmers being too poor to afford tractors. The rows are straight, one after another. It looks easy. Why not? We pull over and ask a farmer if I can try. He loves it! He shows me - left hand on the handle of the plow. Push down on the handle and the metal point of the wooden plow comes up. Pull up on the handle and it digs deeper. Your right hand holds a stick with a leather throng. Swing it around to your right so the oxen go left. Swing it left, they go right. OK, got it, doesn't sound too tough. To say the least, my furrows are not straight and within two minutes I have the poor oxen facing each other and the farmer nearly rolling on the ground with laughter.

A few miles down the road, there's a crowd of people in the middle of it. They seem to be centered on something. We approach slowly. One of the truckers has hit and killed a child. The driver kept going. It happened minutes ago. There's much crying as we creep by.

As we near the next village, three trucks are stopped. We talk with a policeman, who says they have the driver. Wondu says most drivers won't stop for fear of the "local payback" (which would be fatal for the driver). The lack of concern for those on foot is disturbing sometimes. I wonder aloud to Wondu if perhaps the degree of a country's civilization could be judged on how the strong (drivers) treat the weak (pedestrians). He very much agrees - as three old women scamper to get out of the way at the sound of his horn.

Konzo - "King of Kings"

Back in Addis Ababa, a visit to the Sisters of Mother Theresa becomes moving and disturbing. They have 14 such places in Ethiopia. The sisters take people that no one else will. There are TB patients, horribly crippled kids, and many people with AIDS. One of the nuns tells me that half of their patients have AIDS.

The AIDS patients I visit appear to be all men and are housed separately in a large room. The room is filled with what appears to be army cots with barely enough room to walk between them. Two or three horribly thin bodies lie on each cot. Almost all appear to be sleeping. One rises up on his elbow and looks at me. I wave. He craves attention and smiles and waves back. As we leave, I wipe my eyes and the sister notices. She's from Germany. "Ja, ja," she

Died two months ago
(Nice, but not very talkative)

says, "I cry every day." The sisters have their own hearse parked in back. It's used once or twice a day, I'm told.

Southern Ethiopia is very different than the north. It's more tribal, less farming. The new driver, Johnny, is a nervous driver, so I drive. He asks me not to tell the owner of the agency.

We visit many Konso villages and are welcomed in each. In one Johnny asks me: "Do you want to see the king's house?" "Sure!" He died two months ago. "OK."

The paths are lined with stones, branches and logs. Each compound has a formal entry. The king's is no different. The queen's here with her son

Konzo Tribe - King's Son, Queen, and Grandson

and daughter. Balloons and a Polaroid are enthusiastically received. They ask if I would like to meet the king. "Pay to view" of course. Johnny is superstitious and totally turned off. I'm curious.

Johnny negotiates the price down to 30 birr, less than $4 (they started at a 160 birr). The king's guard, who I don't see, is through an enclosure about 30 feet away. He is to prepare the king's body. The death has been kept a secret because first they have to raise money for his funeral. Here you pay people when they come to a funeral.

The king is now ready. I'm led to another enclosure and outside on a chair sits the king in a colorful robe and head covering. Each Konso village has a king. This one, Johnny had told me, was the "king of kings"

Jumping of the Bulls

- very important. His face is all that I can really see and the skin has been covered with a thin coat of honey (commonly used here). Circlets of white ostrich egg cover each eye, with a black dot for the iris. I take several pictures. I like the king. He listens to all my stories.

Johnny's not here. He tells me later that he was freaking out, though he expressed it a little more strongly.

From there we start walking back and a woman invites us up to her home on a nearby hill. She gives us some sorghum beer served in calabashes. It has the consistency of thin creamed corn. The view from her home is beautiful. She's very nice and kind of a flirt. A picture of herself and her children in front of her home is a hit. The neighbors hanging over the branch fence enjoy some beer that I offer out of the generous amount I have left in the calabash. Of all the tribes around, the Konso are the most numerous.

When we get to the Hamar tribal area, we hear there's to be a "bull jumping." Before a young man can get married in Hamar society, he must show his bravery by jumping and running over the back of bulls held by his friends. They tell me he gets only one fall. After some negotiation, the price of attendance drops to 70 birr for me. Several kids befriend me, including 10-year- old who sits with me the rest of the day. Several of the people speak some English, and help me to know what's going on. The

Whip marks

English was learned from visitors; no schools here.

Before the jumping, girls taunt young men to whip them, to show they have courage too. The saplings must hurt but they never show it. The attitude is: "That all you got?" The blood, welts and scars on their backs from previous years are all too real. Finally the bulls are all lined up next to each other. The naked young man runs and jumps on the back of the first bull and continues on across all 13! No falls. Victory! He is successful. Then everyone rather nonchalantly goes on about their social business and celebration.

I invite three especially great kids to join me for a Coke at a little outdoor dive restaurant near my tent-cabin. It turns into a meal for them as they finish my dinner and a little more. The 10-year-old rushes home because it's her job to start the fire for the family meal. She returns shortly to out eat everyone else. She also translates an offer from the friendly waitress at the restaurant. I decline. Yoiks.

Ethiopia - you are my favorite country in Africa. Thank you for your very warm hospitality.

Taunting - to be whipped

Belize - 2004

We are having a great trip - my wife, daughter Tina, her husband Mariano, and their kids, Maddie, Sophie and Ella. I leave them for a couple days to visit a priest in the western end of Belize. I stay overnight with him in kind of a deserted part of some building. The next day he and I travel to attend to several parishes he had not seen in months. The good father says Mass and baptized babies at each stop. At one parish he must have baptized 11 babies, so we were late to the next parish. Didn't matter; life's not run by the clock here.

When we return to his home, the priest relates how satisfied he is with his life. He says many people compliment him on the good work he is doing. He tells them is very happy what he's doing - it's no hardship at all. Nice. What a truly good person. A young friend of the priest stops at the house. I suggest we go buy a beer or two for all of us. After we get the beer at a little store about six blocks away, the friend suggests we take a different route back. When you're a gringo, it's safer that way, he says. Good to know.

The next day a short drive brings me to a group of nuns the young priest had suggested I meet. They're delightful people. Across from the entrance to their buildings, a small house is smoking. It had burned down last night, a complete loss, they say. It was a one-room structure built about 6 feet off the ground, basically on four-by-fours.

The sisters invite me for lunch, which I happily accept, and the poor woman whose home it was stops by. We're introduced and I ask what happened. Her two grandchildren were staying overnight in her home, and one child is afraid of the dark so she lit a candle, which eventually lit some window coverings and the house itself. She got out. After some translation problems, the sisters explain that the children had gotten out but somehow the grandmother thought there was still someone in the house, so she went back in. Big mistake - the roof collapsed on her. She was able to crawl out but, as she showed me (with little modesty), there were two huge raised welts on her back where the burning beams had knocked her down. What a story!

After lunch I drive around and find a little place selling lumber. There are a couple guys there who were friendly and informative. They said it would be cost about $500 to replace the burned structure. Wow - $500 for a person's home? The sisters are given the money with instructions that it's for the rebuilding and not to tell the woman where it came from. Months later, the sisters send me a picture of the new home. It looked nice. What a rewarding way to spend a couple days.

I drive back to rejoin my family and continue enjoying our time together in beautiful Belize.

Haiti - 2005

A very generous friend and I are visiting a compound near Port-au-Prince where several young, idealistic Americans have taken on the project of making, or rather having the hired Haitians make, bio-sand filtration systems.

Getting water for the family

The filtration systems are 42-inch-high by 12-inch-square boxes, with a filter on top, then gravel, and then smaller gravel, then special sand. An outside pipe comes up about two-thirds of the way from inside the bottom. When you pour water in the tip, clear water comes up the pipe from the bottom and out. No on-off spigot is necessary because the two-thirds level is about the level of the water inside. You pour in the amount you want to come out. After a week or so, the bacteria inside chomps up all the bad stuff. The result is pure, drinkable water. One such container serves the needs of about 10 people.

The young people are doing a nice job, one that really helps. Many diseases here result from contaminated water. After seeing how they are made, we visit some homes that actually use the systems. Seeing the families is great – they're friendly and open, and eager to show off how the device works.

Chris, who runs the filtration place, warns us not to go near Cité Soleil, a densely populated slum area next to the international airport, because it's so dangerous. Police won't go there. The United Nations Stabilization Mission had a station there to try to gain control over the violent armed gangs but opted to leave. Now troops and police only go in armored personnel carriers.

Chris says he was shot at twice in one trip and now won't go even near the area. Some violent residents were trying to get him to stop. Robbery and / or kidnapping are the usual motives, he says. All this, and he was just driving by.

The young woman explains the rules for us to stay tonight here at the filtration system compound (These are also posted on the door of the cabin where we are going to sleep.) Odd, they are asking us for money and yet the woman doesn't seem to realize that giving him instructions and being condescending probably isn't the best approach. I can feel it coming. I suggest we turn in for the night but my friend wants more information. Then he loses it. The woman is crying. My friend is perplexed. "They'll never get a cent from me." He later sends them $25,000 for their work, but only through someone else. It's a good cause.

Sewage disposal

Road to Koray

We take a long, bumpy ride to another airport to fly to Jérémie. This airport is actually quite decent, especially after Port-au-Prince. Leaving Jérémie the next day, I am reminded that there are always enterprising people - anywhere. The gravel road is rough. Progress is at maybe 10 mph. Around a bend the road has been cut into the hillside. There's been a landslide and many large stones litter the roadway. It is impassible. Each stone is about the size of a human head.

Helpful people remove stones & replace

There are a few people there who offer to help clear the way. Isn't that nice? I jump out and help, too. Then I notice that the stones have been quite uniformly placed, not like a landslide. They'll be replaced for the next customer.

We visit Corail, where it seems the only industry is bilking the NGOs (non-governmental organizations). Five years ago, some well-meaning Canadians came to help. As they arrived in town, they handed $10 bills out the windows. They didn't ask what was needed, but built some very nice, simple homes with blue roofs. They gave them to the locals, and included paint. The locals sold the paint and then asked for money to tear down their old houses.

The Canadians didn't find out what was needed. Didn't work with the people, and ended up with the worst possible result. Their effort wasn't really appreciated and the culture of "take what you can get" was bolstered.

Not everyone is here expects handouts. A woman, Madame Tata, invites us in and treats us to her moonshine. She and her 12-year-old daughter greet each of us with a kiss on both cheeks. As a parting gift, she gives us a small bottle, along with homegrown vanilla, herbal tea and coffee to take home. Delightful.

There's another woman, Mama Crappo (which means "frog" and Haitians hate frogs) volunteers cleaning, cooking, and running meetings and even church services when the priest isn't here. Maybe there's hope.

Pride is universal. In Corail the homes are never far from an open sewage ditch going to the nearby ocean. Electricity, if any, is sporadic. Most of the shacks I could have built in an afternoon. Many are bad enough to look like I did. No heating or cooling needed. Yet on Sunday, the residents all seem to have a single outfit for Mass. Everyone looks clean and pressed. Their pride is evident.

Cutting wood planks

Poland, Lithuania, Latvia, Estonia, Russia and Finland - 2005

This trip was to get a fleeting glimpse of how the "released" nations of the former Soviet Union were faring since its dissolution in 1991. Plus St. Petersburg and Finland were close.

Poland has so many wonderful churches and the people are very friendly. That being said, it's sad that the two sites that I remember the best are the salt mines at Wieliczka and horrible Auschwitz.

The salt mines are reached by going down hundreds of steps into the earth. Thankfully the way out is on an elevator. Impressions: Wetting one's finger and putting it on the wall and then tasting it. Yup, it's salt alright. Everything's salt, the walls, the floor, the ceilings. To see a good-sized church with a salt altar far underground and filled with beautiful statues all made out of salt is fascinating. A stable underground? It's here. I'm told that there were some mules that had never seen daylight.

Auschwitz is a different story. To experience up close what is an unspeakably horrible place is unforgettable. You see the railroad tracks where trains of boxcars brought the incoming prisoners. They were divided into two groups; one to be worked to death and the other sent to the gas chambers. The barracks had wood slabs for prisoners to sleep on and they were tilted slightly. Why? Prisoners didn't dare leave to urinate because someone else would take their spot, I'm told.

The "Work Shall Make You Free" (in German, of course) sign at the entrance was to keep hope alive and thus trouble down. The ovens, the barracks, the exhibitions of suitcases and other belongings that some expected to be returned to them just make one sick.

Walking across an open area, I realized I was stepping on white sticks poking up from the ground. Looking around I saw thousands, not sticks but bones, white bones. Thousands. Many exhibits give some idea of daily life and death here. How could anyone go through here and not ask how humans can do this to other humans. Millions of Jews and others, including thousands of Catholic priests (this is somewhat unknown), died here just because of who they were.

I leave, I look back. What does any visitor see over the barbed wire fencing, not a hundred feet from the building that had the gas chambers and ovens? It's the commandant's home where he and his wife and their children lived. They say when the ovens were busy you could smell the burning bodies miles away.

Vilnius is the capitol of Lithuania. The Stikliai Hotel is well located in the center of town and more than adequate. There's the Old Town nearby, which was the old Jewish Quarter. Cathedral Square is worth visiting also. There are little stands that sell round loaves of bread with salt, poppy seed or sesame seed. Really good! The Natural History Museum has a great selection, plus interesting information on prehistoric tribes that had lived in the area. As my bus pulls out of Vilnius, though, my mind jumps back to Auschwitz.

Latvia's capitol Riga is more cosmopolitan than Vilnius and very attractive. Although the churches, while beautiful, are not in the same class as Poland and not nearly as ornate. The people are friendly, yet not particularly outgoing. Most people appear trim and in good shape. No one's overweight except old people. Women don't look you in the eye (not just me! – culture, I think). Most of them under 40 wear tight jeans, all sorts of styles but all tight fitting at the top and wide at the bottom. I see more high heels and more makeup than in Poland or Lithuania. Guys are mostly grungy, haven't gotten in style yet. Most speak Latvian and Russian. The younger ones speak English.

On the way here my seat was near the back of the bus in front of seven young people about 18 or 19 years old. One of them, Vicktor, offers me a beer. Their enthusiasm about their future is quite evident. They are Russians living here and traveling home. They have lots of questions for me and all want to get into banking or investments. The three young women don't seem to care as much. Many of the young people I meet bubbled with the same positive attitude. Older people seem unsure of their future.

Estonia's capitol is the gorgeous town of Tallinn. There's no room at the Old House but they did have an apartment, which turned out to be a half a house, for $60! Two bedrooms, a living room with a fireplace, and a kitchen - just right. Tallinn's old city is delightful in spite of being a real tourist haven. Dinner? Excellent salmon, chicken with cheese and pork and oh, yes, of course, caviar. "Doesn't everyone darling?" Cost about $13. Cannot stay long in Tallinn; wish I could.

I hate being a tourist and the worst thing is to admit it. The nice thing about it, though, is that it allows me to read a map in public - everyone else is. At Tallinn's small port there are wonderful old 16th-century walls with foundations going back to the 1200s. A block farther they give way to traffic, regular streets and Soviet-style concrete block apartment buildings.

Oddly enough, because the train makes so many stops, the bus to St. Petersburg is quicker, about nine hours and overnight. St. Petersburg is where Peter the Great showed Europe, after beating the Swedes in the early 1700s, that Russia was a European power - and important. The city, built with the slave labor of Swedish prisoners and peasants, plus taxes on everything, is impressive.

A couple things stand out in my memory. The Hermitage is unparalleled in my experience. Massive, it contains over a thousand rooms and is nearly a half a million square feet. Inspiring, awesome, over the top - sure. Pick your own words. Books have been written; I couldn't and won't.

A hydrofoil takes me across to the Petrodvorets, one of the former summer residences of the czars on the outskirts of St. Petersburg overlooking the Gulf of Finland. The Grand Cascade (of water) leads to the Grand Palace. Set on 1,500 acres, it's as an imposing and attractive approach as there can be. A tour's a must.

It's time to think about dinner and head back to St. Petersburg. After looking up several restaurants, a walk along the river brings me to a huge old boat. It's moored, and advertises that it has a music hall and restaurant. Why not? Part of the bow is the music hall, which is empty. In the other part of the bow resides a beautiful beamed restaurant located on the mile-wide Neva River, across from the Hermitage.

No one else here. Sun slowly setting. A glass of wine in a crystal goblet. Sparkling silverware. Olives, borscht, and salmon (surrounded by mashed potatoes) that has been under the broiler just long enough for a golden brown finish is served under a silver dome. I stand at the window and look at the boats and sunset. Then the pianist starts playing. Desert was good, too.

Only one other party has come in. The young waiter does a very good job. I tell him so and he asks me to write my comments in a register. Gladly.

The train ride to Helsinki, Finland, is uneventful and $66 for the hotel isn't bad except they have a room only for one night.

The tram's only $10 for a three-day pass, and is a good way to get around. Taking a circular route gives me a good taste of the city. A very short boat ride to an island brings me to the zoo, which is just OK but set on a beautiful rock pile of an island. The Lutheran Cathedral (Tuomiokirkko) reflects the skills of many laborers and the Finnish Museum is certainly worth the time.

For a room tonight, there's nothing under a $130 to $160 for a room in the old central part of the city. I talk with an Argentine couple who are both musicians. He tells me he's Jewish and there are now more than a million Jews in Argentina. He earns $400 a month doing research on 16th century music. For $400 a month you can live well in Argentina, he says. Friendly people. They have reservations; I don't. Their hotel just had a cancellation so I get a double room for $60. It's big and very nice - a deal, with breakfast included.

It's about time for a Mexican meal and someone on the tram mentions the Santa Fe, so I get off. A good beer and the beef fajitas are perfect. It's a busy hotel weekend for Helsinki because of boat racing in the harbor. Tour boats, ferries and several ships are in the background. The huge catamarans must be 50-foot long. It's going to be tight and it's a short course - fun to watch. There are many little shops set up at the waterfront, plus there's a hall with many more.

St. Petersburg has the history and the buildings, and sorry to say, seemingly rough, rude people. Helsinki has a few sights and people who go out of their way to be friendly. Most speak English, too. A friendly receptionist at the hotel has looked up the nearest Catholic Church. There are very few in Finland. Luckily, it's on the same tram line. Not knowing when Mass is, I get there at 9:19. Mass is at 9:45 and in Latin! Timing is everything. Latin - it's been a long time and it brings back memories. At least part of the sermon is in English. It's a very small, well-built and well-kept church. Many Asians, maybe Koreans, attend.

The Natural History Museum is next and not much is expected. Pleasant surprise! They have many stuffed animals, including an elephant, in this quite compact museum. They also have a tremendous amount of skeletons. The real surprise is I recognize a male platypus because of the poisonous spur on the rear legs. Next to it is another of only three monotremes in the world, the short-nosed echidna.

The young man at the admission desk comes by, and I point it out to him. He's an enthusiastic graduate student. I mention it's one of the few poisonous mammals in the world. He says he thinks there is another one flight down. Off we go. I ask him if it's a shrew. He doesn't know the word. It looks like it, so he looks it up. A shrew! He said he knew it because it is the only poisonous (in the saliva) animal in Finland. What fun for both of us! Yeah, I know, a little geeky.

Two more cathedrals and a short walk takes me to what they call the Rock Church (formally Temppeliaukio Church), which was built directly into solid rock. It's interesting enough to fight the tour bus crowd for five minutes. Someone in the crowd someone asks where I was from. When Milwaukee was mentioned, he told me that there are 7000 Harley-Davidson riders in Finland!

My two-second analysis:

- Eastern Europe - Enthusiasm for the future, but many complacent, with a lack of outward ambition.
- Russia - Grumpy. A culture of purposely doing as little as possible intermixed with some wanting to get ahead but without being hamstringed by the former.

Turkey - 2006

Funny how some things work out. When we were in Dallas to watch my super son-in-law, Mariano, play soccer, we did a little shopping, too. In one interesting store full of foreign goods, I asked the owner, who had an accent, where he was from.

"Turkey" he said.

"I'm going to be there in two weeks!" I say.

"You have to stay at my Seven Hills Hotel."

The hotel has the perfect location in Istanbul, right between the two of the city's most famous sites. One is the Blue Mosque, built in 1609 and whose architecture is a classic combination of Ottoman and Byzantine. The other, the Hagia Sophia, was built in 537 AD started out as a church, became a mosque in 1453 and is now a museum. It was the largest cathedral in the world for nearly a thousand years. (The first Hagia Sophia was built in 360, the second in 404. Both were destroyed during revolts.)

Even though many Muslims consider pictures taboo, some undamaged Christian symbols remain on the walls, including some crosses and a mosaic of the Holy Family.

The Seven Hills Hotel is full but has a room at its annex a couple blocks away. "Normally the cost is one hundred and ninety dollars, but for Ismail's friend, one hundred."

The rooftop restaurant has a fabulous view of the Blue Mosque, the Hagia Sophia and the Bosphorus, the strait between the Black Sea and the

Mediterranean Sea. It's odd, looking down, to see the broken windows of a rundown building just a few feet from the Four Seasons Hotel. A glass of Turkish wine accompanies dinner. Even though Turkey is a 95 percent Muslim country, it is also the seventh-largest producer of wine. Also odd.

A nice couple at the next table asks me to join them and we have a great talk. They are from San Francisco and have come to visit Croatia for the last five years. They have a 55-foot sailboat that they brought here last year. "Please call us if you come through San Francisco in the winter."

It's Sunday and a taxi takes me to a pedestrian-only street where St. Anthony of Padua Catholic Church is located. There's some Italian influence on the street, and the church choir seems to be Korean. An Italian (maybe) priest with African deacons celebrates the Mass. Many other nationalities are represented.

Church is followed by a walk along the Bosphorus. A guy offers me his whole boat for only $67 an hour, then $55, then $48. He walks me down the pier two blocks and shows me a big boat shared with others for $14 for two hours. I thank him very much for his help.

Many people are out and every bench has a young couple. Some public display of affection is obviously OK - nothing really bad. I take a picture of a girl who is "wearing the veil," a scarf to cover every inch of her hair so as to not improperly tempt men. I do notice her beauty is evident. Her form-fitting clothes are quite common.

An early morning flight the next day brings me to Cappadocia, where a car and driver meet me. I have a reservation at the Cave Hotel for tonight. On the way a visit to an underground cistern with 336 huge supporting pillars built in 532 is interesting. A look down into the water from the slippery wood walkways reveals large carp swimming in the 2-foot deep water. The cistern was discovered in the 16th century when an architect heard that people were getting water by lowering buckets from their basements.

Next is history come alive. To escape the Romans, early Christians went underground . . . way underground. To date, they've discovered 35 underground towns here! The soft rock was carved into passageways, rooms, even stables and churches. (As for the passageways, it would have been better if I was 5-foot tall.) Some towns are eight to nine stories deep. In the two towns my driver-guide and I visit, we explore six stories, all well-lighted. Air vents provide air circulation. Here and there, water trickles down. I'm told that some of the sites are connected for 29 kilometers.

We walk through one passageway where there's a grate covering a hole that's 3-to-4-foot across. Of course the grate wasn't there in the old days and the only light for the Christians and the Romans chasing them were little torches. The Christians knew when to jump, the Romans didn't. Fascinating.

Into the fresh air and to the famous "fairy castles" that are everywhere. They're naturally formed by rain eating away the softer rock under the harder rock, and leaving towers. Some of these tower formations have been carved out and serve as homes and a few churches. Some frescoes in the rock churches have been vandalized - purportedly by Muslims who've scratched the eyes out to "kill" the image - but many remain.

At our next stop, the fourth-generation owner of a pottery factory shows me around. He even has the potter make (throw) a plate. Beautifully made items were for sale. The factory was partially underground.

After a little driving down a rabbit warren of streets, we end up at the Cave Hotel. Its charm is well hidden in a jungle of all types of homes in the surrounding area. The hotel has 18 rooms and the staff tell me four more are being built but that labor is so expensive - $28 day for laborers and double that for a skilled mason. They have reserved a "very special" room for me. Right. Down many steps, through portals and gates, across an alley and now here's a walled garden in front of a cave home.

The garden is padlocked. Another padlock guards the wooden sliding bolt on the door. The good-size living room has a bench at the end with an Oriental rug covering. There's a fireplace and television. It is very special - it's the owner's suite! He's out of town but his shaving cream and sandals are here as is his clothing in the closet. There's a second living room and a kitchen. A bedroom and sitting room make up a second floor. All underground. The only natural light is in the first living room, which has large windows overlooking the garden.

The manager from the Cave Hotel and I get along well and today he's my driver. He suggests a visit to his aunt's home. I had met his uncle earlier in town selling from his small store. The manager-driver's aunt is very gracious and soon brings us tea and cake. Later, we have lunch at a nearby cafe. It's Ramadan when observant Muslims fast during daylight hours. The cafe is one of the few open and it caters to visitors.

We stop at another place, and the driver asks about bread. They will have it later, we are told. They are not keen on pictures, so I take a photo of the pumpkins seeds the baking staff is preparing (and one of the staff). Later we go back and pick up two flat round delicious loaves of bread. No charge! Nice.

The driver and I have become friends, so he pours out his heart about his girlfriend, who is married to someone in the army. It is an arranged marriage, and she promises to divorce her husband when he comes home because they (she and the driver) love each other. The driver's not so sure and is afraid of the husband and the families.

We all have problems, don't we?

Prague (Czech Republic), Bratislava (Slovakia), Budapest (Hungary) and Belgrade (Serbia) - 2006

It's well known that Prague is beautiful. World War II left this capital city of the Czech Republic mostly untouched. The preserved and restored old buildings (at least in the most-visited sections) are great. And there are so many - not just the "important" ones, but ordinary old homes, too.

The Prague Castle is unusual. The fortification is stone underneath, but the stone was sheathed with mortar to present a smooth wall for up to 50-foot high. Constructed along the wall and continuing it are buildings cheek to jowl. Regular windows lead up to the usual pitched roof. From a distance, it appears as a row of buildings.

The towering St. Vitus Cathedral is surrounded by the wall, and at night both the wall and church are floodlit and truly magnificent. The approach from the huge old arched Charles Bridge might be the best. The bridge, like the large street and square, is pedestrian only and is a gathering place at night as well as day.

Several musicians play in the area, hoping for an offering. The one who moved me the most was a lone violinist with sweepingly mournful sounds. He acknowledged my offering along with the others. Quite a group had gathered.

There is a certain excitement with great crowds of people. Here you'll find many young couples and many seasoned travelers, in groups and individually. A majority is from nearby countries and few are Americans.

I sit in the square, just enjoying. A narrow street nearby becomes filled with the drone of a swarm of tourist voices. It reminds me of the running of the bulls, or lemmings maybe. I'm sitting next to a bench with a life-size bronze man; it doesn't take long for their alert scouts to spot him. Before long the swarm surrounds it with their cameras. Time to go.

The railroad station is about 3 kilometers from the center of the city, and after several queries I take the Intercity train to the border city of Břeclav, and then switch to a local line, which is not nearly as nice. Two quick checks of my passport, one for each country, and we're there. A nice Slovak woman who shared the compartment exchanges 200 in Czech money for 200 Slovak.

The railroad station is about 2 kilometers to the historic center of Bratislava, the capital of Slovakia. I walk instead of using the tram or bus. While Prague has more than a million people, Bratislava has about 400,000, and the tourists who couldn't fit into Prague are here. It feels like Prague Junior. The highlight is listening to the Berlin Philharmonic on a large screen in a square surrounded by outdoor restaurants and appreciative crowds.

Earlier I had gotten a ticket for the hydrofoil for Budapest, my next leg of the trip. The Danube River forms a good part of the focus of Bratislava.

Fashion for women, both here and in Prague, tends toward the low-rider, hip-hugger, skin-tight variety, bottomed off with sport shoes or high heels. The pavement is all cobblestone and the heels seem to present a challenge for some. Guys' fashion runs the gamut but is more casual.

In Prague everything is beer, but here in Bratislava one sees the occasional wine glass. There is an excellent dark beer in Prague called Kelt, and I also find a good dark beer here on tap in a Mexican restaurant. Too bad I have already eaten - the food looked good, too. The place also had an old Harley-Davidson, which I take a picture of.

Yesterday the Kampa Garden Hotel room in Prague that I had reserved was a little over a $100. It was clean, had a good location, and the arranged driver took me right to it amid a barrage of interesting facts about his country. (He didn't seem to take a breath, especially after I showed appreciation, and continued in fairly good English.) Tonight, the City Hostel in Bratislava is clean, and includes breakfast in the morning. It gets my business.

Budapest is next, and with my ticket for the hydrofoil already purchased, I'm on my way to the dock. We take off about 10:30.

The captain invites me up to the bridge after I ask him a question. There's only room for four, and I end up spending most of the four hours as a guest of Captain Tibor. He also gives me a tour of the engine room. The hydrofoil has 1,000 horsepower. "It's the fastest thing on the river at forty-five mph," he says. He's very proud, I'm very interested. It makes a good combination. Fun, plus the ride is beautiful, even going through the locks. I'm told the lock doors weigh 500 tons apiece. It takes only five minutes to fill with 15 meters of water.

We pass the largest church in Hungary and the captain gives me many suggestions about his Budapest, some helpful. He mentions hotels as inexpensive as $140 dollars.

The one I found is a hundred. It's a fun place: third floor, buzzer to get in. It's in a good area and the room is clean. A Tram Number 2 runs along the Danube River and I write from a pub at the back of the last car. Excellent Guinness on tap and beet ragout to eat. The castle across the river on a hill is lit, the bridges on either side are outlined with lights, and it's about 70 degrees – a beautiful evening. Wish you were here, sitting across from me. Wish I could capture the moment with a camera. I can't.

In next morning I'm taking a train to Belgrade, in Serbia. In spite of the indifferent attitude of the woman who sold me the ticket, I was nice and smiled and thanked her for all her help. When she was comparing prices - single chair, sleeper with six to a cabin, sleeper with one or two - she finally hinted to take the two to a cabin and that I'd be alone anyway (and it's $50 cheaper). Thank you!

On board, I get talking with a young Swedish doctor who is complaining about being in a six-person compartment because he thought he had asked to be alone. Off we go - smooth and comfortable. I even have a sink with running water and a little welcome bag. Didn't mention that to the doctor.

We arrive right on time in Belgrade. It doesn't look good; I have forgotten they've been through a war here recently. The Hostel Hotel is across the way. There's a bed and single sink in the room, no roommates, and a bath down the hall – for about $30 dollars. Deal. Tram Number 2 makes a circle route, and by the time we make it back I'm ready to leave. Plain old dirty buildings, pieced-together cars. I find out later you can buy a German car in Germany, pay full amount then half again as much in taxes to bring it into Serbia.

The zoo is mostly a 1940s steel-cages type. Pitifully small areas for animals. Oddly, the zoo has one elephant and one giraffe, and at least 50 wolves and thousands of birds, plus some dogs. Some of the dogs are Rhodesian Ridgeback and General Patton's funny-nosed variety. Odd to see dogs in a zoo.

The citadel and the military museum are OK. I stop in a bakery to ask where the Russian church is. The man doesn't speak English and the two girls speak very little. He motions me outside, to point out directions, I think. We get in his old car but it fails to start, so he monkeys under the hood and gets it going. A mile later he parks, walks me around another church I also want to see, and asks the woman in charge to let me in. Wow! Nice. I thank him and with a wave, but he's gone.

The Russian church is a gem and St. Mark's nearby also interesting. St. Mark's is different because it is supported inside by four huge pillars. Each must be 12-foot in diameter.

For dinner later, I'm directed to a little street, pedestrian only, lined with cafes. It's early so I walk the full three blocks or so. A gallery is interesting, and the attendant speaks perfect English and I tell her so. She recommends a Serbian restaurant up the block a hundred feet.

The meal that was served included a plate of pickled peppers (hot), corn-influenced bread (extra good), two beers, and a plate of cucumbers (which I refuse so they bring a plate of tomatoes and coleslaw instead). The mixed grill includes two large pieces of chicken (one wrapped in bacon), three sausages, one slice of ham (didn't look great), beef (with too much fat for me). You get the idea - I didn't order dessert. The restaurant is more than a hundred years old. Soon four guys come in to play Serbian music. The walls are covered with paintings. Nice.

Tomorrow the only train to Bucharest, Romania, leaves at about 4 p.m. and it's a 17-hour trip. A sleeper seems to be a good idea. Forgot I had also been told about another pedestrian street near the one where I had dinner. It's called Silicon Street, named after California's Silicon Valley. There are supposed to be the most beautiful girls there, who have an industry of their own. . .

The next morning I pass several buildings with obvious bullet and rocket holes in the walls. They were bombed in 1999, a nice gentleman explains. He also tells me somewhat proudly that they did shoot down a stealth jet, parts of which are on display at the airport.

Further on, the Ethnographic Museum is well kept with displays also in English, which really helps my enjoyment of it.

I have heard about some ancient baths and wander in that direction. Public baths were a big deal years ago, a real social outing, besides being a necessity. The bath building is old and huge and still very much in business. Why not? Paid the cashier, followed directions - locker room, private locked stalls, key given to me by an attendant. Now it dawns on me I don't have a suit. They rent a suit to me. The place has steam rooms and pools of different temperatures, each about 20-by-30-foot. The hot soak feels so good.

The train is fairly seedy but there are two bunks and no bunkmate. Goodbye, Belgrade. We pass by some grim concrete block apartments, then go between the embattlements, past the citadel and the river and out into the countryside. Corn and cabbage are ready to be harvested. Some older simple homes, small, with red tile roofs, dot the countryside here and there. The crows here have black tails and gray wings and bodies. Some huge farms come into view now, probably a carryover from collective farming days.

Bucharest is fairly friendly, and I tell that to everyone, which results in even more friendliness and helpfulness. The Natural History Museum and numerous impressive churches were interesting. One anthropology museum was closed, but a side entrance is open and I ask to see the director. He couldn't be nicer. He says he closed the museum today because he is prepping for a talk he is to give in Germany.

I mention that I am an anthropologist and he brightens up even more. He asks an assistant to turn on all the lights and take me for a tour. Then he autographs a guide book for me. I wish him the best on his talk. The museum has extensive exhibits and the place is very large. What fun!

The train tomorrow to Istanbul – where I'll catch my flight home - leaves at 1 in the afternoon.

The Forbidden City

China - 2007

This will be a quick stop, not really fair to report in depth on anything I visited, but interesting to me nevertheless. Beijing is big, busy, with plenty of history. The first stop is to the Koryo Tours Office, the agency that arranged my visit to North Korea. More on that to come.

The Forbidden City: Don't you love the name? Well Beijing was forbidden in the old days of the emperor, but visitors are certainly encouraged now. It truly must have been impressive for a visitor of old to meet the emperor in these surroundings. Of course that was the purpose. The Summer Palace on the shore of Kunming Lake was even more fun to visit. The brochure alone boasts of 29 different attractions including the Marble Boat, which, no, doesn't really float but it appears to. It's surrounded by the waters of the lake.

Alongside the lake is Suzhou Market Street, a great walk with fun little shops. Of course I had to get my fortune written on a scroll for only about $3 dollars. "Good fortune as you wish" and "Whatever you think will be successful." Two for one! This trip's gonna be great!

Would even the briefest visit to China be complete without a visit to the Great Wall? It is a short drive to the section of the wall that's near Beijing. Just walking a short distance on the wall shows one the difficulty of building it, along with the intimidating result.

The wall was built to protect against the raiding groups from the north. Construction in the hills and low mountains must have really been difficult

The Great Wall

to deal with, especially without modern earth-moving equipment. The building of the wall started in the 7th century BC and didn't end until almost 2,000 years later. The wall extends over about 13,000 miles! Sections of it have been lost, of course, but the wall remains as one of mankind's greatest constructions. The topography does allow stupendous views.

Back in Beijing, I ask a middle-age man for directions and he not only tells me what direction to go, he takes me most of the way there. He was in New York once, he says, and someone helped him. He was glad he could repay the kindness. A stop in a bar and a short talk with the bartender is good. Somewhere during the conversation, I ask him why all the pictures of Mao are still around.

"Wasn't he responsible for more than five million deaths?"

"Yes, it's true, but everyone makes mistakes . . ."

Fittingly, tonight's hotel will be the little Red Wall Hotel. Many of Beijing's neighborhoods have been eliminated to make way for new skyscrapers. Luckily, some of the old neighborhoods have been retained. Near the hotel is a hutong, an original side street with charming little courtside homes and a few restaurants.

Marble boat

I wander along and pick a place to eat. Few people speak English here, but pointing to what was on another customer's plate works fine. And it was good! Suddenly a voice booms from the next table as a man sings a couple of notes. I turn around and the man is most apologetic in waves of hands and some English.

"You like Chinese opera?"

"No, no" I said "Sing!"

He asks: "You like Chinese Opera?"

"Oh, yes!" (Or I would soon.)

The man and woman with him are friendly, too. It turned out they are with the Chinese opera. The man gets a guitar-type instrument out of a case and the other pulls out a sort of violin - that's the only description I come up with. The woman is a singer. There are several other customers in the little 10-table restaurant. This delightful trio played and sang an hour and a half, one and a half hours! This trip's already great.

Notice the required support pole under the tail

North Korea - 2007

My trip to North Korea starts in Beijing. The agency, Koryo Tours, is located here and is run by former residents of Great Britain. It's a small agency, but it's one of the oldest and most successful in helping visitors get to the Democratic People's Republic of Korea, or the DPRK. (Well, at least the last word in their official name is accurate). We know it simply as North Korea. If you ask most people what is the most secretive, controlled country on earth, they'd say "North Korea" and they'd be right. The agency personnel are quite polite and careful to point out the "dos and don'ts" of visiting North Korea, especially when traveling alone.

North Korea owns two commercial planes and one is down for repairs, I'm told by some people I meet briefly. They tell me that the plane is a copy of an American plane, copied by the Russians, then someone tacked on two more engines to the tail end next to the two already there. It works OK, except that, as someone pointed out, when the plane is loading or unloading, the ground crew fixes a steel pole under the rear fuselage. Why? When people first board in the rear of the plane, their weight, and that of the extra engines, is enough to tip the huge plane backward. Uh huh.

After landing at the airport in Pyongyang, the capital of North Korea, I walk into the rather plain terminal, and two men approach. One of the men asks if I am James Bruce. They introduce themselves as my "guides." I use the quote marks because some people call them government minders,

Pyongyang - no lights at night

which is certainly correct. One asks how I should be addressed. I smile and answer "Jim." He says I may call him "Mr. Kim." OK.

We have our own driver and are on the way into the main part Pyongyang, and the first thing I notice is how few cars and other motorized vehicles there are. No bikes either. Several attractive policewomen are seen directing traffic, except there's almost none. There are no traffic lights. The women direct an oncoming car and do a military right face for the opposing cars, of which there are none. The other thing I notice are the billboards that show a North Korean soldier bayoneting an American. The facial expressions of each are melodramatic. Welcome.

I am taken to the Yanggakdo Hotel (no, I didn't have a choice), which is on an Island in the Taedong River. A pleasant setting; only a few people are here. My minders check me in. My room's on the 35th floor and has a great view of the city. Someone tells me later that it's one of the few floors used in the hotel. The room's fine, clean. There is a large mirror attached solidly and flush to the wall.

Dinner in the dining room is very good - there's little choice as to food, but it's good. A few others are there, including a Korean-American professor from the United States with his family. He's very nice and quite

Main Street - few cars and no bicycles

open to me about conditions here. (The next morning he comes over and has breakfast with me instead of his family.)

After dinner, I go for a short walk. Can't really remember if they said not to leave the hotel or not, but no one stops me so I go to the little golf course across the way. No one's there but everything is open. This is the golf course (the only one in the country) where Kim Jong-il reportedly shot 11 hole-in-ones - the very first time he played!

In the morning, as I am leaving my room I see an Asian man at the elevator. He has opened a window and is taking pictures of the city. He smiles and silently motions to me "shhhh" and continues to take pictures. You're not allowed to take pictures of anything without permission from your minders. I get my camera and take some, too.

At night, there is not a light to be seen in the entire city! Some of the architecture of Pyongyang is amazing, and the guides are proud to show it off – well, that's their job too. They show me a lot in the few days I am here. The length of my stay is limited because I am an American. The overall message the minders share - and the only one visitors are allowed to see - is designed to give the impression that: "We are strong, we are the best and we are fortunate to live in our country."

The North Korean people are told the rest of the world is much worse off. How does anyone know any different? Information is strictly controlled. How many people believe it? Impossible to tell.

Back to the architecture: Among the most amazing is said to be the unfinished Ryugyong Hotel, which resembles very tall pyramid stretched into the sky. At 108 stories, it's imposing, and is among the tallest 20 buildings in the world. The plan for it is to have 3,000 rooms when finished, and to be topped by a revolving restaurant. The shape and the size are impressive. The hotel was supposed to open in June 1989 but in 2007 it still isn't finished and hasn't been worked on for years. I'd read about it and ask my minder to drive past it. "Maybe later," he says.

Later never came. I understand from others that you cannot go anywhere not on a pre-approved schedule. In addition, there is a prescribed route to go to anyplace that has been previously approved.

The Mansudae Art Studio statue of Kim Il-Sung (the Great Leader) is huge. This reminds me of another restriction. Any picture you take must contain the whole statue, including feet. People looking at it are dwarfed. We also visit the Grand People's Study House (central library), the Chollima Statue of a giant flying horse with the "Get your work done quickly" theme, the Korean Revolution Museum (the largest museum in the country), and the Students and Children's Palace (where several children played musical instruments for me).

The Korean Folklore Museum is excellent and the woman in charge is friendly and informative. The Mangyongdae Revolutionary School also has classes of students learning to play several different musical instruments. Department Store No. 1. has many items on display, but I find out later

Propaganda film

that, sadly, most citizens are not allowed to shop there. (The minders don't mention that.) Shoppers need to have a hard-to-get authorization card.

We also see a movie studio, where a man explains what they were producing (it was all propaganda). At the Military Museum there is an exhibition not unlike a toy train set, complete with mountains, roads, moving trucks and tanks. It shows how the North Koreans beat the Americans and forced them to surrender!

USS Pueblo

And speaking of surrender, we also visit the USS Pueblo, the unarmed spy ship that the North Koreans captured from the United States in 1968. An older retired veteran explains how it happened. He had been there. From his tone and the bored look, he has explained it many times. A short video is shown to accompany his talk.

Other places are interesting, too, as is the incessant propaganda. The Juche Tower signifies the independent nature of the North Koreans. (Not mentioned is that without help and trade from the outside, they'd have trouble existing due to the policies of the communist government.) We drive to the Arch of Triumph, which immortalizes Kim Il-Sung's guerrilla victory against the Japanese. The North Koreans claim he started his campaign in 1925 at the age of 13. It is pointed out that the arch was taller than the Arc de Triomphe in Paris . . . by 3 feet.

She claimed the Americans started the war

When we stop to visit, a very forceful employee explains how they crushed the Americans after we had started the war (what we call the Korean War). Toward the end of her talk, she keeps jabbing her finger at my face, saying: "Do you realize America started the war?" Yup, by that time I'd had it.

I pointed my finger back at her and asked' "Do you realize you are the only nation on earth that believes that?" She stands looking at me with her mouth open. My minder rolls his eyes and we go back to the car. I never did mention that there were 32 nations' troops with the United States in the Korean War, under a United Nations mandate.

We're supposed to go see the subway but I decline. I've seen subways before and have found the best are in Moscow. Mr. Lee, one of the minders, says he has seen the ones in Moscow and these are better. He admits later he hasn't seen the ones in Moscow nor been out of North Korea. I have read that the subways here are basically glorified bomb shelters, beautiful and rarely used. Also, before the trip I had seen a video of many people going in and coming out of the subway entrance. Oddly enough, the video was long enough to show the same well-dressed people go in and come out . . . over and over again. Actors.

My minders always meet me in the lobby of the hotel at a prescribed time. One time when I left my room, I notice a door in the hallway next to my room that perhaps is a broom closet. It has no room number and isn't locked. I open the door and instead of a closet, it appears to be a very narrow unfinished – and dark - passageway going along the wall of my room. I step in a few feet to see if I can see a two-way mirror to my room. Then my chicken heart, or common sense, tells me to get out . . . now. And I do.

One of the most impressive sites we visit is the Kumsusan Memorial Palace, which had been Kim Il-Sung's residence. In 1995, a year after his death, it was converted into his mausoleum. It's huge, of course. Few foreigners have been allowed to visit until recently. Moving sidewalks take people through a beautiful hallway lined with granite that's 1-kilometer long! Air jets help remove any dust from visitors' feet.

Reaching the top floor of this four-story building reveals the gigantic room containing the glass coffin of the Great Leader in the center. There are a few other groups of people here, all Koreans, all hushed and very respectful. All circle the coffin, and on each side stop and together bow toward it. My group (three of us) waits its turn and then also circles the coffin and stops at each side. My minders are on either side of me. They bow each time. I take one step back each time. No way I'm bowing. They say nothing. We leave.

We head down to a lower level where there are many desks precisely positioned in a squared semi-circle. Each has a large open book and a chair. This is where you record your amazement and worshipful comments. Each person has an open page. I sit and write couple of my thoughts about the beautiful buildings and the melodramatic setting. I turn the page.

My second minder, who has never pretended to be friendly, grabs the page and turns it back to see what I've written. In an accusing tone, he asks: "What does this melodramatic mean?" I look at him with a little "let me be the teacher" look and explain that it meant a wonderful, over-the-top display of respect (or something like that). He grumbles and turns the page. We move on and I make up my mind to be more careful.

On our way out, small groups of ordinary Koreans are coming in. They all walk in formations, as if trying to echo the military. They all have on their best clothes but the clothes reveal how really poor they are. They all have very somber expressions. None look at me. I mention to Mr. Kim that everyone always looks glum and unfriendly. All of a sudden the next group coming toward us is waving and smiling at me. I swing around and see Mr. Kim motioning for them to smile and wave. He's been caught. He sheepishly grins. I thought it was telling that they all did exactly what he told them to do.

Officially everyone's equal in North Korea. Opposed to that is the understanding that a third of the people support the government, a third is neutral and the remaining third consists of those considered to be enemies of the state. No effort is made to enable, sustain or even acknowledge the last third of the people unless for labor or if they're creating problems. There's also the rule of that if someone has committed an offense, their parents and children are also responsible. All are put in prison.

Nutrition? The average person in North Korea is estimated to be 3 to 4 inches shorter than their relatives in South Korea. A visitor is not allowed to take pictures without permission, and especially not of soldiers. I receive permission to take a picture of two soldiers at the border who just happen to be almost as tall as I am (6 feet), and perhaps they are there just for that purpose.

The people in the elite first third are mostly centered in Pyongyang, and are considered loyal to the leadership. There's more to the leadership than just the leader - many people are in the top command and the leader is just the most important of them. Everyone in the country reports on each other, including those in the elite third. They have no problem getting food or most of anything else they want, depending on their position.

About 10 years before my visit, it was estimated that nearly 10 percent of the population starved because of a bad harvest and inefficiency of the communist government. That's 2 million to 3 million people! Guess which third they came from?

Before the starvation, it was considered a crime to grow your own food. That would have been a statement that the state was not providing enough for you. Following the mass starvation, it has been allowed. Selling food was also an offense before. Afterward? The state now charges a tax for the use of market space on the street.

Food: This reminds me of my experience at a restaurant in Pyongyang. It was quite nice, clean and of course the waitresses were immaculate and attractive. (At the hotel too, the waitresses are obviously selected partly on their good looks. Their makeup is well done and looks the same on each. Impression is everything.) So, as we walked into this restaurant I noticed that all the tables were set, and all had a plastic bottle of water, with an accompanying glass, at each place. Only one other table was occupied. The food was good and much more than I could eat.

During lunch I finished my bottle of water and politely asked for more. The waitress gave me a puzzled, blank expression. No water came, so I reached across to the next table and took a bottle. The waitress came over, grabbed the bottle with a glare and put it back where it was! I questioned Mr. Kim "I can't have more water?" He got up and went to talk with someone. Soon a waitress came over with another bottle of water. The lesson: When a government provides what you need, the government also decides what you need.

Next stop: Panmunjom. It's a beautiful drive to the border - 102 miles – and takes about an hour and a half. The highway is divided and almost

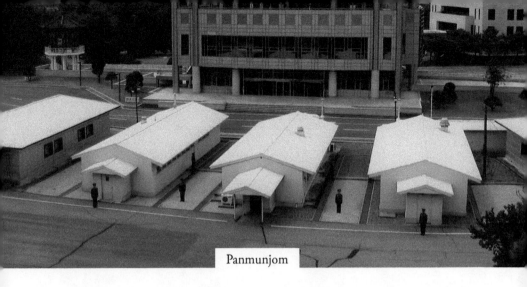

Panmunjom

deserted. There are several huge truck-sized rectangles of concrete balanced on angled pieces of concrete along the route. Each is supported by a small block of concrete underneath. If that bottom piece were to be removed, the huge rectangle would come crashing down and block the whole highway. I ask what it is. Mr. Kim says it's for decoration. Later I find out it was to block the highway in case of an invasion from the south.

The highway is clean, no rubbish anywhere. There are a couple of women up ahead down on their knees cleaning the highway with buckets and scrubbing brushes! We drive around them. They don't even look up. There's a man farther along cutting the grass with a small hand sickle. He's also gathering the cut grass. Mr. Kim explains that each village has the responsibility of taking care of a section of the highway. The grass has to be cut anyway and will help feed the man's animals, possibly a few goats.

We've arrived at Panmunjom, at the border of North and South Korea - the most heavily fortified border in the world. We park at a small building and find a couple of other visitors are there. A short lecture follows. Then we go a short distance to the buildings that actually straddle the border. North and South take turns, very formally, occupying the building. It's the North's turn, so we enter the building. The U.S. Marines and South Koreans are just outside on the South's side. North Korean military personnel are outside on the North's side. The North always has two soldiers who face each other, a safeguard so if one tries to escape the other can kill him.

The inside of the building is mostly bare, except for some tables and

Bravest girl

chairs and the two North Korean soldiers standing at attention. I am shown to a chair, where I sit down. An officer stands next to me. There is also a young woman, the translator. They obviously knew I was coming because she speaks English - and very well. The officer starts his rambling spiel about the war without looking at me, pausing every few sentences so the woman can translate for me.

My two minders have walked away and now lean against the far wall talking to each other. Part of the man's talk relates how I am now sitting in the very chair where the American general surrendered and signed the armistice. I look at woman as she translates with an unbelieving, "Oh, bull!" look. In the middle of her next translation, she looks directly at me and says, "You know I have to say this," in the same voice she uses to translate. I will never forget those words and her look. Bravest girl I've ever met! If the man or the minders knew what she has said, she'd be in prison or shot, and her family with her. Wow! I thought about it all the way back to Pyongyang. Wow!

The next evening we are going to the big event at Kim Il-Sung Stadium, which seats more than 100,000. No pictures are allowed going

Arirang Festival

in because there are some soldiers stationed there. The reason I scheduled my trip at this time was to see Arirang, the famous "mass games," which are mostly synchronized dance and gymnastics. Someone - thank you very much - informed me tickets go for $50 to $300, but to buy the one for fifty because "It's the same seat."

When we arrive, the stadium is filled, not an empty seat anywhere. My two minders and I walk to our seats. Two entire rows are vacant. The three of us are the only ones to sit in those rows. The seats are high up and in the center - the best in the house. Everyone is in a festive mood and seems genuinely enthusiastic, especially when pictures of the leaders appear along with the writings about their victories.

Korea is shown with a dividing line (fault of the Americans). I am given a lot of second looks and I do see a couple other foreigners. The costumes are bright and colorful and the choreography is complicated, with many movements. A huge card section is used for design, pictures, moving waves, and for movies, all promoting the basic themes of Arirang: Two people who love each other and wars - beating the Japanese in 1945, then the Americans (not the UN) in 1953.

There's no competition – it's all display and pageantry, with more than 100,000 participants! Amazing zip lines shoot people on bungee cords to a net hundreds of feet away. Add to that gymnastics, melodrama and music - mostly recorded and coming from loudspeakers.

Thousands and thousands are on the field at any one time - and they are good, really good. I have never seen anything close to this - nor ever expect to again. It's fabulous! The whole event lasts from 8:30 to 10. (Side note: They're planning to stop the games for at least 10 years, so this is likely one of the last ones. Hopefully it will return.)

It was a fitting end to my trip to North Korea - a great show.

Mongolia - 2007

My schedule says my plane should leave Beijing at 9:10 in the morning and get to Ulaanbaatar, the capital of Mongolia, two hours later. It's raining heavily there so the plane can't leave to come pick us up. We passengers all wait in line for three hours ready to check in. Never is there an announcement.

Finally, a couple of small buses arrive to take us to a hotel. I've befriended a Mongolian, Two-bolt, who has just finished his third year of high school in Washington, D.C. He lives there by himself! As we are both singles, the airport employees want us to wait until the end of the line. Two-bolt agrees. We are now a two and get on a bus. We get to sleep just a few hours.

There's no wakeup call the next morning, but when we get up there are vans waiting for us and the other passengers. An agent says she called everyone - but she didn't call anyone we talked to. The plane's now scheduled to leave at 6:10. Well, 8:10 is close enough.

From the plane, Mongolia is all I had pictured: Sweeping views of low mountains that are covered with sparse grasses, as in some parts of Montana. Later I notice the livestock just nip off the top nutritious parts.

There's a sign "Boojum Travel" as I exit and Tsalman, a pleasant 20-year-old Mongolian woman, meets me. She was an exchange student in Boston for six months and her English is pretty good. Her cousin, the driver, is a big hulking, shy guy. I think he said "Hi" once.

Creative entertainment

We see some of the sights in UB, (everyone calls it that). We go to the Winter Palace of Bogd Khan, which has incredible wooden and painted carvings. Next are Gandan, the largest temple, and then the National History Museum, with its large collection of dinosaurs and numerous stuffed birds and animals. In the afternoon, we enjoy a play with gorgeous costumes. All is very impressive and fun.

Tsalman and her cousin drop me off and my first night in the capital is spent in a "guesthouse." Actually it's one bedroom in a two-bedroom apartment with a single bath. The building was a little seedy, but the room is clean. No one's in the other bedroom, although a woman comes in the next morning not knowing I was there. I was just leaving anyway and she was pleasant about the mix-up. Tsalman turns out to be delightful and tries very hard. Was this her first assignment? Never asked. The driver's a good driver.

Tsalman informs me that 95 percent of Mongolians are Buddhists. This will be especially pertinent later.

We have too big of a lunch at a Mongolian barbecue place that is similar to those in the U.S. It is very good so a huge dinner sure won't be needed. The traffic is terrible.

Finally we get out of the city, ending up in the country in a nature preserve at a travelers' ger camp - just what I thought I didn't want. The shower after dinner is good however and the food is fine. My ger is about 18-foot round, and has four beds with a firebox in the center. Quite luxurious. Tsalman asks me if I want the fire started. It's about 50 degrees. Sure. She also asks if I want it started again at 4 in the morning. Sure.

Night comes quickly, as does 4 in the morning. Not fully awake, I thank the two young women who are lighting the fire. One giggles and says, "You're welcome." Very few speak English here, so that may have been Tsalman. (I find out later she also speaks Russian!) I get up about 6 or so and no one else is around yet. Today we're going to visit with a real ger family, and maybe ride horses, camels or yaks, then stay the night.

Throughout the morning, we talk about many things. Tsalman says if she worked in an office like her mother, she would earn about $800 a month, but she likes this better, at $300 a month. Teachers get a $150, she says.

When I arranged this short trip to Mongolia, I specifically mentioned two things: One, I want to travel alone with a guide, and I don't want to see another traveler, much less the dreaded tourist. If I do, the trip's a failure. That request usually separates the usual "We do cruises and all-inclusive resorts" from the people who can really help me find what I want.

And second, when I found a travel agent who seemed to have the Mongolian expertise I was looking for, I suggested staying at a normal hotel would not connect me to the people I wanted to meet. That didn't seem to deter the agent either. We got along well. I added that I didn't care if the guide-translator was a man or woman.

Still, there was some surprise when I found out my guide was going to be Tsalman, this 20-year-old Mongolian woman who had spent six months in a university in the United States!

Tonight Tsalman and I are going to what she calls a popular restaurant. Inside are a few foreigners, so she turns me around and we find another. The first choice has good food, she says - too bad. I haven't said a word but appreciate her sensitivity.

At the next little restaurant there are three young girls that put on a wonderful show in gymnastic balancing and contortions. They must

Fabulous moves

be only about 9 to 12 years old, and do a great job. The few other locals who are here appreciate them as much as we do. Balancing on a pole with one hand, the three are making a pyramid using backbends. The ultimate trick, though, is by the one girl who, from their little platform, bends over backward and picks up an apple with her teeth from the floor a foot below! I would not have believed it possible. The restaurant's food was as good as the show.

Mongolia is located between Russia and China and is largely undeveloped. There are many sheep, goats and open spaces. We drive to a barn where we get some horses to ride out onto the steppes (plains). The horses look healthy enough but quite a bit smaller than I'm used to. The saddles are primitive and the riding style is different. When you trot or canter, you stand up and forward in the saddle.

We have a delightful ride. Tsalman has obviously ridden before. We see other horses, not in a pasture, just free and roaming. We can

The steppes

We're invited to stay for dinner

look around and not see anything for miles except sand, hills and the occasional stream. There are very few signs of man.

Then I see it- a plastic bottle laying there, spoiling the untouched wilderness. There was a time I could pick up something just by leaning out of the saddle. It's worth a try - it's a small horse. I swing down and grab the bottle and am back up into the saddle. I did it! One problem: Grabbing the plastic bottle makes an odd crackling sound.

As the horse moves around, my holding on to the bottle causes it to crackle more. The horse starts bucking, which amounts to nothing more than serious crow hops (as we used to call them) - pretty straight forward up and down. I'm doing OK but the horse doesn't stop. Not worth it. I drop the bottle (maybe it's still there). The horse wins.

We have nice long ride and then return the horses to the people at the barn. Next we're off with our driver to where we are staying tonight. In the distance we see a good-size building with five ger in a row. As we get closer, they look very clean and white. We stop and look around. The inside is immaculate, with the beds all made up. The floor is carpeted! They're for travelers, and dinner will be served in the main house, which even has toilets. Disappointing - nuts, I know, but it's not what I

13-year-old daughter helps prepare dinner

envisioned. Let's go. Of course we don't know where we're going or what we're going to do.

We get to the base of a mountain, which Tsalman and I climb to get a view. Lots of sheep and goats. When we come back down we meet a couple and their 13-year-old daughter. They're camping alongside a stream and have a fire going. Their car and tent are nearby. Would we like to join them for lunch? Lunch? Sure! The couple is very nice, as is their daughter. They offer soup, meat, potatoes and onion, which is all very good. I didn't get to try the pickled vertebrae.

We get talking. I don't remember what kind of work the man says he does but the woman says she is one of the few remaining shamans in Mongolia. Interesting! She explains that the mountain behind them is holy and she says no one is allowed on it, especially women. Whoops. Not only did we climb it before we met them, obviously Tsalman is a woman. What to do! No problem for me but the woman says Tsalman should apologize to the mountain.

We get in a semicircle facing the mountain. The shaman woman gathers up a mouth organ, bracelet with bells, two talons and a pig's tooth. In addition, she wears a special blue dress. Tsalman puts on another

Goat herders' yurts

special dress the woman gives her, then goes to the base of the mountain, bows down and throws rice.

Just when I think it's over, the woman asks me if I want help for my allergy. Tsalman tells me: "She wants to touch you."

"Go ahead, touch me." The woman walks around behind me and massages my head, neck, fingers, and shoulders, and concentrates a lot of pressure on the nose area. It does feel better! I contribute $20 euro to the cause.

I take some pictures of the area and of some horses climbing out of the river. I'd like a picture of this wonderful family but the woman says we cannot take a picture of her because she is a shaman. Pictures of her husband and daughter are fine, though.

We sit by their fire and talk for awhile. Where are we going tonight? Don't know - probably sleep in the van or on the ground. The wife invites us to stay with them and have dinner with them: "Let's go get a goat for dinner." I volunteer to pay for it.

The shaman, Tsalman, the driver and I drive a few miles to a goat herder's ger. Invited inside, the shaman soon has everyone laughing and they're all very friendly. She doesn't know them but that doesn't stop her. We're invited to share some bread and butter. She bargains with the goat herders. I bring out balloons, which are a big hit with the goat herder's children. We sit around and talk in the ger while the goat is being prepared outside. Another couple of men and a woman are here, too.

The shaman spies two skins sewn together hanging on the wall. There's an open top, and liquid inside. The shaman's not shy. The herder invites her – and us - to have some of the liquid. She scoops out a cupful, sips it and offers me a sip. As she's getting everyone a glass, I notice she takes a sip of each before passing them on. She tells me it's Mongolian vodka! We would think of it as fermented mare's milk. It doesn't seem strong. Truthfully, it's not bad tasting at all.

We're all talking and the goat herders are interesting and they sure don't seem to mind the interruption to their lives. Not many visitors out here in the middle of nowhere. Now the shaman is sitting next to me on a couch. Tsalman's on the other side in a chair. The shaman is having a good time and another glass full of vodka. She grabs my knee as she's talking and explains about things that I don't remember. What I do remember is when she starts stroking my leg. No harm - just very friendly.

Then she asks Tsalman to take a picture of us, which she does - the forbidden picture of a shaman! This is so much better than the tourist ger. There was also an arrangement to stay with a private family. Tsalman tells me the private family does it all the time. "It would be spotless!" And somewhat contrived . . .

We get the goat meat and head back across the steppes to the shaman's camp. The meat's cut up, put in a big pot with potatoes and the cooking begins. I cook a little liver with a slice of onion on a stick in the flames under the pot. What else could one want? There's some dried horse manure in a bag hanging nearby. It serves as kindling. I notice the steel wool they use to clean the pot is stored in there, too. What's in the pot's almost done. They've also made some soup, which is passed around in a large cup. It's good, but salty. I eat too much, but I do take some more of the delicious potatoes.

I plan sleeping next to the van, where it's dry and out of the wind. Two pair of pants, three shirts and my windbreaker - it's still going to be cold. Surprise! Tsalman and the driver have already put down the seats in the van to form sort of a bed, not quite flat; the hump goes where my waist is. I have a passable night's sleep. Tsalman and the driver sleep in the shaman family's car.

I'm up about 6, and see many birds, some fairly large, and some similar to great blue herons, but even taller. The mist is burning off and it's going to be a beautiful day. Everyone's up. We finish eating and heat a pot full of water for tea and coffee. Their small table is full of potatoes, meat and packaged cookies. The little girl's name is Bolorsuiti - she writes it for me in my notebook so I'll get it right. She's 13 but looks more like seven to me.

The next day Tsalman mentions that she saw the shaman stroking my leg. Yes she did, I say. Tsalman is very happy. And so am I with my short trip to Mongolia.

Friendly Shaman after
a few Mongolian Vodkas!

Shaman's husband

Italy - 2009

It starts out with a little joke with my granddaughter, Alex. She has just turned 15 and her spring vacation is coming up soon. I ask her if she is going to Daytona Beach for a wild time.

"No Baba" (this is the name she gave me about the time she was learning to talk).

"What are you going to do?"

"Nothing"

I suggest: "Why don't you and I go somewhere?"

"Really?"

After some research, I find it. It would be safe, not too expensive and really interesting. I call her: "Italy!"

She thinks I'm kidding but shortly thereafter, off we go!

The trip begins with a bang. Our first Italian experience is a great fall. About seven hours into the flight, Alex is sitting in front of me in the next row. We had tried to stretch out and sleep - not much luck. She tries to get up to join me in my row and her knees buckle. "My legs were like Jello," she says. To which I respond, "What are you - a baby?"

To make this trip a little different and fun, we stay in a convent in Rome the first night. Even better, the nun who has helped us arrange this is a delight. Unfortunately for me, she doesn't speak much English. Fortunately for me, Alex gets along quite well with her Italian by using her Spanish background. Alex is in charge.

Alex thinks an afternoon nap was in order after the long flight. This provides a great opportunity for me to sneak out. The nun has suggested a little Italian restaurant down the street for tonight's dinner. They are just closing up when I walk in at about 2. The restaurant has six tables and looks clean and very nice. I talk with the owner, mentioning that my 15 year old granddaughter loves Italian cooking and that his restaurant was recommended by the sister at the nearby convent. Smiling and hands waving, he asks: "What does she like?"

"I don't know."

"No matter." He says he'll see us when they open tonight about 8.

When we arrive, two waiters serve a dozen sample plates of Italian food in a circle around Alex. The owner is most enthusiastic about how she likes each dish. (They serve me something too but I am definitely in the background.) I think Alex is impressed. How could she not be? The spread consists of pesto cheese, buffalo mozzarella, grilled vegetables, baked cheese, prosciutto, eggplant, a mound of vegetables, two different kinds of bread, wine, potato pasta, pasta with bacon, pork, potatoes, stracheta (an arugula salad with beef), and custard with strawberries and grapes. After dinner, our waiter, Roberto, insists that we not tip, saying, "Americans pay tips, not Italians." Wonderful people and a wonderful memory for us.

During the next couple days in Rome, we walk and - as Alex says - walk and then walk some more. "We" tried not to walk past any churches, and upon entering few disappoint. Of course, the Vatican is unique, and the rest of our must-do list is long: St. Peter's, the Sistine Chapel, Trevi Fountain, great food, Spanish Steps, gelato, Tiber Island, the pope celebrating Mass, museums, observing the huge crowds, more gelato.

One of the more unique memories (I guess you would say) was climbing inside of the dome at St. Peter's. A rather large woman somehow ended up in front of us and was having quite a hard time making it to the cupola – the ultimate destination. It's kind of scary knowing that you are in a tiny walk space inside of the dome, where you have to lean to one side even to make it. Thank God this woman made it.

Once we have made it to the cupola, we are surprised to find that these gorgeous statues we had seen earlier from the ground in front of St. Peter's are unfinished. Someone must have figured that no one would see their backs up here!

One of Alex's favorite places is Castel Sant'Angelo and Piazza Navona. One of her least favorites: the church elaborately decorated with the dismembered bones of the Capuchin monks of the church's past. A little reminder of our mortality.

We pick up our rental car and head for Florence but, because of traffic, detour and go instead to San Marino, one of two tiny independent countries within Italy's borders. (The smallest country in the world is the Vatican City, also within Italy). After a short visit to the capital, a little hill town also called San Marino, we are off again on the beautiful mountain roads and up the coast. We count nine switchbacks on the way down one road alone.

Tonight it's Alex's turn to find a hotel in the tiny town of Cesena, and soon enough she spies one she likes. It turns out to be perfect. After we plead poverty to the nice receptionist, the suite that she says is normally $95, becomes $90, then, if we pay in cash, $85. It has two bedrooms and breakfast is included. Both are great. Good job Alex!

Three local restaurants are recommended. We look at all three and choose the third. It's 7 p.m. and we're early for dinner, but our waiter is most helpful and even finds a glass of wine for me. (They didn't sell red by the glass.) Alex always has a sip just to make sure it's good. We enjoy the Italian cuisine and we rave about the pasta to the waiter.

After dinner where is Alex? Upstairs making pasta with Grandma. The gelato (which is now almost a must for us) is found nearby. This gelato is special, we're told, because it's made on the premises. It does taste extra good. One of the owners speaks very good English and we find out that he was a United Nations security guard and traveled a lot. When we mentioned Milwaukee, he answered: "Fonz"! (We noticed he dressed like Fonz too). He was cool. He said he was planning a trip to the United States and asked about what he should see. We shared our ideas and he gave us the lowdown on San Marino: "It's where the rich like to be. Like an Italian Monte Carlo."

Early the next day, we're off to Venice. It's just a short drive up the coast and we've reserved a room in a little hotel near the Grand Canal. After turning the car in and getting several directions from friendly shopkeepers, we find the hotel. It's small but clean.

The next day, after wandering for a while taking in all the sights, sounds and smells, we blunder into Piazza San Marco (St. Mark's Square) from the side. The wait in line for the Doges Palace is well worth it. The unbelievable splendor of its paintings, gold and sculptures must have had the desired intimidation effect; it does on us.

On to St. Mark's Basilica, which also is impressive. A long walk down the waterfront then back along a side calle (street) got us to lunch on the piazzo. Then another good walk back to our hotel to rest our feet and plan tomorrow's activities (and tonight's dinner).

Alex is a brat and wants me to tell about me stepping in the dog poop - but I won't. OK, her note: "Stepped in dog poop, almost fell. Hilarious. NOT. :)."

After lunch we explore the Correr Museum, with the colorful history and art of Venice - more than we can absorb. A boat ride on the canal takes us to the train station, where later we'll catch a ride back to Rome the next day. We stop at a little restaurant near the Rialto Bridge. First we try the bruschetta antipasto. Good. Next I have spaghetti and meatballs and Alex has aglio olio – spaghetti tossed with olive oil, garlic and pepper. Both are good. This is followed by a scoop of the best chocolate gelato we've had.

On the way back we take the "scenic route" and stop at a little market to pick up some bread, cheese, water, a little sausage, and apples the size of your head for the train trip to Rome.

The train leaves just after noon and arrives in Rome about 5. We just have time to pick up our bags from the hotel and, on the way back, see just one more church . . .

(Written by Alex and Baba)

Ayman and Tahani family

Israel and the West Bank - 2009

A couple had come to our church, Lumen Christi Catholic Church in Mequon, selling olivewood carvings from the Holy Land. Their daughter lives in Bethlehem. I've always wanted to visit Israel, so I took them to lunch. They were very nice people, and contacted their daughter, Samah, who emailed me.

Samah was nice and a huge help. Nothing like having someone who knows the ropes help you out. Samah is a Palestinian Arab, but a Catholic, not a Muslim. She's one of about 5 percent left of the West Bank Arabs who are Christian.

When I mention to Ayman Khatib about maybe going to Israel, he was excited and most helpful. Ayman is an Arab Muslim originally from the West Bank and now living in Milwaukee. An explanation how we met: A few years before, we had a young woman from Morocco stay with us for a few months while she underwent some operations. Columbia St. Mary's Hospital provided Ayman as an Arabic translator, and we became acquainted.

The Wall - 10 meters high with concertina wire at the top

Ayman invited me to stay with his parents when he and his family go to visit them in the West Bank. Wow. What's better than one person helping? Two! And perhaps even more valuable is the perspective of each. Growing up and in business, Jewish people were always a part of my life. I had Jewish friends. I had dated a Jewish girl. One of my partners was Jewish. Now I had an opportunity to see the things from the "other side."

Samah had just been promoted to be the executive director of the Arab Hotel Association. (The Israelis do not allow it to be called the Palestine Hotel Association.) Her income seems to depend on whatever she can talk the different hotels into giving her. The association has about 90 members. Samah's small office is two worn out, second-story rooms and a bathroom, but it is wonderfully located right across from the walls of Jerusalem's Old City.

From one window, you can see over the ancient walls to the shining Dome of the Rock, an Islamic shrine on the Temple Mount. (Temple Mount is considered a holy site in Judaism, Christianity and Islam.) Samah says the former director left the place in a mess and today is cleanup day. She's a big woman, forceful and outspoken, about 35, nice to me but bitter about the treatment of the Palestinians and perhaps life itself. "We have no problem with the Muslims, we all hate the Jews," she tells me when we first meet.

While Samah and her crew clean, I am go explore. The Old City is fantastic. It's a maze of winding walkways, all stone as are the buildings. Many generations have walked on these walkways, including Jesus Himself. It reminds me a little of Fez Medina in Morocco.

The Old City is charming, with many little doorways to homes and small shops. The people are friendly, yet busy with their own lives. The walkways are so narrow that garbage is picked up by a little tractor, no bigger than a lawn tractor. Practical. In Fez, the garbage was hauled out in bags slung over a donkey's back. Ahh, progress. Most of the women here cover their hair, but the rest sport a mixture of modern pants partly covered by long coats. Mohammed would probably not approve. Samah notes there is a continuing argument about clothes.

I am on my way to see the Church of the Holy Sepulchre in the Christian Quarter of the Old City. Large, polite but pushy crowds pry their way into a line to see and respect the places where Jesus was nailed, died and rose from the dead. I'm here, really here!

I have to separate my thoughts and shield my mind to the bustle and noise surrounding the scene to get any appreciation. Inside, many candles continue to darken the walls to black. The construction of the church was directed by Helena, wife of Roman Emperor Constantine I, about three hundred years after Jesus died and rose again. There's not a huge, singular area inside like most churches, and the entrance to the little square that fronts the church could easily be missed.

The entire Old City covers only 209 acres and this is just a little squib of it. I pray at the Wailing Wall, the only part left of what is believed to have been the ancient great temple built by King Solomon. It's essentially a retaining wall for the courtyard above. It alone is impressive. Some of the stones are as big as small trucks.

There are many Jewish people at the Wall doing their quick bowing motion and praying. Some look around to see what's going on while they recite their prayers. Scrolls are kept in a couple of wardrobes along the wall. Paper kippas (yarmulkes) are available nearby. Women have a

Approach

separate area to the right. All very interesting.

After walking for an hour or so, I head back to Samah's office, which is in full cleaning mode. All the furniture's in the hall. Samah has an assistant get us some lunch and we eat amidst the mess. About 3 p.m., Samah and I take a minibus back to the checkpoint. With the traffic, it takes about an hour. There's smoke in the distance, lots of it, and maybe that's why there's a delay. Garbage fire? Bomb? No one knows. It's interesting to experience not turning on a radio or TV to find out what's going on. Never did find out what happened.

Later in the afternoon, the Church of the Nativity and the Milk Grotto are both interesting to visit, but I'm soon getting "churched out." A lot more walking and it's time for a shower.

Samah's called to invite me to dinner tonight with two of her friends, one she says is an investment broker, and Sammy, a driver. The restaurant is a quiet place outside the bustle. Wonderful. She has some strong views but is certainly trying hard to be a good host. The dinner's good as were the companions, although I felt like the investment broker perhaps has in mind doing some business with me, and that's OK.

The next day I find myself in the car with Samah heading to Jerusalem. The trip should only take about 15 minutes. Soon we arrive back at the checkpoint and go through. There are several revolving gates, concertina wire and walled approaches. Without permission, it would be tough to get close to the person who checks your passport or permit.

We're called forward one at a time. There's a metal detector past the revolving gate and we're still 50 feet from the bulletproof office. They also have what appears to be a hand / fingerprint check for some. The occasional wait is definitely irritating but I understand its purpose. The process is especially intimidating for Arabs. I smile. Usually I'm just waved through. At every opportunity Samah shows her contempt, which no one seems to notice.

Normally at a checkpoint you press your passport (or, for the Palestinians here, a permit to travel) up against the thick glass. The guard enters your numbers into a computer and when nothing objectionable shows up, you may proceed. Checkpoints are usually a hassle for Samah, she says, but today there is little delay. I'm waived through by a bored guard. I notice the guards seldom look you in the eye, concentrating on the numbers and the computer. Approval to proceed is the slightest little nod toward the exit. Blink and you'd miss it. Condescending? Oh yes.

The walled Old City of Jerusalem is where I spend most of my time. The informative Museum of the Tower of David is located in the citadel, part of the defensive wall. The Temple Mount excavations and the museum called the Davidson Center are fascinating. The Temple Mount is believed to be the site for the First and Second Jewish Temples. According to tradition, the First Temple was built by King Solomon in about 957 BC, and destroyed by Babylonians. The Second was started in 538 BC. To quell Jewish revolts, the Romans leveled everything in 70 AD.

All that was left was the stone base on which the temples were built. The huge stone formation that makes up the wall supporting the western part of the platform is now called the Wailing Wall or simply the West Wall. It's the closest the Jewish faithful can get to what were their once great temples and that's where they come to pray.

When the Muslims took control of Jerusalem in the seventh century, they built the Dome of the Rock on the platform which today is a mosque. Non-Muslims are not allowed inside, as the man indicated when I approached. Muslims consider it the third holiest site after Mecca and Medina.

284

Robert the Bruce wanted his heart buried in Jerusalem (1st Crusade)

On the way, a young man in a booth starts talking with me. We get along well. He insists on making several earrings for my family - no charge. What a nice surprise.

Outside the Old City, I catch a tour on the #99 bus circuit. The tour guide provides information and explanations about all the sights, as well as about some places that are no longer here. The talk has obvious sympathies toward the Israelis, such as "The wars we had to fight."

I make a stop at St. Andrew's Church, where a stone in the floor commemorates - ta daa! - King Robert the Bruce of Scotland, who lived during the Crusades era and desired to have his heart buried in Jerusalem. It was. He wasn't. The rest of him is in Scotland. The whole place is very low key. The man at reception desk didn't even know he was wearing a tartan tie. Can you imagine?

Next is the #124 bus to the Bethlehem checkpoint. The cost is 4 shekels (about $1). When I get to the checkpoint, the taxi guy wants 60 shekels to take me into Bethlehem and settles for $30. Still, about $10 for 10 minutes - seriously? He's very friendly, though, and mentions he has relatives in Detroit.

The Israelis claim the recently built Israeli West Bank wall has stopped

Jewish settlement overlooking Khatib's home

terrorist bombings inside the walls, which seems to make sense. Samah says it has nothing to do with the wall. She doesn't say what stopped them, and I silently figure that it probably wasn't the terrorists' good nature. She will not give any credit to anyone connected in any way with the "occupiers." President Bush is bad, of course. "What did he ever do for us?"

I point out that he actually increased the aid to the Palestinians by about $80 million.

"Is that true?"

"Yes."

She thinks about it. I think maybe we're making progress. "Well, it wasn't his money!"

Back to the Bethlehem Hotel, which is very nice. I plan to take a taxi the next day to the Nablus checkpoint where Ayman Khatib - the man I met in Milwaukee whose family lives in the West Bank - will be waiting. When I enter the hotel restaurant, it appears that two busloads of people who will be dining here are arriving. The hotel clerk, when I ask, tells me there are several good restaurants on the street behind the hotel.

I find the street easily, and as I pass a guy sitting on a chair in front of a nice hotel and shop, he speaks to me in English. We get talking and he shows me his shop even after I explain I'm not buying anything. Interesting man - it turns out that he owns not only the shop but the hotel, too. He is Joseph, a Catholic Palestinian. He tells me "You have to meet the Irish priest,"(plus two nuns, also, I discover).

The priest is called and soon comes downstairs from his room. We talk, and I find out he was in business as a farmer in Saudi Arabia, where he made a lot of money there. The nuns with him joke that he lacks subtlety. The priest is very learned and about 70 years old, as are the sisters. The three of them and Joseph insist I have dinner with them. It's a big buffet and everything is excellent. Joseph absolutely refuses any payment at all from me. I find out later that the father and the sisters haven't any money to pay for anything, even the rooms.

Toward the end of our somewhat theological talk, the good father asks me: "What is the ultimate goal of man?" I offer that Saint Thomas Aquinas said it was happiness.

"That's the answer!" Bingo - twice. He agrees with the answer and on top of that it turns out his name is Father Thomas Aquinas! The priest and nuns say they get a lot of direct messages from God but they don't know where they are going next - God hasn't yet told them. Still, it's a great evening - all the better because it was unexpected. And all because I began talking with a guy sitting in a chair in front of a hotel.

The next day Samah meets me and we take a taxi to the "Wall" to meet up with Ayman. The taxi driver passes the phone back to me. It's Ayman, letting me know he will wait on the other side of the wall and see me after I got through security. I say goodbye to Samah and thank her profusely.

Security's no problem. My American passport is a big help. Once I get through the checkpoint, I get a big hug from Ayman, and off we go to his parent's house, where I'll stay for a couple days. To reach it, there's a long gravel driveway that serves several houses, with stony farm fields on either side. A low concrete wall surrounds the house, leaving anywhere from 6 feet to 15 feet on the side. These areas are is jammed with different types of fruit trees and bushes. A walk around the house could provide lunch.

The house is a good-sized, two story, built, of course, of concrete with little frame anywhere. It was intended to be a two-family home, and, therefore, has two living rooms. Space is not a problem, yet "my" bedroom has two beds in addition to mine. Mr. Khatib, Ayman's father, sleeps here, too - kind of dormitory style. He's very nice gentleman, a retired postmaster who speaks some English. His wife is all smiles and always pushing food on me. I joke later that this is not Nablus, it is "Eat, eat."

There are some relatives there, as well, and all make me feel part of the family. Quite a bit of time is spent sitting and talking, eating, drinking – tea, coffee, Spite, water. Ayman and I walk to town to get some hummus. It's a very artistic presentation. Little slivers of cucumber encircle the hummus. Designs are made by dipping a medium-size spoon in olive oil, then into what looks - and tastes - like a mild, orange-colored spice, and finally making connecting half moons in circles in the hummus. We scoop it up with pita. The rest is carried home, with more pita.

By the time we arrive back to the Khatib house, dinner is ready. The house has become crowded - more relatives have arrived. The television's on, there are kids playing, and everyone is snacking. We talk until almost midnight. Ayman has arranged a car and driver for the next day for a drive up toward Nazareth and Galilee. The cost: $300. Ayman doesn't feel comfortable in going past the wall, so I'm on my own with the driver.

The farewell dinner at the Khatibs is special. Ayman has purchased a sheep (the second one, the first wasn't big enough, he said) and had a butcher come over and prepare it. Three equal piles of meat are now sitting on the stone walkway: one for the family, one for neighbors, and one to be distributed by boys on bicycles to poor people in the neighborhood. Which pile goes to which group is not known. Ayman's cost? About $3 a pound, or $450. Wow! Nice, and I find out the celebration is all because of me! They also tell me Samah had called to make sure I got there OK.

Most of the people I've gotten to know are Palestinians. Most are friendly, though a little abrupt at times, but very generous under the all inclusive "You are my guest" culture. All complain about the travel restrictions. None I met see any justification for the wall.

The second greatest complaint they have is about the Israeli settlements. They say in this land the most aggressive Israelis can

Jewish settlement in the West Bank

build on the hilltops in the Palestinian area without any regard for the Palestinians. The Israeli military then guard them, and build fortified roads to them. Essentially, it appears that by attrition and by making life difficult, the Israelis think they will encourage the Palestinians to move somewhere else. But the Palestinians are having a lot more children than the Israelis. A separate Palestinian country would necessarily encompass many Jewish settlements, including their access roads. The situation seems impossible.

Pictures of the late Palestinian leader Yasser Arafat and current leader Mahmoud Abbas are everywhere, along with thousands of posters with pictures of young men, some with weapons, who've been killed in the conflict. The Israeli homes have one or more Israeli flags fluttering their mute defiance. There are lots of weapons. There's one government program to buy back guns for a $1,000 apiece. (I hope it works out better than a program in India where, in an effort to rid an area of rats, the city bought rat tails for 10 cents apiece. The people then bred rats to sell to the city).

The next day Ayman asks me if I would like to visit one of his neighbors. He tells me the reason: the neighbor's son had a twice-botched circumcision. Yoiks! They tell the story, with Ayman interpreting. The boy is a very slim 14 and looks even younger. He's not accepted by many of the other kids because he leaks and has to go home to pee, can't go on a tree like the others. I take the boy's arm and tell him (with Ayman interpreting) about others in the world - the deformed in Guatemala, the dying men in Addis Ababa, others who have even worse problems. I tell him let nothing stop you. It is a sad moment. Tears are flowing. The mother asks if there is any chance of helping him.

I look at her a moment, but what can I say? I'm no doctor. I don't know what to say, so I tell his parents that I will ask at when I return home. (I do. A doctor who happened to be going there later that year goes and sees the boy, but concludes there is little that can be done. The end of the boy's penis was cut off. The doctor did clean up the botched result.)

Back at the Khatib home, I look out the window and see scattered houses going up the hill. Everything is up or down in this hilly area. I see a pleasant view. Ayman and the rest of the Khatibs view the settlers' homes on the top of the hill above them surrounded by walls and barbed wire and see a different picture.

Israel's Premier Ariel Sharon had said "Grab the hilltops" and the settlers did. The army now protects the settlements and their access. The settlements are all over the West Bank, or what the Palestinians call the occupied territories. They range from hastily installed trailers and mobile homes, to full-blown, miniature cities of very nice concrete homes and apartments.

I have just learned from the elder Mr. Khatib - as we sit together under a tree with a beautiful breeze and a temperature of about 80 degrees - that the mountain across from us is Mount Gerizim, where about 700 Samaritans live. They have been there since the second millennium BC and practice an ancient religion that is a variation of Judaism but shares some similarities with Islam. As government officials they were corrupt, Mr. Khatib says, and are now treated as outcasts. Most are older now, he says, and have many deformities due to inbreeding.

Ayman wants me to meet two of the Palestinian governors. Wow, that would be great!   Originally, I was also supposed to meet Jamal Hessan, the mayor of Nablus, too, but he's in an Israeli jail, accused of being part of Hamas (considered a terrorist organization), I'm told.

While at the Khatibs, I need to get some cash and ask about it. Mr. Khatib takes me into Balata, a nearby Palestinian refugee camp, which looks like any other town except the buildings are very close together. As he and I walk the middle of a deserted street, he's met with knowing waves. He's obviously known and respected. (Ayman had told me that his father is respected because as postmaster, he wasn't corrupt. Nice.) We come to a building. It's not a bank; there's no sign. When we enter, a man greets Mr. Khatib and me, but barely glances at my travelers check as he counts out the money.

As we make our way back out of town, Mr. Khatib tells me: "You know, last month it would not have been safe for you here." This gets my attention. He tells me one of the governors drove here in his nice car with two of his bodyguards. Everyone knew he was corrupt and perhaps a spy for the Israelis. Some of the camp residents stopped the car, pulled him out and set fire to the car! He and the bodyguards had to walk home.

Next on our list is a visit to the mother of Tahani, Ayman's wife. She lives a short distance away on a little hill with a great view overlooking Nablus. Ayman's brother-in-law is also there. He's a senior official in the Palestinian Liberation Organization (PLO). Everyone's been very nice to me, but the brother-in-law seems a little cold. Later Ayman whispers: "He just got out. Nine years in an Israeli prison will do that."

His brother-in-law's solution for peace is the usual – the Israelis give back everything to the 1967 line. And he doesn't believe "all that crap about this is their homeland" either. "They were never here."

He does have a newer Jeep and he's nice enough to drive us to meet the governor of the Nablus area. Here the scene is quite different from the last governor's place. There are about 14 guards with automatic weapons. They don't smile. One actually tries to be somewhat intimidating to me and doesn't give me much room to pass by. I give him an amused smile.

The governor himself is a thousand-dollar suit guy. He's pleasant enough but not someone to have a beer – or, rather, tea - with, though we do. He does not impress me. Later I find out that he was the one whose car was burned. Ha! I didn't care for him either.

Back at Tahani's mother's house, there's an ambulance outside. Seems her mother didn't take her diabetes pill. After the medics leave, she says she feels much better but we don't stay, though she had invited us for dinner.

Ayman has arranged to have me picked up by a "fixer" at 5 this afternoon to take me to Bethlehem. The fixer (never did got his name) is going to the Jordanian border, so he will take me all the way to Bethlehem, instead of me switching taxis at the checkpoint. It'll be a long day.

Mr. Khatib has come in with packaged frozen ice cream cones. It's 10:45 in the morning, and it's still "Eat, eat."

Ayman wakes me at 4:45 with a "Hello Jim." I have 15 minutes to get ready. Mr. Khatib has already prepared some hot milk, into which I dip sesame-coated biscuits. I grab a banana, too. The taxi guy is taking three men to Jericho to catch a bus to Jordan.

The landscape is almost all stone, punctuated by sparse, dry grass for the sheep herds. Each of the herds has a donkey to provide protection. The Bedouin shepherds live in temporary shacks.

At the top on some of the hills are Jewish settlements. The buildings are different - newer and condo-looking. They seem to all have shared the same architect. The giveaways that these are Jewish settlements are the fences: barbed wire, concertina wire at the top and searchlights at night. The planted trees are nice, though. What a way to live. Intimidating, and kind of sad, too. They seem to be prisoners almost as much as the Palestinian - just with more travel privileges.

Ayman says the Palestinian police aren't worth much.

"How much authority do they have?" I ask.

"Depends if their gun is loaded," he replies.

He has arranged for a driver, Wisam, to take me to a checkpoint toward Galilee, where a guide will meet me and take me around. It cannot be just anyone. It has to be someone he knows and that has the right permits to travel where I want to go. Cost? About $300 for the day. That was the best deal he could get.

From Galilee we head west to Nazareth. We honk our way to the

The Sea of Galilee

Basilica of the Annunciation where, in Catholic tradition, the angel Gabriel greeted Mary with "Hail Mary full of grace, the Lord is with you." Wow - that must have been a zinger for a young Jewish girl!

This is the biggest church in the Middle East, I'm told, and the complex is located right in the middle of Nazareth with massive stone walls surrounding a mishmash of buildings. The main or upper church has a large circular opening in the floor - open to the floor below. Down below you see the actual grotto, the place the miracle is believed to have taken place, in the home where Mary lived. On the north wall are the remains of the 12-century Crusader Church. Nearby is the apse of a 5th-century Byzantine Church. Outside are the remains of an ancient Jewish mikveh, the ritual immersion bath.

The huge amount of history in Nazareth overwhelms me. To appreciate or absorb even a part, one would have to stay here a lot longer than my schedule allows.

We continue driving west toward the Mediterranean coast to Haifa, passing through Cana on the way, but there's no time to stop. I am interested in seeing the Golan Heights to the north of the Sea of Galilee. Golan is supposed to be beautiful with many trees, streams and unspoiled nature. Wisam, tells me it's too dangerous. (Israel and Syria have long disputed control of the area.)

Haifa, with a population of 270,000, is a pretty city situated on a point on the Mediterranean Sea. Katyusha rockets (made by the Russians) have hit Haifa, Nazareth and other places we have visited, though it's quiet these days. Wisam tells me that at this point we're only 15 miles or so from Lebanon. In Nazareth, the rockets have killed more Arabs than Israelis. When that happens, an apology is immediately made by the ones who fired the rockets. Bet that helps the Arab families who have lost a loved one.

Haifa used to have a substantial amount of heavy industry but is now more high-tech. Signs with many names of international companies sit atop the buildings. The Mount Carmel range overlooks the area. The Bahá'í Hanging Gardens are fabulous, with their highly geometric designs. The colorful terraces overflowing with vegetation cascade down from the top on the hill to a gold-domed shrine. It is the shrine of an ancient religion, I am first told, but learn later the Bahá'í Faith was actually started in the mid 1800s among people in Shiraz, Iran. The religion is based on equality and unity.

Soon we arrive in Tel Aviv, which has a hedonistic feeling very much in touch with its western influences. Nearby is Jaffa, the ancient port city from which Tel Aviv has grown, and its Mahmoudiya Mosque, which is midsize and immaculate but almost devoid of people. I get a couple of curious stares from some men hanging around the outside. Guess I don't look thoroughly Palestinian yet. Maybe it's the cargo pants.

Going to Jericho is interesting. Clinging to a desert canyon cliff is St. George's, an isolated Greek Orthodox monastery. It reminds me of the Tiger's Nest, a mountain temple in Bhutan.

There are more checkpoints to go through. The Palestinian one is easy and the Israeli easy, at least for me. Just below the little Palestinian village of Jiftlik we come to the Israeli checkpoint. We get out, and the car is searched. We wait in line until we are called forward (one at a time) to the bulletproof control booth. I put my open passport up against the glass for the guard to verify.

The young man looks at the passport and with a surprised look up at me, asks, "Who the hell are you?"

I answer: "Who the hell are you?"

He laughs. "What are you doing here?"

I mumble something about hospital equipment and he waves me through without really listening. As we were talking, I notice in perfectly printed graffiti on the wall behind him: "Jiftlik can lick my balls." Classy. It must be a horribly boring job, but with the underlying sobering knowledge that your job is to stop terrorist bombs.

In heading back home to the Khatib home Nablus, we find the checkpoint isn't even manned in our direction. The Israelis don't much care so who goes into the Palestinian territories as who comes out. At the Nablus checkpoint I thank Wisam for taking such good care of me and then pass though with no problem.

Ayman's friend is there waiting to take me to the Khatib's house. It's about 9 or 10 p.m. when we arrive. There's almost no one home; the relatives have gone. It was so busy when I left.

The next morning, Sunday, Ayman's mother, Mrs. Khatib fixes eggs, bread and a good soft cheese dip. We dip the bread into homemade yogurt with olive oil, which is accompanied by tea. Mr. Khatib, Ayman and I walk a couple blocks into town and stop at the home of one of Mr. Khatib's old friends, who informs me he's Catholic! We're invited to come back later and to go to Mass with him, which we do. There are 40 members of this little church. Abby, the son of the priest is introduced. Son? This must be an Eastern Rite Catholic Church, which allows married men to become priests.

Mass is starting. The altar is behind a wall with three arches to emphasize the holiness of where the tabernacle is. They do some other small things differently, like the sign of the cross. "In the name of the Father" is still a touch to the temple, and "to the Son" is still straight down, but the hand goes to the right shoulder first and then left for the "Holy Spirit" part.

Glad I went to an Eastern Rite Mass on 16th Street in Milwaukee years ago - it doesn't seem so strange to me. At communion time, the bread is cut up in small pieces and given out. The Mass is long, hot and all sung, but interesting. I ask Abby about it all later. It's Greek Orthodox, he says.

Next we drive to the PLO headquarters building in Qalqilya, where there are two armed guards outside. Ayman greets them, and one guard politely answers that I am expected. We are introduced to several people

Palestinian Governor's Headquarters

Palestinian Governor

and all are very nice and quite solicitous. The governor of the Qalqilya Governorate is delightful. He shows us maps and tells me about the wall, the Green Line zone (a pine forest area which delineates the pre-1967 the boundaries between Israel and the West Bank), and the problems the governorate faces. He talks about the needs of the hospital that is being built to serve 80,000 to 100,000 people. (They have nothing to furnish it with, he says.)

Before we leave, Ayman, the governor and I have our picture taken. Hanging on the wall behind us are pictures current PLO leader Abbas and the late leader Arafat. In all, there are seven governors, I'm told. This one seems really concerned about the welfare of the people he represents (and of course he'd like some help with that hospital).

Holy Family
Maternity Hospital

Today in Bethlehem I'm to meet Dr. Robert Tabash, director of the Holy Family Hospital, a maternity hospital. As we drive up to the entrance, I see the names of Milwaukeans Dan and Eileen Meehan carved on a stone in the wall, along with others. The hospital is modern, immaculate, and in the process of revitalizing a wing. They need 32 beds, side tables, over-the-bed tables and supplies.

Dan Meehan had donated a 40-foot container full of supplies in 2000. Doctors Tabash and Kentgen show me around, even finding a box with the Meehan shipping label and, on a computer, a picture of the hospital staff unloading the container. They're generous with their time and the overall pace here seems quite relaxed.

The hospital averages three births a day. Although the hospital is Catholic, 90 percent of the patients are Muslim women and girls, and most have had some problems or they wouldn't be here, I'm told. The patients pay what the hospital thinks is fair, taking into consideration their circumstances. Usually, those amounts don't cover expenses.

About 25 staff members are Muslim. However, Dr. Tabash points out, the employment contract, states the hospital will supply the uniforms, which means no veils. Anyone can wear a surgical cap, which they all do, and they all dress the same - no distinctions.

In the Palestinian Territories, only about 1 percent of the Palestinians are Christian and 55 percent of those live in Bethlehem. I receive a great tour of the hospital and complete explanations. Dr. Tabash even has the ambulance give me a ride back to the hotel.

On the way, I stop first at a little restaurant whose owner brings the chef out to explain how he makes everything. He's Mexican! The owner says he can't get avocadoes, so in place they make a "tapenade" with finely chopped olives, anchovies, capers, coriander, garlic and black pepper. Next are two chicken quesadillas and two tortillas, cheddar and salsa. The cost is about $9. Dessert is a chocolate given to me by one of the Muslim patients as she awaited the birth of her baby. Doubly sweet!

At the Khatib home, a 23-year-old woman, Samoon, goes out of her way to talk to me, probably practicing her English. She is engaged to Ayman's nephew, who is also at the home, but a bit shier. She wears an athletic outfit but has every bit of her hair covered. Tahani serves a generous helping of lamb for lunch - delicious with the pita bread, yogurt and water.

In one Palestinian group I visited, after telling me the usual things about how bad the Israelis are, a man says: "But those Jews are very smart, very smart."

I say: "If they're so smart, why didn't they take land that had oil?"

Lots of laughter. Forgive me Lord, but I was in.

This is the day I'm leaving, so I get up about 8 a.m., and soon the others are up, too. Interesting, Mrs. Khatib has her hair covering on for prayers but takes it off to talk to me. Others are in modest pajamas, the kids still sleeping on the floor. Samoon runs to the bedroom screaming after getting seen by me without a hair covering. Ayman rolls his eyes and laughs when I tell him later. Much ado about nothing.

It has been a great trip, a good experience, and it was really made possible by the kindness of Samah, and especially of Ayman and the rest of the Khatibs.

I tell Ayman how much I appreciate how his family has adopted me and allowed me to become a Palestinian for a short time. The sheep and party were in my honor. He says everyone wanted to do everything to make me happy. They did. I am.

All this kindness, all this trouble they go to for me, and yet I know that many Muslim believe the Quran, the word of Allah, forbids Muslims to have friendships with Christians unless the Christians are in authority and the faked friendship is useful. I am torn whether this is the reason or if their beliefs in Islam, like most religious beliefs, are tempered by a good dose of pragmatism. I think, and certainly prefer to think, that they regard me as an honored guest and friend. It works for me.

(A follow-up: After many years of correspondence and some social interaction, one of the last emails I receive from Ayman says: "You know we love you Jim." Hope we meet again in heaven).

Thank you my Muslim friends.

The Squirrels - 2009

There's an old oak tree in our backyard. It must been there forever. It wasn't the biggest oak and it never had as many acorns as some of the others in our yard. That's why it was so strange. In the tree lived groups of squirrels. That's not strange - there are always plenty of acorns around our house.

The strange thing happened years ago. One group of squirrels started fighting with the other and seemed to claim the whole tree. It seemed that they didn't know the other group had been there a long time, too. There was a big fight that went on for days. There've been other fights, too. Why would they fight over this one tree?

When it first happened I was just a little kid and all the squirrels looked alike to me. Then my grandfather pointed out that some of the squirrels had white-tipped ears. He said they were just like some that lived in that tree years ago, when he was a kid. Grandfather smiled and said: "Maybe they thought because their ancestors lived there, they had a right to live there, too." I thought that was silly. How could they know that?

It seemed to us that the white-tipped squirrels, because they always won the fights, kind of lorded it over the others. You could see the others were kind of scared. Still, they would sometimes drop sticks or acorns down on some of the white-tipped ones to hurt them. Then the white-tipped would chase them and sometimes even bite them. This had gone on a long time now. It was crazy. There were plenty of acorns around for all of them.

For a time there was what Grandfather called a stalemate, with certain branches being for one group and certain branches for the other. Few dared cross into the others' territory. But then something new happened. Some white-tipped would climb up branches that were not part of their territory. These branches were higher up and had more sun. The white-tipped were claiming them!

There was a lot of commotion by the other squirrels but they couldn't do much. The white-tipped were stronger. Soon they'd built nests in those higher branches and the branches became part of the white-tipped territory.

It seemed to me that neither the white-tipped nor the others could go almost anywhere without fighting or chasing each other. There was always a lot of tension in that tree. None of them seemed as happy as some of the other squirrels in other trees on our property.

Grandfather said he thought the fight would go on forever. He said:

It's like two prisoners.

Each has half a key,

But each blames the other

For not being free.

I don't know what Grandfather meant, but he's pretty smart. Jimmy, age 11.

(Written after visiting Israel and the West Bank, 2009)

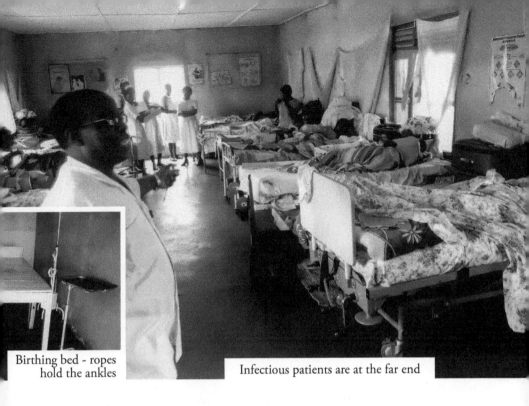

Birthing bed - ropes hold the ankles

Infectious patients are at the far end

Uganda - 2010

Sister Marie Nakitende and I met at a Greater Milwaukee Association meeting. She was very friendly, and I'd never been hugged by a nun before that I can remember. She was selling, but then, so was I.

I like to meet people, especially those from different cultures - it's fascinating. Sister Marie is from Uganda and studying for her doctoral degree at Cardinal Stritch University. We talk, hit it off well, and arrange to meet for lunch. Sister Marie is outgoing and delightful. We have several lunches after that. My daughter Susie meets her and is so nice as to invite her to Thanksgiving dinner. Sister really seems to enjoy being with our family and playing with the kids, who take to her immediately. The only one that doesn't take to her is Molly, the Labrador dog.

A couple of weeks later, Sister Marie receives bad news from home. Her mother is in the public hospital with a heart problem. Of course, Sister Marie is upset at being so far away and unable to do anything.

Uganda's main hospital in the capitol, Kampala, is barely better than staying at home, and possibly dirtier. Health services are free, but there's one doctor for every 22,000 Ugandans and only about 500 "hospitals" in the country. We would call them clinics. How's that socialized medicine workin' for ya?

We give Sister Marie $500 to get her mother transferred to a private hospital where the medical help is better - not great, but better. Her mother eventually recovers nicely.

At our lunches together, I have expressed some interest in Uganda. Sister immediately invites me to visit, and I quickly agree. We arrange to make the trip the following summer, just after she goes to see her parents. It makes sense to give Sister a chance to visit and get settled before I get there.

Long expensive trip to get there - 22 hours and $2,300 later the plane touches down at Entebbe, the city in central Uganda famous for the 1976 successful Israeli commando rescue of passengers on a hijacked plane. Entebbe is about a half hour's drive from Kampala, the capital and real center of everything.

We have arranged through a priest, Father Lawrence, also from Uganda, to have a driver (whose usual job was a mechanic) meet me at the airport and be with me for my stay. The driver will cost $35 a day, plus gas, food for him and $7 a night if we stay overnight someplace. After checking, I find this is a third of the normal price. Sister has said she will meet me at the airport, but that seems uncertain. Driving between Entebbe and Kampala at night is not recommended. As in many countries, night is not the time to be out and about.

Customs is particularly easy especially after I had moved forward to an empty seat in the plane, which was 80 percent full. After customs, as we passengers came out of the restricted area, there was Sister, with a man called Matia - my driver! She's arm waving and hoot-hooing to me (Sister is not shy). She warmly embraces me. My reading about Uganda has indicated that any public display of affection between a man and woman is not allowed. Obviously, Sister has not read that book.

The Catholic Church had made some wise decisions a long time ago here in Uganda. One was that it acquired large chunks of land, including some along the shores of Lake Victoria, the biggest lake in Africa.

Located between Entebbe and Kampala is an area called Nabinonya

Beach. It's dark when we arrive here. After we pass through a corridor of late-night, dimly lit open-air shops, I can barely see the outline of a large number of buildings. We arrive at a place called the Brothers of Christian Instruction. The manager, a nice woman, greets us. The room is clean, the mosquito net, which is supported by poles, has no tears, it includes breakfast, and the price is right - about $15 a night.

The manager and helpers have prepared a meal of beef stew, motoke (a banana or plantain mash), very thin corn "tortillas," bananas, an excellent mixture of diced carrots, cabbage, plus some other stuff in a peanut sauce and bottled water - very good. Several other women arrive and occupy other rooms in the short hall.

It seems that I have a semi-private bath that has an unused door to the little dining room. The other guests share the bath down the hall. My bathroom consists on one sink with cold water, a toilet and two showers, one with a door lined with metal on the shower side and the other with some hooks where a curtain might have been. The floors are covered with shelf paper with many brightly colored patterns. There are tears and holes here and there, but it's basically clean. I believe they use the property as a meeting place, retreats and whatever else comes along. They'd like to expand the use, they say, but don't have a website or advertise in any way.

The next morning I'm up at about 6. It's still dark. I open the door to the dining room and allow a very small frog or toad its freedom. Matia, the driver, says hello about 6:45 and I read and write until about 9.

Last night Sister must have had a nightmare. We heard a yowling wail now and then - weird. The sounds woke up a baby down the hall. In the morning Sister volunteers she had a bad dream, a leopard or some animal was chasing her. We all laugh about it. It apparently woke everyone up. It is suggested by someone that perhaps it would have been better for the rest of us if the leopard caught her. More laughter.

The sight of Lake Victoria and all the birds on the shore is wonderful. There are marabou storks formally walking in the their black and white outfits (nicknamed the "undertakers"), ibis, kingfishers, cormorants, ducks, a small eagle, swallows, hammercocks, egrets, black birds of some type, and more - and they're all intermingled with the monkeys (vervets, perhaps) that are roaming the grounds.

I have asked Sister what tribes she and Matia are from and get no satisfactory answer. They say the Luganda tribe, meaning Uganda. Hmmm . . . I had thought we would stay in her parents' village but we will not. "We would have no transportation if something happened," I'm told.

Odd. I don't ask what could happen or why Matia would not be with us. Sister changes the subject and says her mother is very anxious to meet me. I have asked Sister not to tell anyone where she got the money to pay for a private hospital, but I have a feeling she did.

Question: "What would be an appropriate gift for her?"

Sister bluntly asks how much do I want to spend?

"Twenty or thirty dollars."

"Why don't you just give it to her?"

Maybe.

Uganda's population is about 38 million, and although there are 33 local languages, English is widely spoken. The temperature today, and most days, is about 77 degrees. The exchange rate is about 2,300 shillings for an American dollar, so when $500 is exchanged, you're given an envelope for the inch-thick wad of bills.

About 90 percent of the people are subsistence farmers. Water covers almost 20 percent of Uganda's landmass, and the rich soil makes farming quite productive. Tribal affiliation is still important and the Bantus form the largest ethnic group. About 85 percent of the population is Christian (Catholic and Episcopalian) and there are Muslims (11 percent) and animists in the northeastern part of the country.

Other interesting facts:
- Hoteli means restaurant.
- Chai, as in quite a few places, means tea.
- The word ka ba means king. I use this word several times when I am introduced to men, and find it amusing. "Yes, yes," they say, "You are a king!"
- Only 9 percent of the homes have electricity, malaria is common and "short call" means to urinate.
- Ugali is a stiff maize porridge.

- Putzi are tumba flies that bore into your skin. (Oh, great.)
- Pombe is a millet beer and a Rolex is a fried egg sandwich! Where else in the world can you buy a good Rolex for 50 cents?

Today we're to visit a zoo, supposedly one of the best in Africa. Many zoos are intriguing because of two things: the animals and any information about them; and the housing and surroundings, which tell a lot about how the local people feel about animals.

I've been fortunate enough to have been in more than a hundred zoos from some wonderful zoos where the three objectives of a zoo (education, display and breeding) often fully exist to the display-for-a-buck-type - some quite disturbing. The difference in the animals themselves, such as an elephant in a zoo compared with one out on the plains of the Kalahari, is striking and evident to all but the most superficial viewer. One is active, more muscular, interested in life. The other is a welfare recipient - bored, boring and barely living life.

With that said, Kampala's zoo is nice. The entrance fee is $8 for me and about $2 for Sister and Matia. It's a shame that there are so few visitors. The zoo is beautifully situated right on the shores of Lake Victoria. Although it doesn't have a huge number of animals, the ones it does have are fairly well-housed, with over-grown areas adding a little mystery and adventure to seeing them.

It seems here, as in so much of the world, something is built and then not repaired or kept up. There are some large enclosures, big enough that you have to really look for some of the animals, such as the rhinos, chimps and elands. It's actually more natural and inviting for the visitor this way, and I bet the animals like it better, too. Poor Sister Marie - it seems she is uncomfortable with most of the animals. Something must have happened to her in her childhood.

The traffic on the way back to the city is not good and the narrow roads make it worse. The population of Kampala is about 3 million and it appears as the whole city is on the road today or at the open shops along the way. Exciting!

Out in the country, the rolling hills and lots of greenery remind me very much of Guatemala – so beautiful. We stop at a little buffet place,

Bishop's home and office

but don't stay long because we have an appointment with the bishop of Lugazi at 2 p.m. We get there at 3, of course. "We do not let the clocks rule our lives," they tell me. The bishop is very gracious. Some of the kids and a few adults actually kneel when they greet me.

We are going to see some farmers the diocese has helped. The bishop tells us to use his car and his driver, a delightful monsignor. Three women join us, one with us and the two others in their own car. The three women are part of the parish and are the instructors for the farmers. Matia is dismissed for the day.

My hosts would like to show me what they have been doing to increase production for the farmers. After climbing a few miles of deeply rutted roads, we visit two farmers who are among the 400- plus who the diocese is helping. Both are quite proud of their accomplishments. Pigs provide fertilizer and meat, the drainage ditches provide water, and the cut long grass is used around each plant or tree to discourage weeds and preserve moisture.

The farmers say banana trees take about a year and a half to provide fruit (the bishop later explains that it's about nine months), then the farmers cut it down. When the suckers grow from the roots, they keep a maximum of

Visiting Farmer

three to start the cycle all over again. Other crops include peanuts, coffee, tea, cassava, onions, and potatoes. These are all grown on slightly raised areas about 8-foot square surrounded by hard-packed earth.

The women are interesting and obviously proud of what they have helped accomplish. They are nicely dressed and educated, although it appears that they probably don't actually get into the fields that often. One of them tells me that the pig provides fertilizer to increase production. I offer that in China, human excrement is also used to increase production. "Do they do that here?"

She is shocked: "No, definitely not!" (More on that later.)

Back to the bishop: He takes me on a visit to the just-finished cathedral. (A cathedral is simply the home church of a bishop). The doors are carved wood and beautifully done. The cathedral has a capacity of 1.500, he says, and when they have special masses, some are still standing outside.

We head back to the bishop's house - which is more of a small dormitory with lots of rooms - for tea and cookies, and a shower. The hot water isn't on yet in my room, so the bishop apologizes and graciously tells me to use the shower in his room, and brings me his terrycloth robe for the journey down the hall. What service!

The pace is quite a bit slower here. There are a couple of women in the kitchen and a young nun who is in charge of all cooking. The feeling is less "wait staff" and more "servants." Hierarchy is important here, yet that doesn't rule out compassion. I find out that the woman trimming the edge of the walkways with a knife had no place to live. The bishop had found out and hired her to do small tasks about the place, and now has a place to live too. Nice.

At about 7:45 the next morning, I walk downstairs to the dining room for tea. No one else is there yet except the two young women in the kitchen. They are friendly, yet formal. The kitchen door is always quietly closed behind them. The culture here seems to say that women wait on men, and men are certainly not allowed in the kitchen.

The dining room is about 18-by-12 foot and has two tables and a refrigerator (with water, wine, fruit juice) in the corner. The table has a nice tablecloth and there are lace-bordered napkins next to plastic place mats. Tea, coffee, fancy pots and plates of fruit line the center line of the table. Like many places in Uganda, it's a mix of nice and plastic. Pictures of Mary, Jesus, Saint Francis, a past bishop, and an impala, plus a calendar, decorate the walls. The buffet next to the refrigerator has white labels indicating the contents and location: tea cups, plates, etc.

After breakfast, the bishop's friend, the monsignor, becomes our driver. He's in charge of 20 parishes and outreach centers, and knows all the history of the Lugazi Diocese. He's a good driver and has a delightful sense of humor. The first place he wants to show me is the "university." It's the first indication of his delightful sense of humor.

We pull up and get out at a kindergarten where we are warmly welcomed. I offer a few balloons, which create pandemonium. Then we're off to the local hospital, and the tour of the many wards in different buildings is interesting. All are in pretty sad shape but they are doing what they can with what they have. The staff is certainly willing. I see many patients, the men's and women's wards. I am shown stitches on the belly of one woman who has had a C-section. In one long ward I ask where they put the patients with contagious diseases.

"Oh," the woman says, pointing, "they are at the far end!"

(All that comes to mind is a story about peeing in the pool). I stay at this end. Tours of several schools and a seminary are scheduled after lunch.

Lunch? At the Jinja Nile Resort, no less! There's a huge conference area where the African Peace Conference was just held. The tents are just being taken down. The Libyan dictator Muammar Gaddafi was just here and made a scene by coming from his own tent (flushing toilet and all) by golf cart. His private security guards actually had a shoving match with the local security for not being allowed into the conference hall.

This place is impressive. We are told we cannot go into the hotel area. Right. I ask Matia (he's back) to drive us right down past the troops to the main entrance where I inquire about rooms for the next year. A staff member and I take a golf cart to see some of the rooms. Then Matia and I had a beer on the patio. Did not see Gaddafi.

Matia and I meet up with the others for lunch. While we're eating, a man comes over and introduces himself to the monsignor. He's very nice and respectful to the monsignor and the rest of us. Seems he had been an altar boy for the monsignor years ago. The monsignor doesn't remember him but they have a nice conversation before the man leaves. The four of us finish an excellent meal. Of course, I expect to pay, and am happy to do so, but we soon find out the man - the former altar boy - has already taken care of the check! How very nice.

Next we visit a seminary where three priests join us for tea. Some students introduce themselves. Many people seem shy but are very friendly. Those balloons at the kindergarten earlier quickly got rid of any shyness in the kids. A smile and a question about something they know about helps everywhere else. Most here look you in the eye and then quickly to the side - the normal politeness. Sometimes their voices are so soft that I have trouble hearing. I claim to be hard of hearing so they'll speak up so I can understand what they were saying. I'm an "M zoom," a white guy - assumed to be rich.

After getting back to the bishop's house, a shower really feels great. Before dinner, the bishop says Mass for the six of us in the small chapel. Dinner, reading and writing are next. And speaking of writing - I must have filled out eight visitors' logs during the day. It seems that everywhere you go, you must fill out forms. The ultimate was when the monsignor had to fill out a form for the armed guard at the resort where we had lunch. Included was the question of whether or not he was armed. Would you really admit it? It's about as silly as our signs saying: "No guns allowed on premises."

It's Saturday morning and I awake to the sounds of singing in the chapel down the hall. Nice, but I feel a little guilty not being there. I do make it to breakfast by 8. The bishop is gracious as always, and offers me tea, sugar, milk and everything else.

Some observations:

• What's the cost of bananas on the stalk here? About $2.40 for 50 or so bananas.

• Differences between the United States and Uganda: Gates, walls, fences, and locks on everything here; oddly enough even the interior doors of a private home are locked. The custom is that almost anyone can come into a living room, but bedrooms and the rest of homes are considered private space and, therefore, locked.

• From a distance, some beautiful, large buildings would fit into any American city. Up close, though, even the most recently built ones seem to need repair and the details aren't great. Along the roads, garbage is strewn everywhere.

• Brick homes are commonly topped with corrugated steel roofs, but there are many nicer homes and buildings with clay-colored tile roofs, too.

• Taxis, small vans and boda bodas (small motorcycles) are all over and not known for their safe drivers. Missing another vehicle or person by more than a foot or so is considered wasting space here, as in some other countries.

• Many men's heads are shaved or were shaved a short time ago.

• Fashionable women have variety of braids; some braids are tiny with every other one a reddish color. Some hairdos end in a pony tail.

• Form-fitting long dresses are the fashion for young women; trousers and a shirt for men. Shorts are out.

• The weather? As perfect as was forecast - about 60 to 80 degrees.

After breakfast, Matia drives Sister and me to a local school. It appears that there is a sign for some school every half mile on the main road. Some are private and some are public but, interestingly enough, even the public ones are run by Christians. The school we visit is two long buildings of classrooms at angles to each other and surrounded by packed dirt. Each room opens to the outside. Well-worn and soiled concrete walks help a little when it rains.

There are also some private schools with good architecture, landscaping, and long driveways through imposing entrances. All students pay something - just more at the better schools. The line between public and private is blurred.

It's exam day here so the students are busy. The head of the women's area is named Maria. She is Sister Marie's sister! She is 19 and, I'm told, very bright. She gives me a big warm embrace. Sister says her dream is to get Maria to America for her continuing education. Maria gives me the shortened version of what they teach, which are the normal subjects for students at the secondary level. They have about 400 students here. Everything here and in Uganda generally seems to progress at a relaxed pace.

From the school, we drive out to Sister's parents' home. I am warmly welcomed by her parents with two-handed greetings and many smiles. Two of the middle-aged children kneel to greet me. I kneel back to greet them, which is totally confusing to them and others. Everyone laughs, some a little unsure. We sit and talk, and are joined by other relatives have come over to meet and greet. Balloons make the usual hit and so does a frisbee. Sister's father is in failing health, but mentally sharp. Her mother has trouble walking, but does so for me, I'm told. We have a wonderful visit, including lunch, and don't get back to Kampala until after dark.

Tonight we are staying at St. Augustine's Institute, a retreat and conference center. Quite nice and only $25 - and that includes three meals a day! Gotta love it.

On Sunday, Sister has a family meeting regarding a brother who is getting married. There is much planning to do as many members of both

The Super Market

families stand up and bargain back and forth about who is going to do what. We won't see her until later.

Matia and I go to an open air market on the waterfront. These local markets are great. Matia is interested in buying a fish for his family, and right off the auction dock he secures a nice one, which will be two dinners for his wife and him. There's a pool table right out here in the open, with only a canvas cover for protection. I amble over. Somehow I am talked into playing two out of three games with a local guy. Interestingly, the table is about 5-by-7-foot, with seven yellow balls and seven red ones, plus the eight ball - all smaller than those we Americans are familiar with. We play eight ball, with lots of suggestions from the surrounding kibitzers. Fun people.

Matia says later he saw me take an offered "sweet" from Sister, remove the plastic wrapper and put it in my pocket. He laments the fact that most people in Uganda toss their garbage anywhere. Frankly, the adjoining market and cities look like it. There's a lot of garbage around.

Back to St. Augustine's for dinner, where every dinner includes mashed bananas, potatoes, stew, chai, frioles, and flat tasteless bread. It works.

On Monday I had wanted to see the chimpanzees, about a four-hour

On the way to the market

drive from here. Matia says Sister and the bishop want him to take me to a different place, but near where the chimps are. I agree, and we travel for hours past little towns where the roadways are lined with shops of all kinds and open fields. Often we pass a bicycle being used to carry stalks of bananas. The 5- to 7-foot stalks weigh up to 450 pounds. The bicycles are always walked - no wonder.

Goats and cattle graze just off the road. Wood is collected in bundles of 3-foot lengths and is carried on the head, on bikes or in trucks. Bricks stacked alongside the road are for sale, still in the 10-foot high stacks where they were kiln dried. No mortgages here. When you have save enough money, you buy enough bricks for a few more courses on your home.

We turn left away from where the chimps are and drive to a beautiful place located on a high ridge overlooking Lake Edward on the right and a huge channel on the left. It's called the Mweya Lodge and it's in Queen Elizabeth National Park. What a setting! A half mile across at the edge of the channel there are cape buffalo drinking. I'm told I just missed a tourist boat that skirts the lake for two hours to get a closer look at the animals.

Almost all the guests here at the lodge are white with high-pitched voices. Glad we missed the boat. Way down from the high ridge and the resort is a dock. It's deserted when Matia and I get there, except for three hippos eating off the bottom only about 10 to 15 feet away. We watch them for awhile. Fun; doesn't seem to bother them.

Matia says there is a game drive tomorrow morning for $125 per person if I want to go with the group. I tell him no, that is too much for me and I wouldn't want to go with a group anyway. He has already guessed that. A short time later he tells me he has talked to the head guide and if I can be there at 6:30 in the morning, there is a guide who will take the two of us in our car for $20. We'll be there!

Matia heads to the drivers' dining area at the lodge. My dinner starts off with two Guinness at a table on a terrace overlooking the lake. Lighting is by candlelight, and I dine on tilapia, cauliflower, corn, egg, a lamb chop, asparagus, mashed carrots, potato, chicken, pudding, apple pie and chocolate cake - all good. Some bats are flying around having dinner also, drawn to the bugs attracted by the lights. Other visitors seem too engrossed in their conversations to notice the bats. Maybe that's a good thing. I have a nice talk with Issac and Lazarus, the waiters. There's a semi-tame warthog munching grass about 10 feet away. I hear the familiar sounds of the hippos down at the water's edge. I wish someone were here with me to appreciate it all.

While I was at dinner, the housekeeping staff had pulled the mosquito netting around my bed, turned down the bed, and sprayed the room. The shower's a waterfall of water, so refreshing.

The next morning at 6:30 we meet John the guide who's taking us on our game drive. I tell John, who's very nice, that if he is a really good guide, I'll get to see a leopard. I've never seen one. We all laugh, knowing it isn't really up to him. About 500 feet down the road along the ridge there are three leopards lying in the middle of the road. Wow! I tell John he's really good! We laugh about it all day.

In the next couple of hours we see elephants, kob (resembles an impala), many birds (they claim Uganda has recorded 1,009 species), cape buffalos, lions and warthogs. A baboon comes down the road ahead of us. He's a beggar. When we stop, he squats next to my window like a dog waiting for a treat. I shouldn't - but a balloon mildly interests him.

First he bats it and then punctures it with a claw. Then he picks up the pieces and smells them. Not to his liking, it's quickly ignored. He does like the banana though.

The four-hour trip back to Kampala turns out to be closer to seven, with all the road construction, but well worth it. We leave midmorning. The lodge has packed a lunch for us, which makes the trip go a little faster. Many people, old and young, are hauling jerry cans. It's the preferred way to get water from a central well, spigot or seep. More stalks of green bananas are seen carried on walked bicycles. Dozens of car repair places offer stacks of used tires for sale out front. Other small places sell food, commercially boxed crackers and such as well as fresh killed chickens and other meat hanging from hooks, flies included.

Cars, small motorbikes and trucks belching smoke compete on the roadway with the occasional dog or child running across. No one slows down much for either. Some of the older women sport floor-length dresses that have 4 to 5-inch peaks of cloth standing straight up from the shoulders. The colors are bright and varied on the same dress. (These dresses are called Gomesi and are the traditional dress of the Baganda people.) Bags of charcoal stand stacked waiting for a buyer. Each cylindrical bag is about 2 feet wide and 6 feet long, and topped with long leaves to keep the charcoal in.

On the way, in a deserted country area, we see a man running ahead of us down the road repeatedly firing a shotgun. Matia quickly slows down and stops. There are no other cars in sight, but many young men are running just off the road to the left of us, all dressed in bright yellow shorts and shirts. Another man with another shotgun is running with them.

The man with the gun runs over to our stopped car and asks, rather forcefully, for a ride for a group of them. Matia says no, explains that I have hired him, and tells the man he should be more polite. The man says he is chasing an escaped prisoner and that the others, in yellow, are other prisoners and are helping to catch the escapee. I suggest that we give him and just one of the prisoners a ride. We do. A half mile down the road, they leave us and continue their pursuit up a hill toward a farm. Sort of broke the monotony of a long drive.

Back in Kampala, Matia drops me off at a Catholic B&B - good place, $50 a night. Matia is supposed to pick up Sister Marie and Maria, her sister, who we met the other day at the school where she works. He drops me off at about 6:30 but didn't get back until 9, and Sister, Maria and some other cousin are waiting for us there. The cousin is quite shy and any conversation with her is strained. Maria makes up for it and is very friendly. Sister has picked a nice place for dinner that is not crowded and has music in the background. Because of the nice weather year round, this is an indoor-outdoor arrangement. Good dinner, good conversation.

The next day we have an appointment to meet Jack Norman at 9 a.m. Jack is the head of Catholic Relief Services (CRS) in Uganda. Matia is supposed to pick me up at 8:30, so there should be plenty of time. He arrives at 9:10. I had forgotten about "African time." The security at the gate to the CRS office is somewhat off-putting and officious. I sign in, fill out a form, and am given a visitor tag to be worn. Not really a warm welcome. I bristle a bit.

Across the street is the American Embassy, with large concrete blocks piled up in front and armed Marines backing them up. Jack tells me later that the Catholic Church had owned that property, too, before selling it to the United States. A recent bombing is the reason for the increased security.

Jack is an impressive guy, gracious and informative. Microfinance, where money is given to a parish, doesn't work as well here as does organizing villages to save together and then if someone needs to borrow, the money is there, he explains. The interest on a loan is determined by the people themselves and all the CRS does is get it all started. It's self-funding, and it appears that the people involved are much more into "ownership" of these ideas, therefore making the project more successful.

Other CRS projects include high school education, drug education and testing. Agriculture is another field where education enables the farmers to use fertilizer and better seed to produce better results. Jack says the idea is for the farmers to put themselves out of work. He sounds sincere. I like the idea, and him.

Corruption is rampant in Uganda, Jack says, and building costs are higher because of it. The consensus from people I've talked with is that even the money from the huge discovery of oil in the northern part of the country will never reach the average Ugandan. Jack does relate that young people from many different African countries met recently in a conference here and bolstered each other's opinion that they have had enough. Corruption is out! The problem remains that many of the uneducated are given a few dollars and the crooked politicians are re-elected.

Off to the museum. We have lunch at a restaurant just outside the entrance. Food is good, place is clean. The museum is said to be one of the better ones. The exhibits are good, but dusty and worn, except for a hall of educational posters showing how to build latrines and prevent HIV. I wish the nice women who were so shocked about using human excrement for fertilizer were here. There's a large group of posters showing exactly how to do that. Outside on the grounds, a dozen or so leaf-covered huts have been built to show the various styles of different tribes in the country. Interesting. I thank Sister for all she has done for me and head for Entebbe to catch my plane. I make sure there is no "African time" here. We're early, so Matia and I make a stop near the airport at a park on the shore of Lake Victoria, where there are benches and a little restaurant. The breeze from the lake is refreshing and the setting is perfect.

Thanks Uganda, Sister, Matia, and everyone. It has been wonderful. Hope to see you again.

Burma (Myanmar) - 2012

You've seen them in pictures, they look weird and uncomfortable. In person they're nice women who do look a little weird and are uncomfortable. Longer necks on women were thought to be attractive years ago here in Burma among the Kayan people, so they decided to stretch young women's necks by placing rings of brass around them, forcing the head up. (Wouldn't you bet it was a man's idea?)

The solid brass rings wound around the necks of these now grown older women make the necks appear longer, but to me, not more attractive. Modern x-rays have shown that, contrary to appearance, their necks don't get longer. The brass rings merely push down the collarbones.

Like everywhere, these women have a few things to sell to the occasional passerby. Few foreigners come to this area, I'm told. Several of the women are weaving on back looms. The woven cloth has intricate designs and is used for skirts and blouses. They're beautiful. One woman is helping her husband with the masonry on their new home. Another woman, younger, offers to show us her home, so my guide, Min Min, and I follow. Her home stands about a hundred feet away. She tells us

that the younger women don't believe in using the brass rings, so in a few years there will be none to be seen.

A few facts: Burma, also called Myanmar, is a Texas-sized country with a population of about 53 million. There are many different groups in Burma, including the Karen who had made up 27 percent of the British troops because they were trusted by the British. (I stayed with the Karen people in nearby Thailand about 20 years earlier). A military dictatorship has run this country for many years now. About 70 percent of income is spent for food and 35 percent of the children under the age of 5 are undernourished. Estimates for annual per capita income range from $290 to $435.

Burma's a poor country, but with its centrally planned administration some get along well. Most, though, do not. We drive past a 16-lane highway as nice as any in the United States, but the only traffic we see is an oxcart! I missed a great picture. Central planning wanted a beautiful highway, but few here have the money to buy a car. Even the internet is controlled. I could not email home.

Among the customs are to not touch heads and not point your feet at someone. The fork pushes food to a spoon in the right hand, and you

Shwedagon Stupa

eat from the spoon. At temples, your shoes are removed before entering; you enter on the left, and exit on the right. Giving or receiving anything is done with the left hand fingers supporting the right hand's elbow. Lots for me to learn.

Independence came to Burma after British rule, which lasted from 1885 to 1948. More than a million people have been killed since then in various rebellions. The longest has been the Karen rebellion, which started in 1949 and hasn't completely ended in the northern part of the country. This is the reason I can't visit that area. The military's control of the population was very complete up to the year of my visit.

Last year Burma was rated 164 out of 168 countries for freedom. It seems to be loosening up a little - but very slowly. All the land is owned by the government, which can tell someone to move at any time. As for right now, even all the teak trees in country are owned by the government, even if you planted them.

Aung San Suu Kyi is "the Lady" and is revered. She ran for president in 1988 when the military held elections for the first time in decades. The military leaders thought they would win easily. When she won, they

Volunteer cleaning ladies

confined her to her home. Just months ago, she was set free, but with conditions. We drive past her home. She's still there . . . and still guarded.

The people of Burma are shy but friendly, even here in Yangon, a city of about 5 million. The temples and stupas (Buddhist shrine) are numerous and fantastic. Many of these buildings are covered in gold leaf and shine in the sun. They were sponsored by wealthy citizens. The higher and more spectacular they are is said to mean more karma. A few are higher than 500 feet.

We first visit Yangon's famed Shwedagon Paya, a gilded stupa, 522 feet in total height, which is surrounded by dozens of smaller shrines. Lots of karma! Unlike churches, there's no "inside" to most of them. With shoes and socks off, you walk around the main building on marble or stone terraces.

This is Sunday and a volunteer group of women are sweeping to keep it all clean. Many of the men and women you see wear a longyi, a kind of full length skirt. Great pictures. But just like in Italy, where after seeing so many fabulous churches, one gets "churched out," here, after seeing many, many stupas, I have a new expression: "Stupafied."

Min Min, the guide, and Han, the driver, take me to see numerous gold shops and sidewalk vendors selling food and anything else you might want. The currency here is the kyat, and the official exchange rate is about 820 kyats to the U.S. dollar. I had changed cash (they don't accept traveler's checks) at the airport at that rate, and was told it's the same or a better rate than elsewhere. Leaving, they'll buy back any leftovers for 810 kyats to the dollar. Fair enough.

We arrive at the old colonial Yuzana Garden Hotel, which is attractive and clean. I smilingly ask the clerk if I have the president's room. She smiles back. The room is huge! I have to walk it off. It is 36-by-28 foot with a beautiful herringbone laid wood floor. The separate bath, with marble walls and granite floors, has two steps up to the toilet. It's like a throne! The president should be so lucky.

Looking outside, the traffic is a little different than one would expect. Motorcycles and scooters are not allowed in Yangon because of government regulations. Later, I thank the clerk at the front desk. She smiles.

The name of the nice porter is Mule - don't ya love it? Translates easily. The next day after much talking, Mule invites me to go to his home when I return in a few days. He has a wife and two children. I look at my schedule - can't do it. Really too bad; it would have been interesting. I thank him for his invitation.

There are two ways to get to Nyaungshwe. One's a divided highway

16 lane highway - ox cart just passed

that's faster and skips the populace. Boring. We take the other. We travel through many towns separated by never-ending green rice paddies. Along the way, we see many people walking, bicycling, and on motorbikes and in trucks, and a few cars. There are stacks of cattle dung and bricks, bamboo poles, roof thatching for sale. We see small two-wheeled tractors with farm tires pulling trailers behind where the driver sits. In some areas there are carts pulled by oxen.

The people are universally friendly with the possible exception of those who are too dumbfounded or too shy to return a nod or a hello. Wonderful people! And to think I would have missed all this, especially the people, if we had gone on the highway.

Nyaungshwe, which was the capital at one time, is situated on Inle Lake. It's the only place where I've seen fisherman standing on one foot on the tail of their long-tail boat with one hand on the giant rudder and the other holding a giant paddle propelled by the other leg. The lake and the fishermen are picturesque and rightfully shown on travel posters about Burma. I'm taken by speedboat to the place where I'm staying tonight.

The hotel's great - each of the rooms is on the water and separated from the next. I walk down the dock to my room. The surrounding lake scene is magnificent. Dinner's accompanied by an ABC beer, dark, local and good. Min Min and Han join me. I notice that the waiters who were so friendly before and were practicing their English with me, no longer

hang around when Min Min and Han arrive.

The following night has us in a guesthouse in a nice semi residential neighborhood. Going for a walk alone after dinner, a very thin betel nut user greets me with many gestures and a few English words. (You can always tell a betel nut user by the bright red teeth and gums). He gets across the idea that I should stop on my way back. I do. He invites me to sit with him and two other men outside on a patio-type area in front of their building. It turns out this is a branch of a private forestry company that plants trees.

One of the men is the manager who was with the forest service but now is semi-retired. He says he used to cut trees but now he plants them. Tea is served and we have a nice conversation. As I leave, the manager says if I am staying awhile, to please come over again. Nice people.

The next day Min Min says we can go see the working elephants. It turns out the cost to see the elephants dragging cut trees is going to be $150. The "book" said it was $90. Seriously? The elephants are going to have to do their work without my help.

The Catholic Church is next (many Karen are Christian). It's a beautiful church from the outside but the doors are locked. Around back a window is open and a woman is arranging flowers inside. She not only lets us in, but explains the Stations of the Cross to Min Min, a Buddhist. His idea is

if you lead a good life and respect others, things will turn out fine.

We're invited to meet the priest, who is in the back typing. He's very gracious, too. As we leave, a nun is going in and invites us back for tea and vanilla wafers. She tells us that 23 nuns and 20 novices live here. Another nun joins us and we have a delightful conversation. What fun and all because of walking around a locked door.

We visit some very impressive hotel, can't remember the name. The rooms range from $500 to $600 a night, here in a country where the average income is less than $400 a year. I'd be embarrassed to stay here even if I wanted to spend the money and even if it was in a wealthy country. There's teak throughout the hotel. I'm shown a big apartment that is about 2,500 square feet and includes three bedrooms, a dining room, kitchen and bath. The pool is close and the views of the lake are nice.

On the drive back I see that many homes in the area are quite beautiful and in the Burmese style. Traditionally, the first floor was for the animals and the family lived upstairs. Now in this area, the first floor is for cars, bikes and motorcycles. The older homes are teak - built when teak was cheap. The newer ones are masonry. Old and new both have corrugated metal roofs.

The names of places here are sometimes confusing for a traveler. Spelling is sometimes different for the same place and, to make it worse,

many times the name has been changed periodically.   Burma and Myanmar are two commonly used names for the country itself. Names of people are sometimes repetitive, like Min Min, and they do not consider any as first and last names the way we do.

Skin color is another thing. It seems that everyone here wants to stay as light as possible, and they don't have dark skin to begin with. Umbrellas, especially for women, are common. Even more common is an obvious patch (sometimes on the whole face) of what looks like thick makeup. It might be 3 inches in a rounded square on women's cheeks. They use a powder that comes from wood sold in 6-inch long stick, 2 to 3 inches wide, with the bark still on. They rub it on a stone to create the powder.

As I wait for Min Min and Han, I give away a couple of shirts. I've gotten in the habit of taking older shirts or other clothes (or some I don't like so much) along on a trip like this. At an appropriate time, I give them to people who can probably use them. I find this is very much appreciated and I don't have to carry them home. Seems to make sense.

Driving through Naypyidaw, the new, purpose-built modern capital of Burma, it would be easy to forget you're in one of the poorest nations of the world. Up on a hill, there's the home of the ruling general that

we can see behind walls topped with concertina wire. It seems in any dictatorship or socialist/communist country, most everyone is poor - except those at the top.

The giant Uppatasanti Pagoda is 521 in total height, only one foot shorter that the one in Yangon. It's unique, I'm told, because it's hollow - it has an inside. Before going up the long stairway, we stop to see the white elephants nearby. Interesting; they're what I would call pinkish and have a surprising amount of hair. They're supposed to bring good luck. Instead of the long climb, I find there are four small elevators, one at each corner. Bless the karma of the person responsible for that!

Footwear comes off, as usual. The inside is massive and fabulous, with gold leaf - lots of gold leaf. There are many statues of Buddha, all in the same pose - a sitting position, one hand touching the ground. Being the enlightened one, Buddha taught that he was the only one to discover "the way" without being taught. The Four Noble Truths are:

1. All life is suffering.
2. Suffering comes from selfish desires.
3. Get rid of selfish desires and you will get rid of suffering
4. The Eightfold Path will eliminate selfish desires.

We're going to our hotel along hotel row, where each building is more fabulous that the next. (It seems that not all selfish desires have been eliminated). We arrive at ours, which is not one of the fancier ones but still quite nice. The outside temperature is 99 degrees. Upon arrival, each of us is brought a cold, wet towel to freshen up with, and then a glass of orange juice. Perfect. Funny - some things are really nice, such as the cold towel, the juice and the bathrobe on my bed, yet the shower in a corner of the bathroom, with a shower curtain and a simple drain in the floor, is real ordinary.

The guys will be back at 4:30 this afternoon for a drive around the city. The roads are four to eight lanes wide with very few cars (Han says there is one highway that has 20 lanes.) There are few lane markings, which wouldn't be observed anyway. I never see a directional signal being used.

Gems are a big business here in. There are three conventions a year when buyers from all over the world fill these hotels to buy gems. Burma is the largest supplier of jade and rubies in the world. We discuss the contrast between the enormity of wealth of a very few and the rest of the population. There is no doubt that the hopes of Burma's ordinary people lie in a change in the future. The people are not happy, and most are poor in a land that has much wealth.

U.S. President Barack Obama is announcing his plan on the television. He's talking about how his plan with more taxes will change the behavior of corporations and everyone will be better off. This instead of letting the market force of free choice of the population drive the success of what's best, what's desired and what isn't. Central planning: Show me one place where it works . . . except for a few.

Our next drive takes us up into the hills. I'm told most people who go to Kalaw (a hill town in the Shan State) fly because the road is too bad to drive. We find that the road is under construction. Women in conical hats are the majority of the workers. They're using pick axes and placing stones, bigger on the bottom, then smaller to build a foundation. The roller is next, then hot tar. John McAdam, the Scottish inventor of Macadam (this type of road construction), would be proud. Tough people.

We arrive at Kalaw. It seems nice and I see a couple of other travelers.

Up early, I'm hoping I can get to the daily 6:30 Mass. I head down to the corner, where I arrange a ride on the back of a motorbike. It's only a little more than a mile to Christ the King Church, and I walk in just as the priest enters. There are about a hundred people in church, which fills half of it. Men are on one side, women on the other. There's enthusiastic singing and participation. After Mass, many churchgoers visit the gravesite out front of a revered priest who served from 1931 to 2000. Wow!

I walk on, but soon several young people catch up with me and try out their English. They invite me to their school, the Novitiate of the Christian Brothers, which is very welcoming when we arrive. The brothers even invite me to have breakfast with them and the students. The students are boys are from all over Burma.

The Novitiate is also the organization's headquarters. A big, beautiful church sits in front of the old one. The churches, administration building and dorms sit on a few acres of land. A nun talks with me a bit and then a young Kayan man greets us, and explains some things about the school and organization. He leads us to a locked museum room with artifacts dating back to the 17th century. Everyone is preparing for the yearly gathering of representatives from all over the country. They tell me about 2,000 people will be here soon. Impressive place and impressive people.

They are seeing if the brothers are right for them and vice versa. The head brother graciously gives me a ride back to the hotel on his motorbike after handing me a helmet. My little donation will probably help them in their good work. (They did not ask for anything.)

Next, we're going to Loikaw, the capital of Kayah State in the Karen Hills area. Because of the condition of the road, the trip will take about five hours. The road is only one lane wide. Motorbikes and one car can pass each other, but if there are two cars, one has to pull over - and they do. We stop at some kind of fair, with dancing, music and beautiful costumes.

Shortly afterward, we're reminded that all is not peaceful, especially in the northern part of the country. We pass through a half dozen military checkpoints and are mostly waived through, except at the last one where it takes 20 minutes to get through. The army major seems pleasant enough but is doing his job. Min Min is supposed to have a copy of my passport for them but doesn't, so the official copies everything in my passport. Oh, well.

On the way, Min Min asks someone if there is a pool table or billiards nearby. The man says yes, then jumps on his motorbike and leads us a block and a half away. It's dark in the building, so the man talks with someone else and the lights are turned on.

We have the man teach us the game. There are two types of balls. There's one red ball and other colored ones, marked 1 to 15. The balls are smaller than what I'm familiar with, as are the pockets. The table is huge, much larger than pool tables found in the U.S. Min Min suggests that one of the players now watching us play me. Fun! There are also several 'crutches" to help with the long shots on the huge table. One of the crutches must be 8 feet long. It seems as if the rules keep changing. I lose. Maybe it would have been better to know the rules.

We visit a Buddhist convent, too, where most of the girls come from poor backgrounds or are orphans. They seem to be about 6 to 12 years old, and are just about to have lunch. Everyone seems to know just what to do. Some carry the low tables up a stairs, some get dishes, some bring the food. After a prayer for blessings on the ones who provided the food, all sung, it's time to eat. There is rice, vegetables and juice. The girls get two meals a day - breakfast and lunch. Everyone is shy. Heck, almost everyone in the country is shy, but it's a great visit!

We've settled into a fairly regular routine in the afternoon. Two to four is rest time while it is very hot, (ninety to nine-nine degrees). I notice the construction workers all sit in the shade and rest at that time, too. Then it's back to the pool table. Same opponent is there and the same result. He beats me. Some other people are watching including a little shy boy to whom I gave a blue balloon yesterday. He has the balloon plus two friends. Luckily, I have two more balloons. Sai, my new driver, has gotten a Myanmar beer for each of us. Good fun.

Dinner is at our haunt from last night with the same good chicken, rice and vegetables. Sai says he's driven for 50 people and never had so much fun. Nice to hear.

Odd thing. Driving is on the right side. Most of the cars I've seen have the steering wheel on the right side. The passenger acts as the "lookout" and tells when it's safe to pass. Boats pass on the left. Carryover from the British? Probably.

They have a great game using "cane balls." The men and boys use their feet and heads and a low net, or they play with six guys in a circle. Very coordinated and fun to watch. Mariano, my son-in-law and a super soccer player, would love it. I buy two of the balls, which are woven out of sugar cane. Ingenious.

Min Min says when he was a boy everyone wanted to be a soldier but now most think of soldiers as bad because of all the repression. Last night, I had caught part of a TV program describing the history of "the Lady." The program was not blocked so the military must truly be opening up. There's hope.

My flight is supposed to be at 3:45 in the afternoon. It's now 8:45. What's unbelievable is who I see walking right through security. Sai, my last driver, casually brings a beer for each of us. He's wearing the striped shirt I gave him. After a little more waiting, the plane begins loading. Sai whispers: "God bless you and good luck."

Burma - a few words
- Hello: ming guh la ba
- Yes: hoh'te;
- No: hing in (mahou' pabu)
- Excuse me: quin u ba
- Please: duh say la
- Thank you: gesu ba
- You're welcome: ya ba de
- How are you?: nay gaung' la
- Fine: gaung ba de
- I don't understand: namuh lay boo
- Where: baa le
- Cheers: chi ya
- Beer: biya

- How much: da be lau le
- Wine: waning
- Good: kaun deh condayu
- Animistic spirit: Nat
- Festival: pura
- Delicious: gong' de
- Crazy: ee u

Drive to St. John Paul's School

Uganda - 2016

Kampala is the largest city and capital of Uganda. Situated on the shore of Lake Victoria, the largest lake in Africa. Sister Marie Nakitende has arranged for me to stay at St. Augustine's Institute, like last time I was here in 2010. There are only a few other guests. I think it's used mostly for conferences. At only $25 a night, the price includes food. Sister and the wonderful driver I had last time, Matia, pick me up at the airport and drop me off at St. Augustine's to let me freshen up and rest. We'll have dinner together later. The shower really feels good after the long plane rides from Milwaukee.

Later, when they pick me up again, we have a little time before dinner to tour parts of Kampala and end up at the waterfront, where there's a lot of activity. It's fun to watch the selling of fish (tons of fish) and see the huge pelicans and hammertops pick over the leftovers. This is where Matia bought a fish and I played pool the last time I was here. Everyone's selling everything. I'm the only foreigner here, which is exciting. When we pull up to the restaurant for dinner, they search the car for weapons. There are several other whites at the restaurant. It's a nice place and the food's OK. It costs is $36 for three dinners and four beers.

A friend of Mariano and Tina (my son-in-law and daughter) asked me to look into an outreach project in Nkokonjeru (also called Nko), which

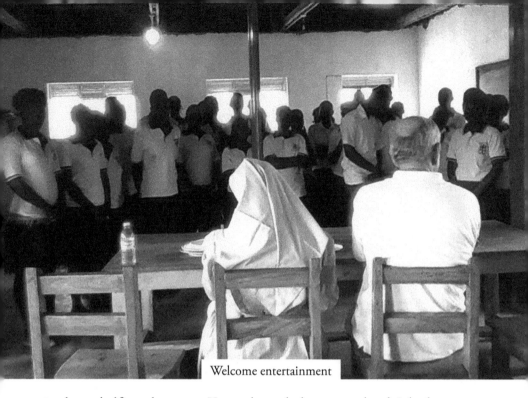

Welcome entertainment

is about halfway between Kampala and the new school I had come to visit. The friend, Beau Engman, and members of St. Eugene Parish in Fox Point (Milwaukee area) are thinking of funding a computer center on the outskirts of the village. They've been corresponding with the villagers, and Beau and his daughter are planning on coming here in the summer. It isn't far out of the way, so I'm happy to go. Meeting the people, touring of their little building and learning about the project are intriguing. It took little time and my report won't say much except how the people impressed me and that the facilities are adequate. I hope it works out well for the village to have people learn about computers and use them in new businesses.

We continue on to the new school. Sister had made friends in Milwaukee when she was earning her doctorate at Cardinal Stritch College. About six of her friends got together to help make her plans for a school a reality. It has been completed just recently - the teachers are teaching, the students are learning, and I am anxious to see it. Sister teaches at a university in Kampala and uses that income to support the school. Fascinating how things can come together. Sister has a vision for a school, and is not hesitant to tell people about it. Several not only think it's a good idea, but finance the project.

School's Courtyard

It's great how different elements come together. Example: The electricity supply is intermittent in Uganda. A generator would really help. A friend, Fred Stratton, is the president of Briggs & Stratton, a large Milwaukee firm that happens to make generators. Maybe he'll know a local dealer in Uganda where we could get a generator. Worth a call, I figure, so I tell him the story. He says he'll look into it. He gets back to me and gives me the name and contact information in Uganda. He's already contacted them! They have the type of generator that's needed and will install it at no charge. Thanks Fred Stratton from the people of the school in Uganda and all who will benefit from your generosity. God bless you. Wow!

Finally, at the end of a long lane, there's the school! Good first impression. The new buildings are in a U shapes with walks between. Everything is neat and clean. I am introduced to each teacher and they explain what they teach. The students are curious about this visitor, but most keep working on their projects. What they're learning is all practical. Everything is with an eye to earning a living in the real world, making a contribution to society. Among the many subjects are masonry, creative sewing, cooking, and hairdressing (of course I had to try on a wig in that class, much to the students' amusement).

St. Augustine Institute - $25/night including 3 meals a day!

Then I see the generator in the middle of the grounds. It's big and has its own locked masonry and steel cage. They're taking no chance that it might disappear some night. It's the most valuable thing on the grounds. I take a picture with Sister Marie to send to Fred. He'll love it.

For a finale, many of the students put on a show for me with skits, singing and dancing. Some were almost professional, while others were looking at those around them to see what to do. Just to try some of the hip motions the students used in their dancing would be painful. We all, with them, have lots of smiles and fun.

Sister has asked me to teach her class at the Uganda Martyrs University in Kampala when I'm here. Today's the day I am to teach the business class. She says there are 95 students waiting to hear from me. Pressure! First I'm introduced to the university's vice chancellor and his staff, who are most welcoming.

Before coming and after Sister asked me to teach her class, I asked my son-in-law, Mike Armitage, if he had any suggestions. Mike had previously been with the FBI. Uganda, like many nations in Africa,

Dance party

Celebration at Sister Marie's parent's home

has more than its share of corruption. The dream of many in a business class is to get job with an international corporation that does business in Uganda. Mike says it might be interesting to the students that the FBI was sometimes asked to perform lie detector tests on prospective employees in Africa regarding corruption.

The students are very receptive and fun. When I mention about the lie detector tests, there are quite a few who give each other looks. Maybe it will do some good. Thanks, Mike. The rest of my time with them is rewarding. I get lots of questions and hopefully my answers are of some benefit to the students. At the end of the hour, at least none were sleeping.

Before going to Sister's family home, Sister, Matia and I attend Mass in the local cathedral. I have to admit, after attending Mass in quite a few countries, it was interesting, but for the first time, not enjoyable. I have to concentrate to remember that I am here to give, not to be entertained. There's a lot of clapping, a lot of music and (in my opinion) too much yelling from the pulpit. It is entertainment, and the cathedral is crowded to the point of people standing in the doorways. Guess it was good for them.

To make it worse, a young woman, Sandra Rodenburg, also staying at St. Augustine's Institute, is with us. Sandra is from Netherlands, and is here to do research at the local hospital. It is Easter weekend and the hospital is closed, so she has nothing to do. Sister has invited her to visit her family, too. Sandra's only 21, but self-confident and outgoing. And she's an agnostic. This was Sandra's introduction to Catholicism? Hmm . . .

On the way to Sister Marie's family home, we pick up her sister, whose name is Maria. (Is that not confusing?) I had met Maria last time, and she's great. Since then, she has gotten married and become a mother. She has her two little children with her. To help out, I often carry one of the kids. Maria's husband is not here. Also on the way, we take a little side trip and hire a boat on Lake Victoria. Not too far away is a spring in the lake that is supposed to be the source of the Nile River. Interesting. Well out onto the lake, there is an upsurge of water from the bottom. When we get back, we have lunch at the restaurant at the dock. To get to the restaurant, we have to go through an airport-type of scanner. I am talking and walk around it. No one seemed to care.

A warm goodbye

Off to Sister's mother's home for Easter lunch and dinner. The extended family is all here and it's difficult to keep straight who is who. There is a lot of welcoming and shaking of hands. Sandra fits in fine, especially with the younger relatives. Maria and a couple others make us feel right at home.

Toward the end of the afternoon, Sister's brother gets up and gives a long talk with some very kind, emotional words for me. Sister's mother has an outgoing personality but cannot speak any English, and she can't get around well either. She was very sick a few years ago but has recovered somewhat and certainly seems to be enjoying the celebration

I will not do a good job speaking at this point – I am too emotional. I ask Sandra to be my spokesperson and to thank them all for the wonderful Easter celebration.

Goodbye, and thank you, Sister Marie, and your family and friends.

My time with you has helped strengthen my knowledge of and appreciation for the world's many people and cultures, as have my journeys to so many other countries over the years. I am grateful I've been given the opportunities to have these incredible, unique experiences.

God bless you all.

About James Bruce

James Frederick Bruce has a business degree in marketing from John Carroll University in Cleveland, Ohio. He worked in residential real estate sales in Milwaukee, Wis., beginning in 1963, and later went on to become president of a real estate company. During his long career as a Realtor, he earned many prestigious designations and founded a title insurance company and mortgage company.

After retiring from the real estate business, he earned a degree in theology and cultural anthropology from Marquette University in Milwaukee.

His travels have taken him to nearly a hundred countries.

CPSIA information can be obtained
at www.ICGtesting.com
Printed in the USA
BVHW092112161219
566650BV00001B/1/P